ANGELS, MOBSTERS
& NARCO-TERRORISTS

The Rising Menace of Global Criminal Empires

Antonio Nicaso & Lee Lamothe

WILEY

John Wiley & Sons Canada, Ltd.

Library and Archives Canada Cataloguing in Publication Data

Nicaso, Antonio
           Angels, mobsters and narco-terrorists : the rising menace of global criminal empires / Antonio Nicaso, Lee Lamothe.

Includes bibliographical references and index.
ISBN-13 978-0-470-83518-4
ISBN 10 0-470-83518-4

1. Organized crime. I. Lamothe, Lee, 1948- II. Title.

HV6441.N52 2005   364.1'06   C2005-902785-1

Production Credits:
Cover design: Mike Chan
Interior text design: Tia Seifert

Printer: Tri-Graphic Printing Ltd.

John Wiley & Sons Canada, Ltd.
6045 Freemont Blvd.
Mississauga, Ontario
L5R 4J3

Printed in Canada

10 9 8 7 6 5 4 3 2 1

For Antonella, Massimo, and Emily—**A.N.**

✳ ✳ ✳

To the memory of
O.P.P. detective-Constable Ron Seaver
1946-2005—**L.L.**

CONTENTS

ACKNOWLEDGMENTS

The authors recognize they're fortunate to have access to some of the most knowledgeable people involved in researching and investigating organized crime. Because of the secretive nature of the players and activities in the underworld, it is important to have a wide array of opinions, information sources, and analysis. A lot of the ideas and events we explore in this book were discussed and even argued over, and having "sounding boards" was key in understanding the activities of "Angels, Mobsters and Narco-Terrorists."

There were several people who spoke confidentially and asked that their identities not be revealed. These people provided documentation, theories, analysis, and directions for research. They include law enforcement personnel, security service operatives, criminals, and criminal lawyers. Their names aren't listed here but their efforts were key to the direction of the book.

Among those we can name are: Adrian Humphreys at the *National Post*, a colleague and good friend who tirelessly provided advice, direction, and no little research assistance in pulling together the diverse elements of this book; Rob Lamberti, of the *Toronto Sun*, who has covered organized crime for the past quarter-century; Paul Cherry of the *Montreal Gazette*, Andre Cedilot of *La Presse*, Richard Dickins, former RCMP Assistant Commissioner and United Nations Country Director in Myanmar, for guided tours throughout southeast Asia and China; Anthony DeStefano, of *Newsday*, for his decades-long perspective on the confusing state of the American La Cosa Nostra's Five Families; Italian Magistrate Nicola Gratteri, who is on the cutting edge of the fight against organized crime; Mario Possamai, an author in his own right and Canada's expert on money laundering; RCMP Chief Superintendent Ben Soave (ret.), who for years has successfully investigated the world's most powerful criminal organizations.

There are, also, scattered throughout the world the people who have helped us for the past twenty years on other projects. It was through their trust and confidence that we were able to pull together this book.

INTRODUCTION

When we published *Global Mafia: The New World Order of Organized Crime* in 1995, we focused on the interplay between various organized crime groups and the cooperative criminal ventures being undertaken throughout the world as mafias, cartels and syndicates found common ground on which to conduct their business. Throughout the book we provided instances of great strides being taken by law enforcement to crack down on these organizations in the wake of the assassinations of Giovanni Falcone and Paolo Borsellino, the famous martyred magistrates of Sicily. Not for decades had outraged public reaction against organized crime been so passionate; not for decades had the will of governments been so promising in combating organized crime. We ended the book with the feeling of hope, that, to paraphrase Winston Churchill, we might have been, if not at the end of organized crime, then certainly at the beginning of the end.

The public's knowledge of the scope of criminal activities has broadened. We know far more about the inner workings of criminal organizations throughout the world. We have new laws and new leaders in the fight against organized crime. Several of the world's most prominent and notorious crime bosses have been jailed, from the Caruanas and Cuntreras to Vyacheslav Ivankov and Cheng Chui Ping. Ever-increasing seizures of criminal assets have been made; drug seizures are in quantities previously unheard of.

But with our knowledge has come indifference, and in effect surrender. With our recognition of the underworld's leaders came something akin to hero worship. New laws failed to stand the test in court; political will has failed those fighting organized crime on the front lines. And for every Caruana, Cuntrera, and Ivankov imprisoned there came new leaders; as a crime group was targeted, new groups emerged. Members of criminal organizations, who previously kept themselves separate either through ignorance, racism, or indifference, met in prisons and found they weren't so different after all. New conspiracies formed, new alliances were made. The increased seizures of assets merely meant that cottage industries of money launderers—often "clean faces" from legitimate financial sectors of the world—could increase their percentages for transactions; lawyers emerged who specialized in hiding assets.

Modern technology that makes our life easier—online banking, ATM machines, the exchange of information—has had an equal effect on the underworld. Using cyberspace, criminal organizations can move their money around and obscure its source; communications are easier and don't require conspirators to cross borders to meet; online banking and ATM machines allow windows for criminals to loot bank accounts.

The underworld in post-9/11 has seen a flood of new players into criminal activities. Countries that once funded terror groups have, in fear of U.S. retaliation, cut off the money supply to insurgent groups. In response several terrorist organizations have turned to drug, weapons and human trafficking to finance their activities. Afghanistan has reemerged as the primary supplier of opium to the world; militia groups in Colombia have all but taken over the cocaine trade. Mexico has deteriorated into a narco-state. Canada continues to be a haven and transit country for criminals and has now become a source country for marijuana. North Korea has turned to drug trafficking to support its nuclear program and to keep the dictatorship afloat.

The territory of the underworld is no longer geographic: it's financial. Every organized crime group in the world is now active *everywhere* in the world. There are Mafiosi, Triad members and outlaw motorcycle gangs in most industrialized countries, from South Africa to Australia. There are Albanian and Chinese criminals in Italy. There are Russian and Israel crime groups in every corner of the globe. Products, whether drugs or people or cigarettes or money, move across a world that has become a free-trade zone—but the free-trade zone only exists for the ease of criminals, not for legislators or law enforcement.

We—all of us—create organized crime. Whether through high taxation on goods or services, or through restricted or banned substances, we want or need access and availability. To eliminate organized crime *from our lives*, we'd have to drastically *change our lives*. We'd have to control or ban everything, or regulate nothing, and that would be impossible. It is in the profit margin between the demand and the supply on which organized crime thrives. If five thousand Fujianese migrants want to emigrate to North America and immigration rules are too strict, someone will bring the migrants halfway across the world and collect a hefty fee. When cigarettes are overly taxed in one jurisdiction, organized crime will create a conduit to source them from a lower-tax jurisdiction. If a dressed packaged chicken costs 10 cents a pound less on one side of a border, someone will exploit that difference by trafficking chickens from the less expensive source.

Each of these ventures requires several components that organized crime is willing to create: sources of supply, transit streams through a border, receivers on the distribution side, and sales teams. Each of these components—remember this industry isn't government regulated and the business cannot be legitimately policed—requires some control over what has now become a criminal organization initiative. At the supply end the aim is to source the product as cheaply as possible to maximize the ultimate profit; the chicken with the 10-cent per pound price difference might be stolen to maximize profits, or might be produced illegally or shipped in unsanitary conditions. The transit of the chickens across a border would likely require some cooperation from Customs officers, thus leading to corruption. At the receiving end, warehousing the chickens requires security to prevent theft by chicken thieves—or competitors—and distributing the chickens into the hands of the people who are going to eat them.

But without a customer willing to buy them at the end of the chain of criminality, there would be no chicken connection at all. But there always is a customer for illicit goods.

Living in a world without organized crime providing services and products is unimaginable—to one degree or another most of us in some way benefit from their presence. And a world run by unregulated organized crime would be equally untenable; the disintegration of government, the judiciary, law enforcement, finance, and taxation would be chaos. So the two worlds co-exist in a constant state of tension—even war.

* * *

The subject of ethnicity or national origin often has to be dealt with in any book about mafias, triads, or cartels. This book doesn't intend to smear the reputation of the hundreds of thousands—or millions—of law-abiding people of the country in which a criminal organization operates; the focus is only on the very, very few who engage in organized criminal activity. This is fair and honest.

However, there is an undeniable ethnic or national component to the *culture* of crime groups: you don't have to be Italian, for example, to *work* with the Italian mafia; you do, however, *have* to be Italian to be part of the culture. Similarly with Chinese Triads: only Chinese people can be members of the Triad; however, everyone may be *permitted* to be involved in their criminal operations. With traditional Outlaw Motorcycle Gangs, with few exceptions, it is accepted that only white males are permitted to become members; however, the new "free trade of crime" is inclusive—blacks to Hispanics to Chinese. Italians are permitted to participate in OMG-related operations. Organized crime is a game every race, creed or color can, and does, play.

But it's important to be very careful, overall, that too much delicacy doesn't prevent a fair examination of criminal operations. Too many investigations by police and even media have been sidelined because a target falls back on cries of racism, or accusations that entire communities are being smeared. Any success by a criminal to hide behind his ethnicity or community is a failure for anyone attempting to expose their activities.

So, for the purposes of this book—as for our previous projects— we reiterate: in the references we make regarding ethnic or national character, we're referring to the criminals, not the race or nation.

* * *

This book isn't intended to be the end-all and be-all book of organized crime and criminal syndicates. It's a broad overview, primarily focusing on how much, or how little, things have changed since we last took a wide look at the subject 10 years ago. Some of the chapters or sections might inspire writers and journalists to take a closer look at a particular phenomenon; this we welcome and whole-heartedly encourage. An in-depth look into the criminal activities of the North Korean government would be intriguing, to say the least. An historical review of the early years of the *'ndrangheta* outside of Italy, too, would be fascinating and valuable. A coherent look at the culture—and not solely the criminal activities of some members—of the Hells Angels and other OMGs would be groundbreaking. The role of "clean faces"—outwardly upstanding members of the legal, political, and financial sectors—would likely be stunning to many citizens.

All these are viable projects and should be taken beyond our sometimes-cursory examinations; the bringing of a fresh eye and perspective in any of these areas could deepen the knowledge available about organized crime and criminal syndicates.

Finally, a note on terminology: The term *Mafia*, with a capital *M*, refers to the Sicilian Mafia, or Cosa Nostra. The term *mafia*, with a lowercase *m*, refers to organizations in the generic sense, the word *mafia* having entered modern usage to mean a closed clique or exclusive group: for example, "the Hollywood mafia" refers to the power people in Hollywood as a group of insiders or practitioners. *La Cosa Nostra*, or *LCN*, refers to the Americanized version of organized crime; "the American mafia" is also appropriate.

PART
ONE
Italian Organized Crime

'Ndrangheta

The remote town of Platì is nestled in the Aspromonte Mountain of Calabria, the Italian mainland's southernmost province. The sign announcing the town is riddled with gunfire, rendering it almost illegible. On the road leading to Platì, is a monument to a murdered policeman. Often the sounds of gunshots can be heard as wild boar are hunted in the scrub; men carrying long-barreled shotguns walk along the edge of the road, braces of wild birds slung over their shoulders. There are protected marijuana fields, one of them containing more then half a million plants. There are abandoned shacks and caves where kidnap victims have been bound with chains and beaten and held for ransom. One, who escaped and made it to Platì, expected to be saved. But the townspeople simply contacted the kidnappers who came to pick up their lost victim.

Platì is home to about 3,800 citizens who share fewer than two dozen surnames, and four of these family names are among the most notorious in the underworld: Barbaro, Trimboli, Agresta, and Perre.[1] Almost everybody in town is related, either by marriage or blood. Finding informants in Platì is impossible, but there's no lack of information: marriage announcements are regularly posted on the town council's notice board, and often the groom is a wanted fugitive.

In town politics strange things happen, but no one complains. In April 2001 the council allocated funds to make improvements around the fiumara Buonamico, a nearby river. In fact, the item is in the town minutes as "a three-year plan for public works ... for the re-vitalization of the area used by absconders from justice."

Less than 10 percent of the people pay their taxes; in 2000 only 131 homeowners paid property tax, and in 2001 and 2002 that number declined even further. Unemployment runs as high as 80 percent.

Honor killings still occur in Platì. There are arranged marriages. There are secret initiation ceremonies with archaic phrases whispered by candlelight, a sliced fingertip and the mingling of blood. There's a system of behavior that has nothing to do with the values society abides by beyond the mountain.

There's one main street running through Platì, and when an unfamiliar vehicle drives through the streets, everyone stops and stares. Mouths close and eyes fill with suspicion. Groups of men gather. "Closed" signs go up and windows are shuttered.

Platì is not far away from the town of San Luca[2]—the *casa madre* of the Honored Society of Calabria, the *'ndrangheta*. While San Luca is the spiritual—even religious—heart of the Honored Society, Platì is the economic one. If not for the modern clothing of the citizens, the expensive cars cruising the streets, and the helicopters hovering over the mountain looking for fugitives, Platì might still be a backward little town in pre-1860 Calabria.

It is from this town and a few dozen others that a formidable global criminal enterprise emerged. The outlaw comforts of Platì, however, could not last forever.

* * *

The early days of the *'ndrangheta*—a Greek word for manliness and heroism, similar in meaning to that of *mafia* in Sicily—are shrouded in legend and secrecy. A popular tale is that three knights from Spain,— Osso, Mastrosso, and Carcagnosso—fled their country after they killed a nobleman who raped a female relative. They went to Sicily, Naples, and Calabria, respectively, founding the Sicilian Mafia, the Camorra, and the *'ndrangheta*. While the tale may be mythic, the three knights are mentioned prominently in the initiation rituals of the *'ndrangheta*.[3]

The *'ndrangheta* was more likely rooted in the culture and remoteness of towns and villages of Calabria. In a place where government interest or involvement was minimal, it was only natural that strong men—as in Sicily—emerged to effectively control citizens' activities. Some leaders were beneficent; others were tyrannical. But all were violent, having to first prove their manliness by committing homicide, preferably in public, and preferably being acquitted of the ensuing charges.

Rules and regulations of behavior were followed by *'ndranghetisti*; oaths and ceremonies were conducted to initiate new members; and conclaves were held to discuss criminal operations in various regions.

In the 1800s the Calabrian mafia was called the *picciotteria* or Honored Society. In 1892 more than 150 men from several villages were charged for mafia-like activities; in the same year almost 100 were charged in an investigation that spread across the province. Both cases showed that more than a century ago the criminal chiefs of the villages at least knew one another, and on occasion worked together.

Many people from the South left during successive waves of migration in the late 1800s and early 1900s, among them 'ndranghetisti on the run from the law or vendettas. As they settled in new countries, primarily in North America, they took with them the roots of future generations of criminals.

After World War II the Calabrian clans—Honored Societies—began to grow rich on Italian reconstruction contracts and black marketeering. For the bosses of the 'ndrangheta the flow of government money into the region increased their power: their control over the workforce, their influence in land transactions, their control of votes, and the traditional fear they engendered in the populace. Virtually every city, town, and village in Calabria had a criminal clan that controled many facets of life. Unlike the Sicilian and American mafias, the 'ndrangheta was built upon the family nucleus of blood relatives and intermarriages. It was, as a result, almost impenetrable; for a brother to inform on a brother would be infamy.

* * *

Italian secret societies in North America are as old as Italian immigration itself. The "mafia," the "Black Hand," the Camorra and the "Society" were used interchangeably. While some of the groups preyed on law-abiding immigrants, others, like the *padrone*, actually provided services beneficial to starting a new life, but of course the services both increased the groups' profits as well as their power in the communities. The line between the *padrone* system and organized crime often blurred. Under the *padrone* system—*padrone* means boss—an established member of the Italian colony was able to liaise between the new arrival and the new society. The *padrone* provided or arranged housing, loans, jobs, and social activities, settled disputes and governed relationships, and generally made the life of the new immigrant easier. As in Sicily and Calabria, the *padrone* accumulated wealth and favors, and as the community grew and members became eligible to vote, the *padrone* often traded these votes to politicians in return for favors. This increased his personal power in the wider society. He accumulated wealth by chipping a small piece off each negotiation; for example, if the *padrone* provided two dozen workers to strip a fruit orchard, he might make a few pennies per worker. In a dispute between two businessmen, he might receive a "gift" from each side for resolving it.

Although some criminal leaders emerged from the role of *padrone*, the system wasn't a criminal organization per se, but rather a parallel entity that greatly reduced the role of the government in the Italian colonies. The forward-thinking *padroni* saw the benefit of reasonably happy immigrants, who would write to relatives and thus generate more clients for them. Others, though, concentrated less on furthering their community and instead made themselves as much profit as possible from everyone who came into contact with the immigrant, from the steamship company that sold them tickets to the businessman who hired their labor.

More sinister was the Society—essentially the early version of the *'ndrangheta*—in North America. The Society was much whispered about before it came to the public's notice, and even then it was made out to be more sinister than it actually was. Early Societies were found in both Canada and the U.S. and were often confused with Black Hand extortion operations. Black Handers were never a cohesive group; in fact, many Black Hand extortions were merely ad hoc and indifferent threats. Like the *padrone*, however, many Black Handers did become major mafia players.

In essence, the Societies founded at the beginning of the 1900s were structured organizations that followed the rituals, secret oaths, and initiations of today's *'ndrangheta* groups. Around a hard nucleus of leaders were regular members, *picciotti*. Regular donations were expected from members to allow a common fund to be accumulated; the fund was used for the furtherance of the Society and to support members who were in trouble with the law or otherwise unable to support themselves or their families.

One of the earliest recognized *'ndrangheta*-like Societies in the U.S. was found in rural Pennsylvania in 1906. It was built around a Calabrian immigrant named Rocco Racco, who hailed from the east coast of Southern Italy. Much ignored by organized-crime researchers, the story of the Honored Society in Pennsylvania in the early 1900s is an invaluable part of North America's criminal history. The case resulted in the first execution of a major mafia figure in America, and was the first time a mafia clan was penetrated by a law agency—the famous Pinkertons.[4]

The Society—whose full name would be the Honored Society of Calabria—headed by the aforementioned Rocco Racco was ensconced in an Italian community in the limestone quarry town of Hillsville, Pennsylvania, near the Ohio state line. The foundation of the group was extortion, practiced upon other Italian immigrants. The Racco group was secretive, not only the secrecy of organized crime groups but also that of many new and insulated immigrant colonies popping up across America. Seldom did any reports of mafia-like activities within the colony emerge; it was only when a conflict arose between Rocco Racco and a game warden that the details of the Society become public.

The early Italian immigrants to America were primarily rural people from the southern province of Calabria and the island of Sicily. They were in the habit of hunting and gathering their needs from nature. Self-sufficiency was one of the primary traits of the newcomers: fish from the sea, birds from the sky, animals from the forest. This was particularly true in areas of Italy where much of the land—the usable, arable land— was owned by wealthy landowners, and wages were poor. A wild boar taken down could provide food for a family for several meals. A brace of birds could provide foods ranging from roasts to soups. But what in Italy might be called sustenance shopping was in some parts of America called poaching.

Many of the Italian migrants in Pennsylvania worked in the quarries and mines, on the railway, or in mills. Their jobs were usually of the lowest rank, requiring physical strength and stamina. At the end of the 1800s Italians and other European immigrants flooded into the area looking for work, and by 1906 Hillsville's population of 1500 comprised an estimated 900 Italians. The area around the town was abundant with game, from rabbits to groundhogs to large flocks of birds in the sky. For the Italian immigrants, this presented not only an opportunity for sustenance hunting—wages at the bottom of the employment chain were minimal at best—but for recreation similar to the informal but convivial hunting parties back in their home towns. One of the prime complaints the non-immigrant citizens had about the Italian colonies, beyond their strange language, different cooking practices and ingredients, and remoteness, was their tendency to ignore game laws.

In response to the Italian hunting habits, several pieces of legislation were enacted. One required that non-residents—Italians, Poles, and other immigrants—buy a $10 license, a license that state residents wouldn't have to acquire until almost 10 years later. And, legislation decreed, non-residents who didn't have a license would be fined $25 if found in the fields or woods with a gun. Added to that were fines for various violations, including hunting on Sunday and having possession of "non-game birds"—songbirds, thrushes, and warblers, for example, which were considered delicacies in Italian cooking. The fine against a single unlicensed immigrant hunter could reach $60 or $70 for each apprehension. For people earning $1.65 a day, this was a significant financial blow.

The rules exacerbated tensions in the region. Crime had risen in the area, primarily the theft of livestock from farms. Local landowners were intimidated by Italian hunting parties on their property, or crossing nearby, armed with rifles and shotguns. A farmer who let an enforcement officer use his telephone to get assistance in arresting an Italian later found one of his cows shot dead, along with a warning note written in Italian. The farmers and landowners expressed terror, and posted guards at night.

In 1903 Seely Houk was appointed deputy game protector of Lawrence County, which included Hillsville. No salary was attached to the job—Houk would earn half of each fine he levied. By all accounts he was a big, tough man who was quick on the draw, and he quickly gained a reputation for being aggressive, even brutal, in protecting game laws and creating a salary for himself. You didn't have to be poaching or even carrying a gun. Houk would make the arrest, lay the charge, and ensure conviction and a fine. Predictably, there were threats on his life, most of them from Italian immigrants.

On April 24, 1906, Seely Houk was found dead in the Mahoning River. He'd died of shotgun blasts; his body had been weighted down with rocks and was discovered only when the spring runoff subsided. He'd been dead for three weeks.

Suspicion immediately fell on the Italian community—there had been several public threats to "kill the son-of-a-bitch"—and a few suspects were identified but later ruled out. Detectives from the Pinkerton Agency were brought in to unravel the case. An undercover agent was put into the Hillsville Italian community, posing as a laborer working in the rock quarries while living in a rooming house.

It was determined that several months before Seely Houk's body was found an Italian immigrant named Luigi Ritorto had borrowed a gun and dog from his employer, store owner Rocco Racco, and went hunting, unlicensed. Ritorto ran into Houk, who was out doing his rounds. As Ritorto fled, he heard a shot and kept going. The next day Rocco Racco found his dog dead of a gunshot wound at the scene. He swore revenge on Houk, and this was taken seriously; Racco, it was known, had founded a secret group of Italian immigrants known as "the Society" or the "Association." In the public's imagination it was known as the *Mano Nera*, the Black Hand.

During his 18 months undercover in Hillsville, the Pinkerton agent, known as Operative #89S, discovered the Society and its activities. He became, in fact, a senior member of Racco's Society. He learned that the Society—and remember, this was almost a hundred years ago, long before informants in Italy divulged essentially the same facts—used an oral examination for "petitioners," prospective members who wished to join; the agent recounted his own initiation. He found that the Society placed itself in the traditional mafia position: between the owners and workers, between the providers of goods and services and the client. The Society profited from both. It collected funds from members and used them to assist those down on their luck through injury, disease, or arrest. It also mediated disputes between Italian residents in the area. In the turf wars between the Society members in Hillsville and other, similar groups in surrounding towns, Rocco Racco had gained a reputation for violence as he led forays against his enemies.

Little is known about Rocco Racco's past, but some reports suggest that he came from Locride on the eastern coast of Italy, an area not far from San Luca, and that he was likely a *'ndrangheta* member before leaving Calabria. In America he formed his group with his closest relatives as part of his inner circle. In the tradition of the *'ndrangheta* he presented two faces to the outside world. One was that of a benevolent shopkeeper, heavily involved in religious activities in Hillsville and godfather to several children born in the Italian colony. The other was that of a violent man who made life-and-death decisions not only among the members of his Society but throughout the colony. Vice was his domain, particularly gambling and bootlegging. But extortion was the primary revenue stream.

In his book *The Hunter's Game*, Louis S. Warren describes the fate of one man who didn't pay extortion to Racco's Society: "Those who refused to make payments might face the ordeal of Nick Ciurelo. Having repeatedly refused to pay a $100 'initiation fee' into the Society, he endured a beating by dozens of Society men who then took turns spitting on him before they painted him head to toe with a broom dipped in a bucket of excrement."[5] Warren also notes that although several members of the colony paid weekly "dues" to the Society, they weren't actually members, never attending meetings or becoming involved in the Society's activities. "When protection from the Society could be acquired only by joining, men joined."

The beginning of the end of Racco's leadership came about as the result of a strike by Hillsville quarry workers. While the owners hired the local mafia—including Racco—to protect their property from vandalism and their workers from violence, two other senior Society leaders, Ferdinando Surace and Giuseppe Bagnato, sided with the striking workers. Accusing Racco of working for the wrong side—and later of sleeping with another Society member's wife—they arranged a trial, bringing *'ndrangheta* leaders to Hillsville from as far away as New York. On March 10, 1906, Racco was found guilty of adultery as accused and sentenced to death. Only by paying Surace and Bagnato hundreds of dollars was Racco allowed to live.

When Racco was condemned by the Society, Seely Houk had already been dead a week, although his weighted-down body was still below the surface of the Mahoning River. And so by the time his body was found and the investigation begun, Racco had essentially become isolated from his former colleagues. Pinkerton investigators penetrated the town with several undercover agents, including operative #89S. Society members told investigators that Racco was Houk's murderer, that he and his brother-in-law, Vincenzo Murdocca, had set up an ambush to kill the deputy game protector.

Racco was arrested and tried. Surace, who was once his rival for control of the Society and had since replaced him as temporary leader, testified that Racco had confessed to the slaying. Other Society members backed Surace up.

But Operative #89S, who had infiltrated Racco's Society to its very leadership, had doubts about his guilt. He'd never been able to tie Racco to the Houk murder, despite having insinuated himself into the deepest parts of the Italian colony, and told his superiors that another suspect had been ignored by state investigators.

On October 26, 1909, Rocco Racco, convicted of murder, was taken to the gallows. He was unflinching; for three minutes he stood with dignity as a priest blessed him and gave him the final rites of the Church. As Racco waited for the drop, he maintained his innocence. In broken English he said: "No guilty of murdering Selee Houk. I never saw no man killed. But I forgive everybody who was against me; the judge, jurymen, lawyers, witness and the pardon board. I die innocent and I'm happy because no murder is on my soul. I'm going to heaven."

Twelve minutes later he was dead, the first Italian gang boss to be executed in America. Clearly his allegiance to the Society that had turned on him was greater than his allegiance to the truth or to God. Fourteen years later it appeared that a mistake had been made in his case when a warrant was taken out for a "Jim Murdock"—who was actually Vincenzo Murdocca—who had been identified but never charged as a second shooter in the ambush.[6] Murdocca by then had vanished and was believed to have returned to Italy.

Whether Murdocca was being sought as the sole killer of Houk—in which case Rocco Racco may have been innocent—or was suspected of being an accomplice, was never determined.

Hillsville had become widely known as "Hellsville," and the probe into the Houk murder did little to slow the Society's activities. Giuseppe Bagnato, who'd participated in the investigation and prosecution of Racco, had an agenda of his own and effectively took over from Surace as leader of the Society. He or his followers would stand at the paymasters' wickets at companies employing Italians and force the workers to hand over a percentage of their wages—some paid as much as 50 percent. Pay office clerks and bank tellers often noted that some workers had cuts across their face or bruises from beatings. Some workers, it was noted, didn't get extorted, and it was clear they were Society men. Several honest workers simply disappeared—murdered, authorities believed, for not cooperating with the Society, or kidnapped and held until they produced their life savings. One man had accumulated $11,000 after several years of scrimping and saving. Bagnato had him kidnapped and tortured until he produced the cash. When United States Steel Corporation detectives working with Italian-speaking investigators from Pittsburgh flooded into the Hillsville area and began probing the Society's activities, Bagnato fled—with the $11,000—back to Calabria. Two detectives followed him but were unable to locate him overseas.

After Bagnato escaped and Racco was hanged, the Society's activities—at least publicly—waned. But the power of the early 'ndrangheta among laborers soon re-emerged, with new leaders appearing from both within the communities as well as in successive waves of new immigrants.

And public and media perception of the culture of the Italian colonies didn't improve much. In the breathy prose of the time, the local newspaper summarized the effects of the successful police investigations in Hillsville:

> Now that most of the bad men are in jail … the long suffering foreign residents of the village are talking and they reveal a great system of persecution and hold up practiced by the Black Hand. The superstitious Italian had no chance at all. [The extortions were paid] in order that spirits might be kept away from the house. When they refused or were slow in paying the most unearthly noises would be sounded … all sorts of mysterious lights would be flashed—the work of the angered spirits—and the terrorized and ignorant Italian was glad to pay to the bosses and be able to live in peace for another week....

* * *

In Canada, similar events were unfolding in Northern Ontario. The widespread migration of Italians, primarily from the Calabria region in the late 1800s, brought a hardworking workforce of mostly male immigrants to North America who sought to earn a living wage and, perhaps, save enough money to bring their families across the ocean. They took the lowest of the laborers' jobs. Brought to Canada and the U.S. under the *padrone* system, many were victimized before they arrived. Every step of their hard journey was profitable for someone: shipping companies, staff aboard the ships, the *padroni* who found them jobs and took a "crumb" of their wages while selling their sweat to pulp and paper, mining, and railway companies.

Across the rugged reaches of Northern Ontario tens of thousands of laborers took the most physically demanding jobs. They worked in rock quarries, for the railway, timber, and mining companies. It was a hard life that could break the spirit of the most obdurate man. Accidents, suicides from boredom or depression, and homesickness for their families and villages all conspired with endless hours of work and little recreation. The life of the immigrant was to work and to save and then to either return home with a nest egg or to bring family members to join him. Even getting a decent wage was a battle; other ethnic groups with the same aims and goals competed with the Italians, offering to work for a few pennies less.

And while most were honest, hardworking individuals, the stresses of being far from home at the mercy of a new country with often confusing social norms could lead to violence. A fight over a card game could lead to murder; grudges could lead to personal feuds. Many of the men charged with violent crimes across Ontario's north in the first three decades of the 1900s, archival files show, were perhaps not coincidentally the parents or grandparents of leading members of *'ndrangheta* families operating today in southern Ontario and Montreal.

With the immigrants came too the *'ndrangheta*. As in Hillsville, several men formed Societies; they either created their own based on the criminal tradition of the Honored Society back in Calabria or they were already members who moved to prey on the expatriate workforce. As the Italian colony grew, so too did the *'ndrangheta*. Many aspects of Italian immigrant life were influenced or controlled by the Society, from vice crimes and job opportunities to room and board and social relationships. Like the other Societies, extortion was the mainstay of the organization. Members were extorted into joining up and into paying regular dues—and, as in Hillsville, many dues-paying members were merely victims and never participated in criminal activities; they simply wanted to be left alone. But in a closed colony where outside police forces seldom penetrated, the Society was all things: the taxman, the enforcer, and the provider.

One of the earliest, if not the first, sects of the Italian Societies was formed in Fort Frances in the early 1900s. Originally considered a minor Black Hand gang, a comparison between its activities and those of what would later be recognized as the 'ndrangheta—the Honored Society—shows almost identical traits. When police investigated a wave of violence—arsons, bombings, and beatings—they were told of secret ceremonies where oaths were sworn and blood was spilled. They learned of a closed circle of men who crouched over a large knife and muttered a formulaic rhythm of arcane poetry and hugged and kissed each other. And the similarities with events in Pennsylvania and Minnesota at almost exactly the same time indicate the Society's international reach.

Francesco Tino[7] was a point man for the Honored Societies in Ontario. Of obscure origin, Tino came to Canada in the early 1900s—likely sometime between 1903 and 1905. He initially spent a few months in Montreal; a year later he turned up in Sault Ste. Marie, Ontario, and shortly later arrived in Fort Frances after fleeing Fort William, where he was wanted for the murder of another Italian migrant.[8] Tino was much feared by the Italian colonies he visited as he wandered from town to town looking for victims and trying to form Societies. His right-hand man, Francesco Muro, who arrived from Italy at around the same time as Tino, also spent some months in Montreal before the pair showed up in Fort Frances. They set about extorting Italians of all classes:

> *On or about December 7th, 1908, Louis Belluz, an Italian Baker, who has conducted a shop in Fort Frances since November last, received a letter written in red ink in the Italian language demanding the payment-over of a certain amount of money. ... According to the statement of Belluz the letter demands the sum*

of $100 and in the event of non-payment, his buildings were to be burned and himself burned to death. …

Tino told Aggie Gordon, the common-law wife of another Society member, that "[the letter] was to get $50.00 from the Baker … if he didn't pay he'd lose his neck" and that he "would take the Baker's head off" if he refused. In fact, Belluz did refuse to pay; he contacted the police and nothing happened to him. And for Tino and Muro it was a shot in the dark that failed; they simply moved on to the vast and increasing victim pool of migrants flooding into the area.

The primary means of extortion—as in Pennsylvania a few years later as well as in such Canadian cities as Toronto, Montreal, and Windsor—was to force victims into joining the "Society men," thereby ensuring they paid regular dues and remained under the control of the groups' leaders. And while most of t hose extorted into joining did so only as a means of protection, others took to their roles and emerged as criminal operators in their own right.

One of the earliest Society men to be debriefed by law enforcement in the Belluz case was Nicholas Bessanti—his first name was likely spelled "Nicola" with any number of spellings for the last—who lived with Aggie Gordon, "aged about thirty, and a half-breed with some education," in a freight shed at the foot of Portage Avenue. The details in his statement—likely taken in 1908 or 1909, decades before the inner workings of the Honored Society of Calabria, or the *'ndrangheta*, were revealed to Italian justice authorities—are telling.

In December 1908 there existed an Italian Secret Society in Fort Frances composed of 15 or 16 members. Frank Tino was leader, Frank Muro was 2nd in authority. I was forced to join the Society. The fee was $35.00 but I only paid $10.00. In joining the Society we took a solemn oath that we would obey our leader's orders; would rob, burn or kill as he directed; that we would protect one another from the hands of the law; to disobey these orders we would expect to be punished by death or otherwise as decided upon by the Society. The Society met every Saturday night in the west end of the freight shed and there they decided what to do to raise money.

In addition to Tino and Muro, Bessanti identified the Society members as "Pettrey, Mike, Frank Paoui, Dommick Murdoc, Joe Ross, Antonio Haenio, Carmine Domic, Salvestor Tino, Nick Salidine, and Frank Dusanti." (Few of the names seem to be correctly spelled—Murdoc was likely Martoccia, Murdocco, or Martocca, names that appeared on the manifests of ships arriving from Italy at the turn of the century. Joe Ross was likely Giuseppe Rossi; Dusante appears in court records as Disante.) A note by the interrogator reads: "We think that Tino has been forming these Secret Societies and exacting toll from the members as fees." At the time the statement was taken most members named by Bessanti were in custody for Society-related crimes, either in Duluth and Hibbing, Minnesota, or at Port Arthur, Fort William, or Fort Frances, Ontario.

Several of the men, including Tino, were charged in the extortion of Belluz the baker. In a July 1909 trial at Fort Frances, the court was told that the Society oath was sworn over "a huge knife two feet long ... and each one was sworn to do as he was told or suffer death by having his head cut off. ..." Tino put on no defense, but he did use a pipe hole in the jail to whisper blood-curdling threats against Aggie Gordon who was also in custody. There were also threats made against the policeman who arrested the Society members. Tino was convicted and sentenced to five years in prison. His father, Salvador Tino, was convicted and jailed for three years. Aggie Gordon got six months in custody. The fate of the remainder of the Society is unknown.

Black Hand extortions, which had been committed against Italian migrants for many years, continued unabated. While the Black Hand was thought of as a "mafia," most of the members were found to be individuals or small bands of criminals operating independently. The Fort Frances case, in which a victim came forward and an early *pentito* emerged, was one of the few times when the term "Society"— the *'ndrangheta* or Honored Society of Calabria—was recognized as a criminal organization with a hierarchy, rules, and a ceremony.

Throughout the early growth of Italian-based organized crime groups in North America, the hidden hand of the Honored Society was in evidence. For example, during the transition of early immigrant Italian gangs into the American Cosa Nostra families, there were signs that the balance of power was being influenced, the fear being that gangsters of Sicilian descent would dominate. Antonio Macri, the powerful 'ndrangheta boss of Siderno, made efforts to ensure that Calabrian criminals were fairly represented in LCN; so too did Calabrian-born Albert Anastasia and Frank Costello attempt to wield influence in the American mafia. Their influence, however, was largely unsuccessful; almost without exception it was Sicilian–Americans who rose to the "godfather" ranks of the American Cosa Nostra. Canada, which had received a predominantly Calabrian immigrant stream, fared better; criminal operations in several cities, notably Montreal, Toronto, and Hamilton, were led by Calabrian-born criminals, although in every case they answered to an American LCN family dominated by Sicilians.

So it was no surprise that in Canada the growth and power of 'ndrangheta was far more substantial than that of the Sicilian Mafia. Early indications of a modern "criminal Society" began emerging in the press and in police reports in the 1950s, 1960s, and 1970s in the wake of a series of gangland murders, bombings, extortions, and drug investigations. With the exception of some Sicilian heroin trafficking probes, the bulk of the crimes investigated were traced to Canadian 'ndrangheta groups with ties to either the American LCN or back to Calabria, notably the towns of Siderno and Plati.

* * *

For many years law-enforcement agencies targeted the so-called Siderno Group, a crime organization from the Locride area on Calabria's east coast. One of the tragedies of Siderno is that, while outside of Italy it is equated with powerful organized crime groups, its history shows a strong social movement for workers' rights. Siderno was also a source of labor who evinced a strong work ethic in both North America and Europe. Many of the most hardworking workers in North America in the late 1800s and early 1900s hailed from the much-maligned small town on the Ionian Sea. The trend continued through the 20th century into the 1950s.

It was during the wave of immigration of laborers in the 1950s that the current leaders of the Canadian 'ndrangheta clans became powerful. The clans are led by an amalgamation of aging *dons* who have been responsible for the bulk of organized-crime activities in the 1960s, 1970s, and 1980s.

It was in Canada that police in the 1970s seized a copy of the 'ndrangheta code; it was also in Canada that RCMP officer John Persichetti was initiated into the 'ndrangheta in 1985, a very rare occurrence that has been little reported. The entire ceremony, conducted in a highrise apartment in London, Ontario, was captured on videotape during an investigation dubbed Project Oaf. The targets of Project Oaf were Giovanni (John) and Saverio (Sam) Zangari, who planned to set up their own 'ndrina, or cell, and intended to "attach" themselves to the Rocco Zito[9] clan in Toronto. The capture near Toronto in June 2005 of Antonio Commisso, the head of the 'ndrangheta of Siderno who had successfully run from a mafia-association conviction in Italy, points how 'ndrangheta members are protected by the Toronto families.

With a strong network of crime cells, as well as being home to decendants of some of the most prominent 'ndrangheta figures, it's no surprise that Canadian 'ndranghetisti are well respected in the Calabrian underworld. During a six-year battle between two families in Calabria that claimed hundreds of lives in the 1980s, it was the Toronto-based Zito, a convicted killer and loan shark, who was reportedly part of a group of men, including Sicilian mafia bosses, who provided guidance in mediating the murderous dispute. And when Girolamo "Mommo" Piromalli, a powerful 'ndranghetista in Gioia Tauro, assumed the newly created and powerful rank of santista, he said the rank had been given to him directly by 'ndrangheta clan in Toronto. When, a powerful associate of the Montreal Mafia killed two Calabrian gangsters hiding out in Toronto, the assassin himself was killed by the 'ndrangheta, with no retaliation or complaint from the Sicilian-based Montreal group.

Throughout the world—particularly in Canada and in Australia where 'ndranghetisti are generally from Platì—the families of Calabria have emerged as major players in the underworld. Several reports say the 'ndrangheta has in fact eclipsed the Sicilian Mafia in several activities, notably drug trafficking.

One of the keys is the bloodthirsty mindset and drive for profits exemplified by the 'ndrangheta of Platì.

* * *

The turning point in the fortunes of the Platì mafia—and ultimately the entire 'ndrangheta—was brought about by the kidnapping trade in the 1970s. Prior to that time, the town was already notorious in many countries for its immigrants who became involved in the Italian underworld. In Canada, Rocco Perri (previously Perre) emerged as the "Canadian Al Capone" during Prohibition days. Several former Platì residents have turned up in the United States, some linked to La Cosa Nostra, with many operating as traditional Calabrian clans within the Italian communities, mostly on the East Coast. Australia too received a large number of emigrants from Platì, and today the ties between the 'ndrangheta of Australia and Platì remain strong. There are also groups of 'ndrangheta cells in South America, mostly in Brazil, that still swear allegiance to their *casa madre*, the "mother home" in Calabria.

Until the 1970s the primary activities of the 'ndrangheta of Platì were extortion, thefts, robberies, cattle rustling, and frauds committed against the government. Even outposts in North America and Australia were populated by serial extortionists, low-level drug traders, and operators of gaming houses. But in the 1970s kidnapping provided the most profitable income for the Platì 'ndrangheta. Teams of men went north to the financial centers of Italy and, working in conjunction with Platì-born criminal groups already in place, abducted wealthy victims. The most famous was 15-year-old John Paul Getty III—an heir of the multibillion-dollar Getty oil family—who was taken from Rome; he was bound and blindfolded and taken south to the Platì area. For five months he was held hostage, mostly because his family believed he might have staged his own kidnapping to get more money out of his tight-fisted grandfather. The kidnappers kept him on the move, hiding him in a series of huts and caves in the wilderness of the Aspromonte mountains. When the payment demands didn't yield prompt results, the kidnappers sat the boy on a block of wood and slashed an ear off with a razor. The ear, accompanied by a photograph of Getty, convinced the family to pay almost $3 million in ransom.

Getty may have been the most famous victim of the Platì kidnappers, but there were dozens of others, most of whom yielded massive ransoms.[10] In the nearby town of Bovalino there's a section known as "Paul Getty Town" because it was built almost entirely from kidnap ransoms.

The banknotes used to pay the kidnappers were tracked by police throughout the 1980s and led them to notorious Platì families in several European and North America cities as well as to members of other Italian criminal organizations. The funds were used to operate legitimate businesses, including supermarkets, export-import agencies, and restaurants. But by following the ransom notes' trail, police were also able to determine the national and international scope of the Platì drug networks. Operations were uncovered in northern Italy and Germany, Holland and France, North America, and Australia.

While the 'ndrangheta was able to enter the drug trade with its ransom revenue, it was also aided by events in Sicily, where both internal warfare and judicial pressures were being brought against the Sicilian Mafia. 'Ndrangheta members began showing up in heroin-trafficking investigations, where they were used as distributors by the Sicilian traffickers; the leaders of the groups were often overseas Sicilian *Mafiosi* who fled Sicily because of the warfare and increasingly successful investigations. In the U.S. and Canada, investigators noted that several Sicilian-based organizations included Calabrian criminals. Canada in particular, where the relationship between 'ndrangheta members and the Sicilians was strong, saw a sharp increase in heroin conspiracies with a Sicilian–Calabrian component.

In 1979 a meeting of 'ndranghetisti, including local as well as Canadian and American members, was held in Calabria to discuss the group's involvement in the heroin trade in conjunction with the Sicilian Mafia. The Canadian end of the network would involve members in the Toronto region. Several Calabrian mafia families would take part in the trade, each committing money, expertise, and overseas connections. Trafficking initiatives were undertaken with varying degrees of success. Still, significant profits were made, to be reinvested in both Canada and Italy, particularly in the local economies in Calabria.

Throughout the 1980s and 1990s the 'ndrangheta continued to grow, almost completely unnoticed in the U.S. where the American Cosa Nostra and Sicilian Mafia were almost constantly being probed. Conversely, in Canada, where the 'ndrangheta had long been the primary target of law enforcement, a wealth of information gathered during almost 40 years of wiretaps and surveillances was key to identifying groups, members, and criminal activities. The clans from the eastern coast of Calabria emerged as key operators in the heroin trade. Toronto was crucial to the intercontinental drug trade: a "barter" system was set up whereby cocaine from North America, where it was plentiful, was shipped to Europe, where it was scarce; in return the same organizations sent easily obtained heroin to North America. Investigators found 'ndrangheta members, Sicilian Mafia members, and Colombian cartel smugglers all working together in several Canadian and U.S. cities.

In one far-flung case, police in Toronto tied the heroin network directly to the kidnappings in Italy. When Vincenzo Restagno, a 'ndrangheta trafficker, arrived at Toronto's Pearson International Airport in early 1989 with $330,000 worth of Italian lira in a shoebox, he was questioned about the money and released. But before turning him loose the Combined Forces Special Enforcement Unit copied down the currency's serial numbers as well as the pages of Restagno's notebook. Restagno took the money to a travel agency and laundered it by having it wire-transferred to a Bank of America branch in New York City. A trace on the serial numbers showed it was part of a large ransom paid for a recent kidnapping in Italy. The notebook was also valuable to investigators; it contained names of dozens of key 'ndrangheta players in Europe, Canada, and the U.S. Restagno was later arrested in the U.S. and sent to prison.

A strong source of intelligence about the 'ndrangheta traffickers came from Vittorio Ierinò when he was in custody in Italy for kidnapping. Ierinò, who regularly traveled to Toronto where his son was being treated for cystic fibrosis, began cooperating with police and revealed the ties between the 'ndrangheta families in Canada and their counterpart in Calabria, particularly in the Locride area. Ierinò also gave valuable information about 'ndrangheta members and cells in the U.S., including linkages between families in several cities and the architects of the kidnapping trade. Then, mysteriously, he retracted his entire testimony, and several suspects in Canada were never charged.

Profits from heroin and cocaine trafficking strengthened the Calabrian crime groups' international reach and allowed them to branch out into vast criminal enterprises across the world. In the 20 years since the kidnap rackets began flowing money into the coffers of the 'ndrangheta families, the Calabrian clans have surpassed the Sicily Mafia in the international drug trade. A series of high-profile arrests of Sicilian *Mafiosi*, as well as the bloody extermination of members throughout Sicily and the resulting flood of *pentiti*, have all allowed the 'ndrangheta to become more powerful than was ever imagined.[11]

In 2004, denouncing the 'ndrangheta as "the most powerful and dangerous criminal organization in Italy because of its viciousness," the Italian interior minister announced the arrest of more than a hundred suspects after a lengthy probe.

'Ndrangheta clans have been found operating in Poland with local organized crime groups and the Russian Mafia, where they launder profits from Eastern and Central European drug trafficking, mostly through investment in restaurants and pizzerias. By forming liaisons with Russian organized-crime groups, they smuggle precious metals and firearms into Europe. Police in both countries have identified two specific Calabrian bosses who they believe were setting up a new drug pipeline to bring Turkish heroin to Europe.

The operations of the 'ndrangheta go beyond the merely criminal. Several covert investigations involving terrorist organizations—some of them still secret today—have 'ndrangheta links. In 1999, for example, Italian authorities in a joint investigation with the British secret service seized a boat off the Adriatic coast. Details of the still-secret and ongoing investigation are scarce, but the seizure was huge, involving firearms and military matériel being transported to the IRA via 'ndrangheta clans.

And in the early 2000s Italian magistrates Luigi Maffia and Roberto Pennisi commented on another link between terrorists and the 'ndrangheta: "People from the east coast, the Pesce clan of Rosarno, imported nerve gas from Croatia. They buried it in a secret location in the Gioia Tauro area." The magistrates reported that the nerve gas was imported in a scheme involving Eastern European organized crime. "It was a Russian gangster who provided the nerve gas to one of the people [we investigated]," the magistrates said. "We were investigating people for the international trade of weapons and we heard them say on the phone that they had the gas from the Russian but didn't know what to do with it. The other speaker said, 'Hide it somewhere. I'll let you know.'"

The gas was never recovered.

When Operation Decollo, a probe into drug trafficking in several countries, ended in January 2004, police found further involvement between 'ndrangheta and terrorists; the mafia was directly involved with paramilitary groups in Colombia and the ETA terror group in Spain. Those groups had traditionally focused their involvement in the drug trade on protection for traffickers. But, according to national anti-mafia prosecutor Pierluigi Vigna, that had changed: "Once, the terrorist groups financed themselves by protecting the drug traffickers," he said. "Now they directly participate in the trade operations of profits of those activities."

By 2005 the area around Locri on Calabria's east coast was deemed the narco-capital of Italy. Links were discovered between the eastern 'ndrangheta and Colombian, Turkish, German, Dutch, Belgium, and French criminal organizations. Two investigations—"Borsalino" and "Super Gordo"—yielded players in several countries, including Canada. Arrests in Calabria were made in Platì, Marina di Gioiosa, and San Luca, all key towns in the growth of the 'ndrangheta.

The sheer financial power of the 'ndrangheta emerged when officials in Belgium and Italy determined that the flow of profits was actually exceeding legitimate investments in some areas. One neighborhood in Brussels, for example, had been entirely bought up by drug-trafficking proceeds in the tens of millions of euro. Two clans—Arnone and Bellocco, of the Rosarno area, both linked to the San Luca families—were involved in an array of property purchases and laundered 28 million euro, mainly drug profits, in local real estate. The 'ndrangheta sold drugs worth more than $45 million a day in the Brussels district. Warrants were taken out for 47 suspects, most of them members of, or connected to, the 'ndrangheta families in Calabria.

In Germany, police found that 'ndrangheta members owned or controlled more than 300 pizzerias. And in Rome the clans owned millions of euros' worth of real estate, some of which a convent of nuns was managing; the same crime group was negotiating the purchase of an exclusive private school.

The gargantuan web of criminal investment and influence astounded many financial investigators. And at the root of the laundered billions was a seemingly impregnable small town in the shadow of the Aspromonte mountains.

★ ★ ★

In December 2001 Italian authorities, led by anti-mafia magistrate Nicolá Gratteri, began a stunning series of successes against the *'ndrangheta*—and their main target was the impenetrable stronghold of the Platì clans.

Gratteri, who travels with armored vehicles and a squad of armed bodyguards, had been frustrated at the seeming impossibility of attacking Platì, the heart of the Honored Society. His primary target was Giuseppe Barbaro, whose clan, the most powerful in Platì, was heavily involved in the international drug trade. Barbaro—nicknamed "the Vanished"—had been a fugitive from kidnapping and murder charges for 11 years.

Gratteri set about establishing a plan that would allow him to find out what was going on in Platì. Sending in police patrols was unfeasible; by the time the officers made their way up the winding road to the town the fugitives would be long gone. And so, working from a detailed map of Platì, Gratteri had remote cameras mounted at several strategic points around the town and focused on well-traveled streets, laneways, and entrances to houses. In this way he was able to monitor the residents' movements, documenting each person along with each house he or she visited and at what time of day. Often, over several years, they saw the wives or other relatives of wanted *'ndranghetisti* pass along the streets and laneways and disappear into seemingly empty houses.

Using the information from the remote cameras, the houses were raided. In one—where Barbaro's wife had visited—they found a warm cup of coffee but no one at home. In another, nothing at all, until one officer noticed that the kitchen tiles in both houses were the same and were smaller than most. The sink was removed and the officers drilled into the wall. They found a tunnel entrance operated by a hydraulic lift system. In the room under the kitchen were a mattress, a refrigerator, and a television set. Giuseppe Barbaro was found and taken into custody. His arrest was a victory for Gratteri, but there were more to come.

In July 2002, after working with military land surveyors, Gratteri called down another raid on Platì. More than a hundred paramilitary police were lowered into the tunnels under the town. They found a network of connecting passageways, some of them even big enough to accommodate trucks. The network ran parallel to the town's sewage system—and the work had been paid for by Platì council's infrastructure money for "public improvements." Rooms had been built and there were ventilation systems, televisions and video players, and beds and chesterfields. Various entryways were bolt-locked from the inside and operated by remote-control devices. Emergency exits ran out of the subterranean warren to the nearby river, into farmers' fields, or up into barns. Ominously, police found signs that, over the years, kidnap victims had likely been hidden in the tunnels and chained to rings in the walls while their families scrambled to gather ransom money.

More than a year later, in November 2003, Platì was almost back to its normal closed self when Gratteri struck again. In an impressive display of force, he sent hundreds of masked and heavily armed *carabinieri* officers into the village in the middle of the night. Trucks filled with raiding teams raced up the road to Platì and helicopters dropped officers into the center of the village. They effectively occupied Platì and began rounding up suspected *'ndrangheta* members and their associates. By the end of the day everyone in town had a relative among the 103 people in custody. The criminal infrastructure of Platì was destroyed; fugitive *'ndranghetisti* and former mayors were arrested, along with a dozen local councillors, and a prominent doctor.

"The structure of *'ndrangheta* in Platì is based on the family," Gratteri says. "As a criminal organization, the *'ndrangheta* of Platì is a completely closed circle. It controls the very breathing of the village; it's the nutrient for every child. And even those few who are not part of that world are terrified to speak out."

The people of Platì were stunned at what they called an invasion and occupation. "We are here like in shock," Maria Barbaro told her uncle in Australia during a wiretapped telephone call at 7:30 a.m. the following day. "We look like bin Laden in a war zone. ... You cannot understand what's going on; people look like dogs, like they've been hit by a curse. What are we to do?"

"Why?" her uncle said. "Is no one in charge of the organization?"

"No. They took with them yesterday ... two men." The impact seemed to overwhelm her. "You cannot imagine what they are doing. They broke doors, they're under houses."

Gratteri was pleased at the conversation. The most impenetrable stronghold of the 'ndrangheta had been penetrated. Plati's notorious reputation as the "new Corleone" had been shredded. That police had actually entered the town, taken it over, and walked in their dirty, heavy boots through the homes of some of Italy's most feared criminals constituted a major victory.

And it wasn't only the crime figures who felt the effect of Gratteri's Operation Marine. The fallout from the tunnel raids was crippling for Plati's politicians when it was learned that hundreds of thousands of dollars' worth of construction and other services had been provided to 'ndrangheta members and their families. The town council was found to be, if not a criminal organization itself, then a tool of the mafia. After the raids the entire council was fired and an outsider was brought in to run Plati.

Gratteri believes the Calabrian mafia could be done in quickly and relatively easily. He told the *Telegraph of London*: "I could take the 'ndrangheta apart like a plaything in three or four days. But I would have to be supported by the politicians and by laws which are proportional to the reality. I'm working in circumstances in which I arrest the same person a dozen times in a year. I believe in the iron fist."

Gratteri's forcefulness and determination in attacking the 'ndrangheta hasn't been without consequence; in June 2005, Italian military police in collaboration with the secret service recorded conversations between jailed 'ndrangheta boss Vincenzo Macrì and his son-in-law. Authorities overheard details of a plot to assassinate Gratteri. Acting on information from the recording, raiding parties seized plastique explosives linked to a detonator, rocket launchers, grenades and an automatic rifle. Several suspects were arrested.

Sicilian Mafia

Although the 'ndrangheta has arguably become the most active Italian-based crime group, the Sicilian Mafia has begun to resurge, particularly in the global narcotics trade. Reinventing itself after more than a decade of disarray, police crackdowns, and infighting, the Cosa Nostra has formed new partnerships—notably with the 'ndrangheta as well as other international criminal organizations—and draws much of its income from "outpost" families located throughout the world. In Europe, North America, the Caribbean, South America, South Africa and Eastern Europe, members of the Sicilian Mafia are re-emerging in crimes ranging from drug trafficking to money laundering, and from migrant smuggling to the trade in military weaponry.

While the 'ndrangheta has emerged in the forefront of criminal activities around the world, the Sicilian Mafia has made strong new moves into Canada and the United States, capitalizing on a weak criminal justice system in Canada and the successful attacks in America on La Cosa Nostra by law enforcement. Working from bases in Venezula and Brazil, the Siclian Mafia appears to be on its way to regaining its former status as the world's most powerful criminal organization. As well, because American law enforcement has been so successful in taking down several leaders of the LCN, police have monitored the movements of Sicilian heroin traffickers traveling from Sicily to the U.S. through Canada. The traffickers are believed to be tasked with re-building the drug pipelines from Europe into the U.S.

This ebb and flow of the Sicilian Mafia's powers has led to talk of the "new" Mafia and the "old" Mafia. In essence, there is only *the* Mafia. Changes are made, the leadership shifts, the external structure undergoes adjustment. But the core of the criminal organization is as it has ever been: changing and adapting, and always profit- and power-seeking.

* * *

Many legends surround the origin of the word "mafia." One holds that it's an acronym of a resistance slogan during the 1262 invasion of Sicily: *"Morte alla Francia Italia Anela!"* ("Death to the French Is Italy's Cry!").

This theory is easily disproved, since in 1262 there was no country known as Italy. Another belief has it that a Sicilian mother, whose daughter was raped and killed by a French soldier, cried: "Ma fia, my fia" or "my daughter, my daughter."

The first publication of the word "mafia" occurred in 1862 when Sicilian playwrights Giuseppe Rizzotto and Gaspare Mosca used it in their play *I Mafiusi della Vicaria*, or "The Mafia in the Vicarage." The story centered on the lives of reclusive members of a secret criminal society in Palermo's prisons. As with the "real" Mafia, the prison sect members had their own secret symbols, communicated with hand gestures for security, and had a structure of command.

In 1868 the word "mafia" was registered in the Sicilian dictionary of Traina. It was said to have been imported by Piedmontese bureaucrats and soldiers after the unification of Italy in 1861. According to Traina, the word had Tuscan roots, wherein *maffia*—with two *f*s—means poverty. A scholar of Sicilian popular culture, Giuseppe Pitré, denied the existence of Mafia as a sect or organization and said that *mafia* meant one's self-respect and sense of personal justice. Other scholars suggested the word was derived from a combination of the Arabic words *mihfal*, meaning an assembly, and *mahyas*, meaning bravado, defiance, and boastfulness. A man might be termed *mafioso* without being a criminal; he simply looks after his needs and the needs of his family, is ready to defend his rights from being wronged, and is prepared to act— violently and homicidally if necessary—to protect his dignity and self-respect. These definitions were well-received by Sicilian society, giving self-justification to any number of anti-social or criminal acts. In truth, these traits, even absent of criminal activity, are nonetheless anti-social concepts that refuse to bow before the laws of either church or state. That such men could come into conflict with the law—particularly if they're engaged in criminal activities—makes a strong underpinning for a cohesive mafia-like mindset.

Sicilians, who've seen their island invaded almost continuously for centuries, have nurtured a strong sense of personal worth, group loyalty, and family protection. Faced with invaders from several countries, it's only natural that any resistance will form around the most capable, the strongest, and the most violent. And if those people are already committed to an organization, the perceived strength is magnified.

Where government collects taxes but doesn't provide adequate law enforcement and judicial and social services, the downtrodden and slighted will turn to a mafia-like group for protection; this allows the *Mafiosi* to accumulate power, wealth, and respect.

And so, as invaders left Sicily, there remained behind a parallel informal "government" of unelected men who had all the power of the state and could force politicians to deal with them. They positioned themselves so that they could mediate disputes between, for example, landowners and workers; they could even bless a marriage or prevent it. Largely left to itself by the central government, Sicily and Southern Italy became a patchwork of fiefdoms, each ruled—sometimes benevolently, sometimes not—by men who were able to govern over the problems of daily life.

This was equally true in Sicily and in Calabria, where ordinary citizens were regarded merely as slave labor and so were exploited by landowners and the government. The ruling elites to the north were indifferent at best and racist at worst, leaving a power vacuum in the south that mafia were only too willing to fill.

* * *

Whatever the true roots of the Sicilian Mafia are, and whatever the origin of the name, the organization is the most cohesive and active of all the criminal groups in the world, with the possible exception of Chinese Triads. The Sicilian Mafia has endured oppression by governments and armies, survived incredibly bloody internecine warfare, and sullied the accusations of informants. In times of power and prosperity, the Sicilian Mafia has extended its reach around the world, at times influencing, if not controlling, international drug trafficking. And after periodic government crackdowns the Sicilian Mafia has always been able to quietly regroup and bide its time. It has never disappeared.[12]

The origin of this powerful organization is tightly linked to the effects of the land reform that followed the abrogation of feudalism in 1812.

Foreign governments—Arab, Norman, French, Spanish, Piedmontese—for centuries relied on local upper classes to manage public affairs, with power residing exclusively in a few noble families that were seen as predatory tax collectors with no sense of justice and moderation. Each family ruled over a large extension of land (*latifondo*) and maintained an army to protect the fields and police the peasants. It was, ironically, this original group of guardians that would form the Mafia organizations we see today. For as the invaders left and times of relative peace descended, the cadre-like mafias demanded that adherence to their power be greater than to any other body—greater than to the church, the state, or the family. The Mafia became a parallel structure in society, characterized by sworn oaths of loyalty and rituals.

In its early days in the 1800s and 1900s, the Sicilian Mafia was largely a rural phenomenon. The island was divided: on the one hand was a miserable peasant population working for slave wages, and on the other was a territorial nobility of absentee landlords reaping huge profits from their land while living in luxury far from the fields.

Between the two extremes was the Mafia. They offered justice and protection to the peasants while at the same time keeping the peasants under control for the landowners. This is what's called the "excellent Mafia position": inserting themselves and their power between opposing parties and benefiting from both sides.

The government was of no help: isolation, both geographical and in mindset, put many villages and towns far from the attention of the powers that ran Italy. To bring about order, the strongest and best-connected men in the towns and villages assumed the duties usually provided by government. Early Mafia *dons* often resembled peasants in appearance, wearing homespun clothes and living in modest houses. And with a well-balanced blend of personal strength and a willingness to exercise extreme violence, they accumulated power simply by being accessible to the community to help resolve difficulties between parties. Early *dons* were seldom paid with money, there being little to go around in the poverty-stricken villages. Instead, they were accorded respect, power, and perhaps the periodic gift of a goat.

The *dons* of the remote Sicilian provinces put on a public face of modesty. When Calogero Vizzini, the *don* of Villalba, a small town in western Sicily, was asked by a journalist if he could have his photograph taken, he said: "Me! In a photograph? I'm nobody, I'm just an ordinary citizen. ... People think I say little out of caution, but if I say little it's because I know little. I live in a small village."[13]

It was in the countryside that the Mafia thrived. By nurturing the respect and fear of the citizenry, Mafia clans were able to control the votes of towns and villages. Politicians found they couldn't get elected without the help of the old quiet *dons* who could deliver blocs of votes. People looked to the Mafiosi for guidance in complicated things like politics—they were uneducated and in any case had little time for ideas or events that couldn't advance their daily struggle to put food on the table.

Through indifference, neglect, and ignorance, then, the central government had essentially delivered much of the island of Sicily into the hands of the Mafia. And in return the Mafia was used by the government to fight communist and trade union groups, often with bloody result.

∗ ∗ ∗

While all the *dons* of the early rural Mafia knew each other, there was no cohesive, island-wide formal association. In the cities, particularly Palermo, many Mafia groups were closely associated. The cities were split up into zones of influence by various clans, and extortion was practiced in almost every part of the city. Gambling was organized; political corruption was rampant. Scandals were covered up, murders went uninvestigated, huge bribes—and effective threats—were made to police and politicians. And just as the rural Mafia had become the purveyors of votes, so too did the urban Mafia accumulate sufficient power in the cities' neighborhoods to influence the outcome of elections.

The secret societies were an open secret. Some were cartels of businessmen or builders, some were union-like associations of suppliers of goods or services. But clearly there were what today would be considered a mafia.

While some scholars have denied the existence of the Mafia as an organization, Mafia-like groups were reported as early as 1838 when, in a letter sent to the Minister of Justice, the General-Prosecutor of Trapani, Pietro Ulloa (1802–1879), wrote about the existence of a brotherhood with links to prominent people of the area. The tasks of these *unions* or *fraternities*—or "small Governments inside the Government," as Ulloa defined them—were control of cattle stealing; proposal of "mediation" between thieves and victims of thefts, and, more generally, between laborers and employees, workers and proprietors; settlement of quarrels; protection of affiliates; and corruption of government officials.

In Agrigento, another prosecutor, Alessandro Mirabile, was convinced that the Mafia was an organization with strict rules and regulations. He based his belief on a memorandum written by Bernardino Verro, who in his youth had been a member of the Mafia but had since become a socialist and later mayor of Corleone. (For his tenacious fight against the Mafia, Verro was assassinated in 1915.) And in an 1886 report written by Palermo's police chief, Giuseppe Alongi, the formal process of joining the Mafia was already known well:

> *The prospective member was vetted for a number of years, his activities and personal bearing, his family background, his "manliness" noted. When it was felt he was ready, he was approached and taken before a council of Mafiosi. He stands in front of a table on which is displayed the paper image of a saint. He offers his right hand to his two friends who draw enough blood from it to wet the effigy, on which he swears his oath: "I pledge my honor to be faithful to the Mafia, as the Mafia is faithful to me. As the saint and a few drops of my blood were burned, so will I give all my blood to the Mafia, when my ashes and my blood will return to their original condition." The initiate then burns the effigy with the flame of a candle. ... From that moment he is a member [who is] indissolubly tied to the association and he will be chosen to carry out the next killing ordered by the council.[14]*

An anonymous Mafioso, in a book titled **Men of Respect**, wrote in 1991 that the oath has only one meaning; the members being initiated "thought they were promising something, [but] this is not what the [oath] was about. I understood this, being older than them and knowing what was going on. It is a threat—the men sitting around the table aren't saying, 'Swear to be loyal for all time'; they are saying, 'If you are disloyal, you will die.'"

Over time many young men were initiated into Cosa Nostra. Some of them were the sons of older members who had an inside track but weren't automatically successful in joining, and some were active criminals who'd worked for a *cosca*—a family—as an associated member or who were seen to have the necessary "bones."

Once initiated, the new member has joined a *cosca*. In a cold-eyed view, ignoring the possibility of honor or fealty, he has in fact been enticed into joining a pyramid scheme; he's been given a "license" to operate a "criminal franchise." There's enormous pressure on him to "send up" a portion of his earnings to his higher-ups and to build a network of associates who'll earn money on his behalf. Eventually he may propose some of his associates as members of the organization, thereby increasing his own power and benefiting from their earnings, gaining a little more as he continues to pass his portion—and the new members' portions—up the pyramid. And as with any pyramid scheme, the goal of course is to rise to the top and receive small portions of everyone's earnings while doing little yourself except attending to administrative duties.

In a less cold-eyed view, the new member has joined a fraternity that allows him to commit criminal operations, usually in a specific field or territory. He gains, and keeps, the respect of the people around him, enjoys a social and cultural life, makes a reasonable living, and is ensconsed within a network of kinship that enables him to exercise his natural skills and anti-social beliefs.

* * *

Although early Mafia clans were often said at the time to be low-class bands of neighborhood criminals, their level of influence became apparent in the Notarbartolo Scandal in 1893. Emanuele Notarbartolo, the former mayor of Palermo and former director of the Bank of Sicily, moved to expel the crooked politicians, Mafiosi, and shady businessmen from the bank's board of directors. The response of the politicians–businessmen–Mafiosi axis was immediate; Notarbartolo was shot dead. And the subsequent investigation revealed the sheer top-to-bottom reach of the Mafia. The shooter, Giuseppe Fontana, had received the order to kill from Raffaele Palazzolo, a standing member of parliament who had feared Notarbartolo would discover wrong-doing at the bank that would incriminate him. At trial both men were acquitted, owing primarily to the influence of the highest politicians in Italy, including Francesco Crispi, the prime minister. For Sicilians—and most of Italy—who had watched the trial unfold, the acquittals were indications that the Mafia had reached into the highest political spheres in the country.

The government responded, not by going after corrupt politicians or businessmen, but by cracking down on the Mafia. Bosses went underground, and some left the country altogether. In fact, many historians believe that the Notarbartolo scandal led to the birth of the American Cosa Nostra. Don Vito Cascio Ferro, one of the most powerful Sicilian Mafia bosses, was among those who fled Italy; he went to America, where he became a voracious extortionist among the growing Italian communities there.

As it would always do in the future, when the pressure was on, the Mafia simply lay low and waited things out. It didn't take long. Within a few years the pressure eased up and then disappeared, enabling the Mafia to continue with its business activities.

In the 1920s and 1930s, dictator Benito Mussolini, enraged that parts of Italy were under the control of someone other than himself, sent his most powerful police official, Cesare Mori, to the island to destroy the Mafia. Mafiosi, those suspected to be such, and those seen as general enemies of the fascist government were rounded up wholesale. Some were hanged in public squares; others were lined up and shot in cold blood. Thousands were imprisoned. Mori, known as the Iron Prefect, was ruthless in his purge. But Mussolini's terror campaign targeted only the visible and lower-level members of Cosa Nostra; those in the gray area between Mafia and government were left unscathed, and after Mussolini's death re-emerged with increased powers.

Mafia members who weren't captured went underground or, again, many fled to the U.S., arriving in time to capitalize on Prohibition and to insert themselves into the growing underground of American organized crime.

The next event that affected Mafia power was World War II. With the death of Mussolini, the Allied victors unwittingly—although many believe it was with full awareness—returned the Mafia to full ranks and power. The Allies opened the prisons and freed "anti-Mussolini" prisoners, but of course, with the prospect of freedom at hand, everybody in prison was anti-Mussolini. And although many of the prisoners were crime bosses who'd been rounded up during the purge of the Iron Prefect, the Allies were unable—or unwilling—to differentiate between criminals and political prisoners and installed Mafiosi in positions of power, particularly in the rural areas. The modest Calogero Vizzini, of "I'm just an ordinary citizen" fame, became the mayor of Villalba. Giuseppe Genco Russo, another powerful Cosa Nostra figure, became mayor of Mussomeli. Michele Navarra, a doctor and the Mafia boss of Corleone, was given the lucrative job of collecting abandoned automobiles. American Cosa Nostra boss Vito Genovese, who'd been deported from the U.S., was made an interpreter; his position with the military was instrumental in assisting criminal activities on the island.

And so, as always, they and the other freed bosses created positions where they could accumulate the most power, respect, and money: in this case as go-betweens for citizens and the occupational army.

Not everyone was blind to the Mafia's elevation to power in post-war Sicily. Lord Rennel, the head of the Allied military government, wrote in a dispatch to London: "I fear that in their enthusiasm to remove the fascist administrative heads and municipal functionaries from the rural localities, my officials, in some cases because of ignorance of the local society, have chosen a certain number of Mafia heads … My difficulty resides at this point in the Sicilian code of honour, or *omertà*. …"

The power handed to the Mafia led to a change in the style of the Families. With massive profits to be made from post-war construction projects in the cities, many of the rural bosses moved to capitalize on new streams of income. Arrangements were made to provide labor from the countryside, and alliances between rural and urban clans—never completely formalized—were firmed up. The cities and neighborhoods were divided into zones of influence, both criminal and commercial. The supply of material needed in the restructuring of the cities was organized, with price fixing, false invoicing, and outright theft and diversion providing rivers of revenue.

The rebuilding of the cities, particularly Palermo, engendered huge profits and led to ongoing gang wars that left hundreds dead in the streets. The immense flow of money began turning the Mafia from a pseudo-benevolent organization into a hungry, ruthless, greed-driven organization. The shift from the countryside to the cities was a sea change for the Mafia. While every town or village still had a *don*, almost all of the most powerful *Mafiosi* now had interests in the cities. The old ways of honor—if they ever truly existed—began to die out. Respect was now measured in dollars; power was now measured in blood.

And the boost in power provided by the Allies, combined with the huge war chests accumulated by the criminal organizations, led directly to the Mafia's first coordinated assault on the drug markets of North America.

* * *

The backbone of the modern Cosa Nostra is narcotics. Fueled by the rich profits from Sicily's rebuilding and strengthened by the sheer number of Sicilian criminals who'd emigrated to the U.S. during the various crackdowns, the heroin trade became the Families' next initiative.

The initial move that brought the Sicilians into the trade was the infamous 1957 meeting at Palermo's Grand Hotel des Palmes. Members of the American Cosa Nostra, headed by Sicilian–American Cosa Nostra boss Joe Bonanno, met with prominent Sicilian Mafiosi. Several matters were discussed. For one, it was proposed that Cosa Nostra take control over the violence wracking Sicilian cities as clans battled for construction contracts; this could be achieved by forming a group similar to the American "Commission" to settle disputes. The *Cupola*—a board of control made up of members of all Families—was subsequently created in Sicily, and would act much as the American LCN Commission but with some made-in-Sicily changes.

But the primary reason for the four-day conclave was organizing the international heroin trade. The Sicilians would act as suppliers for the consumers—the Americans—and Bonanno Family members in Canada and Mexico would maintain the pipeline. Arrangements were made regarding its details—price, quantities, purity, and dispute resolution.

A second meeting was held a month later at the home of LCN member Joseph Barbara in upstate New York. Some of the same American mafia leaders who'd attended the Palermo meeting were in attendance, as well as a small number of Canadian LCN members. While some problems in New York City's underworld were discussed, the primary reason for the meeting was to talk about the disbursement of heroin once it had been routed through Canada and was across the U.S. border.[15]

When the transcontinental heroin pipeline was up and running, it resulted in some tension between Families in Sicily. Since the Families who were involved were able to pour their heroin profits into massive building and construction projects, those Families who'd stayed out of the trade found their power eroding in the face of huge profits accumulating to other Families. Wars broke out between the trafficking and non-trafficking groups, and in the end the former, unsurprisingly, won. With their increasing wealth they were able to corrupt politicians, control markets and prices, and influence the price of real estate in Palermo. In just a few generations the Sicilian Mafia had transformed itself from village or neighborhood organizations into major players on the international stage. They became the new aristocracy of Sicily.

Over time, with power and wealth came envy and greed. The key to controlling the Families—the ones in the drug trade as well as the ones who weren't—was to control the *Cupola*. And so it was that Salvatore "Toto" Riina, a peasant *Mafiosi* from the village of Corleone, set out to take it over. Through a series of maneuvers ranging from double-crossing his friends to assassinating hundreds of both friends and his enemies, Riina first wrested control of the governing council and then launched a campaign of terror against the state itself, targeting politicians, police, judges, and journalists.

His most spectacular crime was the 1992 murders of anti-Mafia magistrates Giovanni Falcone and Paolo Borsellino—in Falcone's case, a bombing that also claimed the lives of the magistrate's wife and bodyguards, and in Borsellino's case, an assassination in which five of his bodyguards also died. Both magistrates had been the most successful investigators of the Mafia ever. They had orchestrated the largest probes into the Mafia, had turned up the most key informants, and had worked on international cases in conjunction with law enforcement officials throughout the world. When they were killed they were trying to centralize anti-Mafia investigations across Italy.

In the strong public backlash against both the Mafia and the politicians who protected them, *pentiti*—informants—came forward in unprecedented numbers. Although Riina went into hiding, he still ran the Families. Then in 1993 he was arrested, tried, and sentenced to life in prison. His replacement, fellow Corleone Mafioso Bernardo Provenzano, hasn't been seen in more than 40 years but is believed to operate from a series of safe houses throughout Sicily.[16]

* * *

Internationally, the most prominent and active of the Sicilian Mafia groups are the ones from Agrigento, in western Sicily. While Toto Riina was doing battle with both enemies and friends for control of the *Cupola* and waging a war on the Italian State, the business of heroin trafficking continued unabated.

The largest and most well-known heroin trafficking case was the Pizza Connection, an international smuggling and money laundering operation that stretched from Sicily to Canada and into the U.S. The Pizza Connection moved tens, if not hundreds, of millions of dollars' worth of heroin in the early 1970s, much of it through a network of seemingly down-market pizzerias in the U.S. and Canada. Similar networks were set up in Western Europe.

The key players behind the Pizza pipeline were broadly called the Agrigento Mafia, an interrelated or interweaved series of clans from several villages and towns in the province of Agrigento. Several Mafia groups make up the Agrigento Mafia—from the town of Siculiana came the Caruana-Cuntreras; from Cattolica Eraclea came Gerlando Sciascia and Rizzuto Families. Together they had created a vast international conspiracy, mostly through intermarriages and a web of godfatherships.

The activities of the Agrigento Mafia have been documented in arrest and intelligence reports going back more than 50 years. Giovanni Mira, a Sicilian-born trafficker, was involved in the prolific Caneba heroin organization in the 1950s, shipping suitcases and anchovie cans filled with multi-kilo loads of heroin to Canadian traffickers, including Giuseppe Indelicato, a native of Siculiana who had set himself up in North America. The list of Agrigento traffickers seems endless: Nicola

Gentile, who was involved in trafficking with the notorious Leonardo Caruana in Europe; Gerlando Sciascia, who was sent to North America in the 1970s to coordinate the Sicily–New York heroin network; Alfonso Caruana and his brothers who flooded the UK with drugs in the 1980s, essentially creating a trafficking-money laundering network through several countries; the Cuntrera brothers, Pasquale, Gaspare, Paolo, and Liborio, who were the hub of the transit of cocaine out of Colombia through Venezuela in the 1980s and 1990s.

Of the clans in the Agrigento Mafia, the most powerful and intelligent was the Caruana-Cuntreras, known as the Siculiana group, although some members are from other Agrigento towns.

The Caruanas and Cuntreras were among several dozen Mafia clans that left Sicily in the 1960s, fanning out across the world and setting up an interlinked series of drug-trafficking cells. The Cuntreras briefly settled in Montreal before moving on to Venezuela. The Caruanas set up in the UK, Brazil, and Venezuela before settling in Canada. Working with other notorious trafficking groups—the Gambinos, formerly of Sicily, the Napoli brothers, the Inzerillos—all were perfectly positioned to take advantage of the shift in trafficking from the French and Corsican mobs of the 1950s and 1960s to the Sicilian organizations.

So notorious did the the Caruana-Cunteras become, that the FBI made a detailed intelligence report about them, "The Caruana/Cuntrera Sicilian Mafia Organization Racketeering Enterprise Investigation Intelligence Profile." It listed dozens of members of the clans and included their connections with several criminal organizations in a dozen countries. A family tree provided with the report showed the dizzying interrelationships between the Caruanas and the Cuntreras and surnames of global traffickers well-known to international drug investigators, including Napoli, Gambino, Vella, Cammaleri, Mongiovi, Cuffaro, Di Mora, Renda, and Rizzuto.

"If you drew an associative chart of the Caruana-Cuntrera Organization and drew one line to each business, family, or criminal contact, you'd have the names of literally hundreds of men in the narcotics trade," a U.S. federal agent said. "And if you then did an associative chart of each of those, you'd have lines drawn to essentially every major city in every country in the world."

The key to the success of the Caruana-Cunteras is best said in the words of Alfonso Caruana himself: "If you shoot, you make enemies; if you share, you make friends."

But that isn't to say there's no violence connected to the Siculiana Family. Several family members and associates were killed during the treachery of Toto Riina. And many enemies of the Siculiana Family were killed during retaliations and infighting in Sicily, Europe, and Canada. The unsolved 1981 assassination of Giuseppe Settecase, the old-style boss of Agrigento, is believed to have been carried out by gunmen from Siculiana in a bid to take control of the Sicily to Canada heroin trade. The Siculiana Family, led by the Caruana-Cuntreras, worked through the Rizzuto crime family of Montreal in the 1970s to eliminate the Cotroni-Violi family, an outpost of the Bonannos in New York. The Cotroni-Violis—particularly the stubborn Paolo Violi—weren't amenable to allowing the Pizza Connection drugs to pass through Montreal. After lengthy negotiations involving international Mafia leaders, the Siculiana Family resorted to violence, leaving Violi dead in 1978.

The Siculiana Mafia has suffered setbacks as well as successes. Gerlando Sciascia, a key player in the Agrigento–Montreal–New York City axis was murdered; Joe LoPresti, another key operator for the Agrigento Mafia, was also slain. In 1992 the Cuntrera brothers were extradited from their "safe" haven in Venezuela to Sicily where they were slapped into prison; in 1998 Alfonso Caruana and his two brothers, Gerlando and Pasquale, were arrested on narcotics charges in Toronto and later convicted and jailed.

And as the overall Mafia constantly changes and adapts, the Agrigento Families too continue to operate vast intercontinental drug networks, primarily in cocaine. Liaisons are in place with cooperative crime groups in Colombia, Mexico, the U.S., Europe, and even into Eastern Europe. While the Caruana brothers in Canada have all been released from jail—kingpin Alfonso Caruana has reached his parole date but is being held pending extradition to Italy—younger members of the Siculiana Family continue to exercise considerable power in several Canadian cities as well as internationally. They have able advisors woven throughout their families and are able to receive guidance as they continue the family tradition.

The most prominent Mafia clan in Canada is the Rizzuto Family, nominally headed by the elderly Nicoló Rizzuto, a life-long drug trafficker with global connections. Semi-retired, Nick Rizzuto is among the most respected leaders of Sicilian crime families in North America. His power—now passed on to his son, Vito—is rooted in the heady days of the 1970s when the Pizza Connection was being set up. Rizzuto was the pointman for the Sicilian heroin traffickers who were blocked by Paolo Violi in their efforts to use Montreal as a conduit for drugs into the U.S. and the repatriation of drug profits through the Canadian banking system. The elimination of Paolo Violi by members of the Siculiana-Rizzuto clans effectively opened the gateway to the American drug market, yielding hundreds of millions of dollars in profits for the Agrigento Mafia.

As Nick Rizzuto grew older and entered semi-retirement, his son Vito took the reins of power. Variously described as "the Canadian John Gotti" because of his classic Italian looks, sleek clothing and his soft-spoken style, Vito Rizzuto is the epitome of the modern global gangster. He speaks several languages and is comfortable in most countries of the world. Until his arrest in 2004, on a request for extradition filed by American authorities who want to extradite him to New York to face murder-related charges, he lived in a mansion on Montreal's "mafia row," an exclusive enclave where prominent members of the Siculiana and Agrigento Mafiosi have homes.

Vito Rizzuto's incarceration pending extradition has led to an unstable situation in the Canadian underworld. Several cases of arson and violence—including the machine-gunning of a Toronto restaurant in an attempt to murder a Sicilian drug trafficker moving into the area—are believed to be related to a lack of leadership among the Sicilian-Canadian clans.

The drug and money pipelines of the Agrigento Mafia are well maintained. In Venezuela, where Nick Rizzuto served a lengthy sentence for possession of cocaine, remnants of the Caruana-Cuntrera Family continue to send massive cocaine shipments into Canada and the U.S. Several shipments, numbering in the hundreds and thousands of kilos, have been forwarded on to Europe. The money launderers of the Agrigento Mafia—most specifically the Siculiana portion of the group—have deeply penetrated the Canadian banking and financial fields and continually repatriate drug profits to offshore havens.

In the United States, relatives and associates of the Caruanas, Cuntreras, and Rizzutos are thoroughly enmeshed in La Cosa Nostra Families, operating essentially as a separate organization within LCN.

La Cosa Nostra

The Italians in America didn't invent American organized crime. Organized crime was in America long before the first Italian immigrant. It's as old as America itself. Slave traders, pirates, extortionists, horse thieves, con men, pimps and prostitutes, and Wild West bank robbers and cattle rustlers all have a place in the criminal history of the U.S. The roots of the historic criminal gangs in America are the same as those of modern groups: supply of services, supply of goods, and outlaw mentality. Commerce brought crime, whether it was pirates plying their trade against transportation companies off the coasts of America or land frauds and the corruption of public officials.

It was in the cities of the East, as urban centers developed, that criminal initiatives became organized. As immigrants arrived in America from disparate countries of the world, they often ghettoized and kept to themselves, both replicating their compact and frequently isolated towns and communities at home and banding together for comfort and protection in places where customs and language were unfamiliar and impenetrable. And among the immigrants, whether from Ireland or England or the cities of Europe, came a small number of criminals. They were often natural leaders who could surround themselves with associates; hence the creation of gangs. Some emerged as community arbiters, arranging jobs and loans, settling disputes, and governing the supply of goods, from liquor and prostitutes to laborers and votes. They were accepted as leaders simply because they took initiative and were able to enforce their demands. An immigrant with few belongings and unable to speak rudimentary English had no hope of applying for a loan to start a business or renting an apartment to raise his family in. In each community a local leader would intercede on his behalf, and in return the migrant had to give him his loyalty and, as the communities developed, his vote in local politics. These votes gave the leader a tradable commodity with which to extend his power into the wider society, and thus were crucial to the spread of organized crime.

In the late 1800s Irish gangs came together. At first they stuck to their home turf, operating in parts of neighborhoods where they practiced extortion and supplied vice-related goods and services. Next came the Jewish gangsters who, as the Irish moved up and out, made themselves a place at the bottom of the American ladder.

But while the Irish and Jewish criminals gained some notoriety, it was the word "mafia" that captured the American imagination.

By the late 1880s, New Orleans boasted one of the earliest Italian colonies. The Louisiana climate was familiar to the Southern Italians who flocked to America; they were reminded of the towns and villages of Calabria and Sicily. And criminals who'd fled the crackdowns on organized crime in Italy fit in easily among the honest immigrants. Two prominent groups evolved in New Orleans—the Provenzanos and the Matrangas. These family-based organizations were at war with each other almost from the beginning. The resulting violence led to a series of vendetta murders, and that led to publicity. And publicity led in turn to a wave of anti-Italian sentiment that demonized the entire community. The word "mafia" was heard aloud on street corners and read in newspaper headlines. There was talk of secret blood-oath societies and the activities of an "infernal order" at work in the colony.

There had been some history of mafia-like activities in New Orleans. In July 1881, David Hennessy, the young and popular police chief of the city, had arrested one of the most notorious Sicilian bandits in the world, Giuseppe Esposito. Esposito had been involved in the 1876 kidnapping of John F. Rose, an Englishman abducted while sightseeing in the Sicilian countryside. To encourage Rose's family to pay a ransom, Esposito sent them one of his ears; then he sent the other one, along with an offer to send Rose's nose next. The family paid up and Rose was released. But the savage details of the incident sparked an uproar in England. The Sicilian authorities cracked down on banditry and organized a massive manhunt to capture Esposito. He was picked up by authorities in Sicily, but escaped. And in 1879, after landing by ship in New York City, he turned up in New Orleans where he married and raised a family. An informant in the Italian colony tipped off police and Chief Hennessy arrested the fugitive. Esposito was deported to Italy and sentenced to life in prison. The informant was shot dead on a New Orleans street.

Hennessy's reputation as a law-and-order crime buster grew in the wake of his successful capture of a fugitive wanted on international warrants. As the battle between the Provenzanos and Matrangas turned into a campaign of murder and intimidation for control of the busy docks, the city looked to Hennessy for leadership. He swiftly identified the main players and took six members of the Provenzano group into custody on various charges. However, all were eventually found not guilty.

Even with the feud between the two clans temporarily settled, crime continued in the Italian colony. Dark tales appeared in the media about the existence of a mafia and other secret societies. Hennessy kept up his pressure on the gangs—his methods were less than civilized and many heads were broken during his crackdown—but his campaign came to an abrupt end on October 15, 1890. Just before midnight he was walking near his home when he was ambushed by gunmen. Mortally wounded, as he was dying he was asked who'd shot him. "The dagos," he reportedly said, using a common slang for Italians and other Mediterranean people.

The assassination of a popular young police chief who was famous for battling the mafia sparked outrage across New Orleans. With news-papers feeding anti-Italian sentiment, a grand jury was convened and it brought indictments against 19 Italians, most of them for murder. On February 16, 1891, four months after the Hennessy slaying, nine Italians were brought to trial. Most of the accused had dozens of witnesses who provided alibis for them at the time of the killing; the majority of these, however, were discredited on cross-examination. Six of the accused were found not guilty and the jury couldn't settle on a verdict for the other three. Inside the courtroom the spectators went wild with disbelief; the jury needed a heavily armed escort to leave the building.

This time the newspapers went after the jury and the judicial system, even though information was appearing that the Hennessy murder had more to do with political corruption in New Orleans than with his campaign against the mafia. It was also clear that some of the accused—prominent mafia figures—had made attempts to bribe and intimidate the jury. But for the residents of the city it didn't matter: the Italians were mafia and the mafia was evil and un-American. Their admired police chief had been shot down, and in typical "Italian" style, it was said: in ambush, from behind, after dark. The day after the trial thousands of citizens, led by a crusading newspaper editor and other pillars of society, descended on Parish Prison where the Italians were still being held for their own safety. The prison guards opened the doors to the cells and told the Italians to do their best to defend themselves. Then the guards stepped back and the mob flooded in. One by one the Italians were beaten or shot to death; two were hanged from lampposts. Among the 11 who were killed were four Italian prisoners who had nothing whatsoever to do with the Hennessy case.

* * *

Throughout the rest of the century and into the 1900s the Black Hand became synonymous with the Mafia in North America. Throughout the U.S. and Canada, Italian businessmen received extortion letters signed *Mano Nera*—the Black Hand. Letters decorated with sinister drawings of bullets, nooses, and threats demanded payment of money in exchange for peace and quiet. There were beatings and bombings connected to the extortions. While never a cohesive criminal group, the Black Hand took on the proportions of a major far-reaching organization. Mafiosi and other organized crime figures were involved in many of the incidents, and many later became major underworld figures. But the activities of the Black Hand were freelance operations, often carried out in an ad hoc fashion.

A side industry was the recruitment of new members into "associations"—thinly disguised mafia groups usually made up of immigrants from Sicily, Calabria, and Naples. In the Italian colonies of America and Canada, crime groups were discovered extorting Italian businessmen into joining their "Societies" or "Families." In return for making a lump-sum payment and paying annual "dues," victims would be protected from crime. New members would also be allowed to commit their own extortions and to bring new members into the group.

All these events were forerunners to the birth in 1920 of the American mafia, La Cosa Nostra, precipitated by the passing of the Volstead Act that brought about Prohibition. Positioning itself in the traditional role of illicit-goods supplier, LCN grew powerful on the profits made in the bootlegging industry. What had been a loosely knit underworld made up of Italians, Jews, and Irish criminals found a common source for profits: booze. And with the profits came struggles both inside the Italian contingent and with the Jewish and Irish immigrants. With almost-instant millionaires protecting their operations, widespread corruption broke out in several American cities as politicians and police were paid to look the other way. The new entrepreneurial criminals were welcomed by a thirsty public; many mobsters, like Al Capone in Chicago, became folk heroes, and for the first time the criminals had the general public on their side.

In the early 1930s a gang war broke out in New York City between two old-world mafia bosses—so-called Mustache Petes. On one side was Joe "The Boss" Masseria; on the other was his archrival Salvatore Maranzano. The first part of the war ended when Masseria was shot dead at a Coney Island eatery; Maranzano named himself "boss of all bosses" and set up the infrastructure of LCN that survives today. Territorial lines were drawn and a hierarchy of bosses, lieutenants, and soldiers was formulated. The center of power in the underworld would be New York City and the ultimate leader would be Maranzano.

For Salvatore "Lucky" Luciano, a powerful and charismatic Italian racketeer who had many Jewish and Irish colleagues, Maranzano's plan was a sound one—except, that is, for the "boss of all bosses" part and the subjugation of non-Italians. And so Luciano, who'd killed Masseria for Maranzano, set about planning Maranzano's murder. With the Mustache Petes out of the way, Luciano quickly consolidated the old men's followers. He set up a commission-like group of LCN leaders of major American cities consisting of himself, Vincent Mangano, Joe Bonanno, Joe Profaci, Al Capone, and Frank Milano, the boss of Cleveland. The "commission" would arbitrate disputes, settle differences, and assign territory. Jews and Irish members were welcomed as profit-making associates, but the core of La Cosa Nostra—"this thing of ours"—would be solidly Italian, and over time primarily Sicilian.

Based on the swearing-in ceremonies of Italian mafia groups, LCN members underwent an initiation process that swore them to silence about the groups and their operations and bound them to one another as brothers. Throughout the Prohibition era the groups—now called "Families"—made millions of dollars in the bootlegging trade. After Prohibition was repealed, LCN Families had huge war chests and they branched out into many illegitimate and legitimate fields, ranging from gambling, drug trafficking, and labor racketeering to food services, waste management, and construction.

Few outsiders had much idea about what constituted the American "mafia," although the public was well aware that there was a criminal organization that allegedly had national reach. When mobster Joe Valachi turned informant and testified in 1962 before a Senate Investigations subcommittee, he detailed the membership of several American crime families, as well as their activities. There was a flurry of attention from politicians, police, and the media, but LCN simply retreated from high-profile activities until the heat passed.

LCN families are essentially regional. Some have national reach—mostly into Florida and Las Vegas—and some whose operations stretched into Canada or into Mexico could even be considered international. But on the global stage they have never become powerful and are the weakest of the Italian-based organized crime groups. Even in the global drug trade, LCN Families are merely recipients of drugs, not direct importers or financiers. Their assistance, when needed to facilitate Sicilian Mafia drug shipments, is usually provided without much more than finacial negotiations.

Since at least the 1950s the Bonanno Family had an outpost in Montreal through the Cotroni and later the Cotroni-Violi organization; the Stefano Magaddino Family of Buffalo had their outposts in Toronto, Hamilton, Niagara Falls, and down the Niagara Peninsula. The Zerilli Family of Detroit controlled Windsor. These were typical north–south lines of loyalty. Other American families—including the Russell Buffalino family of Pittson, Pennsylvania—had interests in Toronto, as did various crews from northern New York State and parts of Michigan. LCN figures active as far away as California and Las Vegas had financial interests in illegal gambling operations that sucked gambling money from southern Ontario. The encroachment of Montreal LCN-related figures into Toronto was always a point of contention between Joe Bonanno and Stefano Magaddino, his cousin.

The American LCN had Canadian connections with several criminal organizations, primarily to the Luppino and Papalia groups in Hamilton; the Zito group in Toronto; and the Cotroni-Violi organization of Montreal.[17] Representation of the Buffalo LCN—the Joe Todaro Family took over after the death of Stefano Magaddino—alternated between Paul Volpe and John Papalia. Both men were reported to be soldiers in the Buffalo LCN. Within Canada they were considered, in the media and in public imagination, to be *capos*, although in reality they were likely low-ranking soldiers. Both were later murdered in gangland fashion.

Coordinated attacks on America's La Cosa Nostra in the 1980s led one United States Attorney in Massachusetts to dub the decade "the golden age of law enforcement." By the mid-1980s there were more than 3,500 convictions of organized crime figures and associates, with $15 million in fines levied and $387 million in assets, drugs, and other contraband seized. Across America special organized crime task forces were formed; throughout a network of 26 cities these units, often working with anti-drug task forces, besieged LCN operations. The number of FBI agents mandated to fight organized crime was increased by 20 percent, and U.S. Attorneys began using the Racketeer Influenced and Corrupt Organizations Act—RICO—against criminal organizations. Under RICO, offenders found guilty received sentences of up to 20 years and $25,000 fines. RICO allowed prosecutors to pull diverse crimes together into a single case to show a pattern of racketeering enterprises. Funding was increased for wiretapping and room probe operations; this led to an increase in informants who essentially convicted themselves through their own conversations.

But as U.S. authorities were finally getting a firm hold on LCN activities, off-stage events were coming together to alter the face of American organized crime. A series of meetings, rooted in decisions made among Bonanno Family members and Sicilian Mafiosi in 1957 in Palermo, were under way to create a drug pipeline that would supply the U.S. drug marketplace with unheard-of quantities of heroin. In Trapani,

Agrigento, and Palermo provinces, and in Toronto and Montreal, conspiracies and murders were being conducted that would smooth the way for Sicilian heroin traffickers to use Canada as a gateway to the U.S.

At the time, these mysterious meetings and the murders in Sicily, Montreal, and New York City were seen as isolated events. In New York, the 1976 murder of Peter Licata and the 1979 murder of Carmine Galante, both prominent Bonanno Family bosses, were considered local incidents; similarly, the 1978 murder of Montreal gangster Paolo Violi was viewed as a local matter. In both cities new players anchored themselves—Sicilian Mafioso Salvatore Catalano on Licata's turf in New York, the Rizzuto Family in Montreal. And a series of meetings were held along College Street, in Toronto's Little Italy, and at Windsor, on the Canadian side of the border opposite Detroit, in which long-time and low-key Sicilian drug traffickers meticulously laid out what would become known as the Pizza Connection scheme. The Sicilians rapidly consolidated important transit routes into the U.S.—at Montreal, the Niagara Peninsula via Toronto, and at Windsor–Detroit—and on both sides of the border set up a seemingly disparate chain of pizza shops. But all had one factor in common: Sicilian ownership.

In America the FBI wiretaps on LCN targets were hearing rumbles about the new network. Its members were referred to as "Zips" because of their fast-speaking Sicilian dialect; there was bitterness and threats against them. Surveillance teams also noted new faces in old LCN hangouts—the killers of Galante and Violi, for example, were Sicilians who would later emerge as prime players in the Pizza Connection. In 1980, as the connection was running full tilt, police monitored the wedding reception of Giuseppe Bono, a leader in the organization, and noted that those present were almost exclusively Sicilians and almost exclusively drug traffickers. Among the guests was Canada's Vito Rizzuto, whose Family had organized the murder of Paolo Violi and several Montreal Sicilian members.

As the Pizza investigation continued, massive exports of cash from of Canada and the U.S. were recorded as the Pizza players repatriated their profits to Europe and the Caribbean. Heroin purchases were made throughout the investigation, with each buy leading to another portion of the network that stretched through big cities and small towns as far away as the American Midwest.

Then, in April 1984, almost 10 years after the Pizza pipeline was first planned, the FBI raided dozens of homes and businesses and rounded up key suspects. Mafia boss Gaetano Badalamenti, who had relatives in Detroit and Windsor and who'd supplied some of the heroin to the American distributors, was extradited from Spain to the U.S. to stand trial as the lead accused. He was convicted and sentenced to life in prison, where he died in 2004. Several other accused either vanished or were found murdered, the Sicilian organizers having prevented informants from jeopardizing the rest of the network in both the U.S. and in Canada.

For the American LCN, the incursion of the Sicilian Mafia or their traditional turf was difficult to live down. While other New York families were on the edges of the heroin scheme, it was the Bonanno Family that effectively became an outpost for a foreign criminal organization, a status that continues to this day. The Canadian Family—the Rizzutos— is still represented in American government criminal organizational charts as an outpost of the Bonannos, but in reality it's the Rizzutos who oversee the Sicilian Mafia's interests in the American drug marketplace.

* * *

The 1980s and 1990s were productive and largely successful for the FBI. After the dismemberment of the Pizza Connection, even though the primary targets had been Sicilian Mafiosi, the list of falling LCN criminals went on. Philadelphia Family boss John Stanfa and other high-ranking members of that area's LCN Family were convicted on RICO charges. The following year it was the Genovese Family's turn, with indictments coming down against the acting boss, the acting underboss, the *consigliere*, and 16 other members and associates of the Family. GAMTAX, a long-term probe into the Detroit LCN, led to the arrests on RICO charges of 17 members and associates, virtually eliminating the entire structure.

Then on March 6, 1996, the FBI initiated Operation Button Down targeting the American Cosa Nostra—which it described as the number-one criminal threat in the U.S. The modus operandi of Button Down was to organize and execute a coordinated attack on the primary LCN families that had been identified in more than 20 cities. Several had been hard hit prior to 1996 and were believed to be in the stages of rebuilding. The five-year Button Down plan was under the umbrella of the Organized Crime Program Plan (OCPP), which was broadly mandated to go after Italian, Asian, African, and Eurasian groups, including those from Russia, Ukraine, and Poland.

By the end of the first year, Button Down officers had indicted and/or convicted a total of 4 bosses, 3 underbosses, 3 *consigliere*, 46 *capos*, 48 soldiers, and 331 associates and seized more than $116 million. And by December 1998 another 53 LCN members and associates were indicted or convicted in labor racketeering cases, including indictments against the Gambino and Genovese Families. In total, 3 bosses, 1 underboss, 1 *consigliere*, 20 *capos*, 26 soldiers, and 270 associates were arrested.

The Button Down office was involved in cases involving LCN activities across America, including Las Vegas, Buffalo, New York, Youngstown, and Pittsburgh. In all, almost 1,000 LCN members and their associates were charged. According to the FBI, the effect of Button Down is in the numbers: active Families in the U.S. were reduced from a whopping 24 to nine.

But while the successes of the 1990s were solid, their downside was the rise of non-LCN groups in several areas of criminal activity, primarily the emergence of Albanian organized crime in the heroin industry in New York City. Other areas saw a noticeable encroachment on the edges of other Families' operations, particularly in ethnic gaming operations.

But if the 1990s were difficult for America's Cosa Nostra, what was to come in the new millennium was far worse; 2004 and 2005 would become known as the Years of the Rat. And, some said, LCN might never recover.

* * *

The focused attacks on American LCN groups, no matter how successful, could simply be deemed the cost of business in the underworld if it wasn't for the harsh sentencing and asset seizure. Convictions under U.S. anti-organized crime laws could, after all, represent death sentences for most of the aging *capos* and underbosses rounded up on conspiracy charges.

In addition, a well-functioning witness protection program helped keep informants secure and willing to talk; funding was sufficient for the attendant translators, transcribers, infrastructure; and technical resources that were needed were provided.

In Canada, however, where focused investigations of major international Mafia cases have been successful, the second phase—sentencing—and the third phase—parole—effectively undo all the work at the front end. Long and expensive investigations, which are usually cut short by crises when funding runs out, seem to hit a judicial wall when they get to court. In criminal cases, pleas are bargained to reduce charges and limit prosecutions of co-defendants. Asset seizures are negotiated in the manner of a Turkish bazaar, with the government settling for pennies on the dollar. Sentencing is extremely light in comparison to the U.S. and, because in Canada drug trafficking is viewed as a non-violent crime, some of the world's most notorious narcotics violators are eligible for parole at the earliest date.[18]

The difference between the two jurisdictions, in short, is the difference between playing softball and playing hardball.

Joe Massino was long hailed as "The Last Don" and the last of a generation of stand-up guys who followed the old ways. The head of the Bonanno Family—which he insisted be called "The Massino Family"—he had come up the traditional way, operating as a killer, hijacker, and strong arm for the Family. He rose to *capo* under Carmine Galante; and when Galante was murdered in 1979 it sparked a vicious internecine war that split the Family in half. After several murders—three of them at the same time in 1981, committed by Massino himself and members of the Canadian Sicilian Mafia—Philip Rastelli, whom Massino supported, won leadership. Under Rastelli the Bonannos prospered, growing rich on millions of dollars of "crumbs" that spilled out of the Sicilian Mafia-run Pizza Connection, as well as labor racketeering, gambling, and extortion.

The Bonanno Family had had a series of hard knocks. In the 1970s the FBI had successfully inserted an agent into the Family; six years later the FBI brought down a host of indictments. Several Family members were caught up in the Pizza Connections case. Then in 1986, Massino was convicted and jailed for the Bonanno Family's involvement in a Teamsters local.

It appeared to observers that the end of the Bonanno Family had finally arrived: powerful members were dead or in jail; their prestige in the underworld had become a joke; they were under investigation after allowing themselves to become puppets of the Sicilian Mafia—original boss Joe Bonanno's legacy—and were taking orders from both overseas and in Canada; and the coveted seat the Bonanno Family had long had on the ruling Commission was gone.

When Philip Rastelli died in 1991, Massino was the only logical choice to take the reins. He'd been on the winning side and he'd gotten his hands dirty arranging and participating in several murders. When he was released from prison in 1993 he took control, naming his brother-in-law Salvatore Vitale as underboss and the aging Anthony Spero as *consigliere*. Massino set about rebuilding the Family, intensifying its involvement in racketeering, gambling, loan sharking, and in drug trafficking—the Sicilian pipeline had, even after the Pizza Connection case, kept up a steady stream of narcotics into New York City. Massino, aware that many of the successful cases against La Cosa Nostra were based on electronic surveillance, concentrated his efforts on secrecy and discretion. When referring to him in conversation, Family members were told to touch their ears rather than say his name. The Bonannos rapidly became a viable Family once more, and it was reported they were given back their seat on the Commission.

The decline and later collapse of the Family began when *consigliere* Spero was indicted on murder and racketing charges; his replacement too was arrested a year later on murder, conspiracy, extortion, gambling, and drug-trafficking charges. Then, in January 2003, Massino himself was arrested on several murder charges. It was revealed that the government had eight turncoat-witnesses against him, including his brother-in-law, former underboss Salvatore Vitale.

Among the charges against Massino were the slayings of the three *capos*, the murder of a Pizza Connection defendant whose body was cut in half and stuffed into two drums of glue, and the murder of Mafioso Gerlando Sciascia,[19] a key player in the "Sicily to Canada to New York" heroin connection. In July 2004 Massino was found guilty on all murder counts, plus arson, money laundering, and extortion. He was facing life in prison without parole.

At the end of January 2005, however, word leaked out that Massino himself had become an informant. Threatened with the death penalty for the Gerlando Sciascia murder, and faced with having $10 million in assets, including his mother's house, seized, "The Last Don" had turned government informant. He'd even worn a listening device in jail while talking to another LCN member, Vincent Basciano.

The effects were immediate. Acting on Massino's information, FBI agents dug up a parking lot in Queens, New York, and found the remains of two of the three captains killed in 1981—the first body had been found years earlier. Basciano was arrested largely based on Massino's wire recording, and was charged with plotting to kill a U.S. attorney.

Massino was the first LCN boss to turn on the organization, and the fallout was widespread. Mafia watchers filled organized crime chat rooms with rants of disbelief; they later turned to disdain and even hatred that Massino had betrayed his code. There was glee among investigators, and some predicted the end of the Cosa Nostra. Even Massino's family—his blood family—reacted in horror and shame.

"He is a bitter, tortured man who now stands alone," his daughter, Adeline, told *Newsday* reporter Anthony DeStefano in an exclusive interview. "We supported my dad through the trial but now feel it impossible to support or condone his actions any further." She told DeStefano that her father had been embittered about his old friends turning against him since he began cooperating. "There has been tremendous support between my parents for a long time.... For personal reasons, my mother will never support him again."

In February 2005, in events believed caused by Massino's about-face, several key Bonanno Family members pleaded guilty to federal racketeering charges. Anthony Urso, former acting underboss, Louis Restivo, a soldier, and former underboss Joseph Cammarano all pleaded guilty to murder and other offenses. The three men are all of advanced age.

In Canada the fall of the Bonanno Family had major repercussions. Vito Rizzuto, known among government lawyers as the "Godfather of the Canadian Mafia," was arrested on RICO charges. He is in custody in Canada vigorously fighting an extradition request from the U.S.

In addition to the arrest and pending extradition of Rizzuto, a former high-ranking federal politician was named in the *New York Daily News* as a "made" member of the Bonannos. The *Daily News* relied on an unreleased FBI document and informent in publishing the allegations surrounding Mr. Gagliano.

Alfonso Gagliano,[20] Canadian former public works minister and former ambassador to Denmark, reacted with anger and disbelief when it was reported that his photograph had been picked out of a photo display by LCN informant Frank Lino. According to an FBI document dated March 3–29, 2004, Lino, who's described as an "individual who is in a position to testify," provided the following information:

The INDIVIDUAL was shown a picture of ALFONSO GAGLIANO. The INDIVIDUAL stated that he recognized GAGLIANO from his trip to Montreal, Canada in the early 1990s. The INDIVIDUAL advised that GAGLIANO was introduced to him as a soldier in the Bonanno family by JOE LOPRESTI, another Bonanno member in CANADA. At a dinner LOPRESTI bragged to the INDIVIDUAL that the Montreal Bonannos had such extensive connections including that of GAGLIANO, a politician. The INDIVIDUAL socialized with GAGLIANO when he was hanging out with VITO RIZZUTO. ...

and:

The INDIVIDUAL made a second trip to Montreal in the 1990s. ... At this meeting, the Canadian Bonannos were informed of MASSINO's new position as Boss of the Bonanno family. LOPRESTI introduced a politician, ALFONSO GAGLIANO, as a soldier in the Bonanno family. ...

Gagliano was furious at Lino's unsubstantiated allegation. He told a Canadian national TV network that while he may have unknowingly crossed paths socially with organized crime figures, he was never involved in criminal activities. "What really amazed me in all this, is that here is somebody [Lino] that practically did it all wrong—he's accused of six murders, extortion, cheating, lying," Gagliano told the network. "This is something that touches the heart and soul of my personality. My integrity."

Documents filed in the Rizzuto extradition case show a mafia connection to the Canadian government. Specifically, a transcript of the debriefing of informant Oreste Pagano on September 21, 1999, reveals links between Mafia boss Alfonso Caruana and an unnamed government official. Asked if there was "a strong association with the mafia and the [Canadian] government," Pagano, a convicted drug dealer, referred to a conversation he had with Alfonoso Caruana: [21]

"We spoke once about it that there was a person who was going into the Canadian government and was from the same village as Alfonso. ..."

"What village is that?"

"Siculiana."

The name of the politician involved wasn't disclosed.

* * *

Meanwhile, as the collapse of the Bonanno Family was under way, U.S. police were targeting the other American families. Several indictments were brought against members, and in some cases upper echelon leaders, of the Gambino, Genovese, Colombo, and Lucchese groups.

There are predictions that America's Cosa Nostra is in a fatal decline; that with informants emerging at the very top of the Families a restructuring will take place with more informal, smaller organizations evolving and carrying on the day-to-day business in a more secretive manner. Non-Italian crime groups will be brought closer to the Families to conduct the more public of their activities, and LCN will live on a steady stream of "tributes" paid as a "franchise fee" by emerging organizations. But La Cosa Nostra has weathered severe storms and crackdowns before and has always hidden itself away, waiting for a new leader, a new regime, to form.

In 2004 there were rumors in the underworld that either Vito Rizzuto or Vincent Basciano—the man who was taped while in custody with Joe Massino—would take the reins of the family. Rizzuto, who's loath to enter the U.S. under any circumstances, would run the Sicilian wing—the drug importers—of the Bonannos from Montreal; alternatively, Basciano would step into Massino's shoes. With both men in custody—Rizzuto pending extradition and Basciano facing murder conspiracy charges—the Sicilian organizers of the drug trade living in Venezuela and Sicily are expected to protect their members in New York City at the expense of maintaining the rest of the Family.

Camorra

The name *Camorra*—the criminal organizations that operate throughout the city of Naples and surrounding areas of Italy—was once more well known than *Mafia* or **Black Hand**. The name, which means "extortion," conjures images of secret sects, mysterious occult powers, bloodthirsty revenge, and an invincible brotherhood. In the hearts of early Italian settlers in North America, the sinister hiss of the word alone could instill terror. And to the world outside the Italian colonies, all crime was *Camorra*, whether the crimes were committed by the Societies of Calabria or the Mafia of Sicily. The Camorra was for a long time a convenient target for their prejudices and fears about the immigrants flooding their homeland.

The roots of Camorra are believed to have been planted as far back as the 16th century, when the Spanish monarchy ruled Naples. A criminal brotherhood called the *Garduna*, a transplant from Spain, brought with it secret ceremonies, oaths, hand-sign communication, and a communal fund to assist members. In a time when life was cheap, one of the tests of loyalty for prospective members was to commit a murder.

There was a romantic aspect to the early Camorra. The members were cocky and had curious methods of communications. When a policeman would arrive they mewed like cats; a rooster-like crowing meant that a victim was in the area. A sigh meant "be silent," that there was someone nearby, listening.

The phenomenon of the secret society spread throughout the Naples area; soon there were dozens, if not hundreds, of similar groups, all under the umbrella of Camorra. Ranks were created: under a Grand Ruling Council were *caporegime*, who headed a group of soldiers, *camorristi* who engaged in road robberies, took "protection" from businesses, and supplied illegal substances at cheap prices. In addition to extorting money from legitimate businessmen and shop owners, they governed legions of pickpockets, thieves, prostitutes, and gambling houses of the city and its environs. Strong, independent criminals were urged—often extorted—into joining and committing a portion of their profits to the brotherhood.

Unlike the Mafia in Sicily or the 'ndrangheta in Calabria, the Camorra was an urban-based organization. It grew rich and powerful on the vast wealth the cities had to offer. Prostitution, generally looked down upon as "unmanly" by Sicilian and Calabrian criminals, was a mainstay for the Camorra. They operated brothels and collected money from pimps and prostitutes alike.

The government was pleased that the Camorra wasn't a political organization and did little to interfere with its activities. At times *camorristi* were even used to keep order in neighborhoods and to spy on political rivals. After the unification of Italy in 1861, imprisoned *camorristi* were set free, sparking a crime wave that lasted almost 10 years. By then the Camorra was out of control and wielded huge power. The government cracked down with wholesale roundups, and soon *camorristi* again filled the prisons.

A government inquiry in 1900 found different levels of criminal activity in Naples. There were elegant and sophisticated members of the Camorra who moved effortlessly through the political and financial sectors, well-connected men who committed blackmail and extortion. There were street-level gangsters who were formed into neighborhood extortion rings to collect tribute from shopkeepers, barge operators, and even beggars. The inquiry was told that many members had been recruited in prison and had to serve one year of apprenticeship to a *camorrista*; if he showed courage and willingness to serve blindly, he would be invited to join at the low rank of *picciotto di sgarro*, which he would hold for three years.

Several ceremonies were described to the inquiry, and most had to do with either courage or fealty. One ceremony involved a mock duel in which the initiate was wounded in the arm; another had the initiate trying to pick up a coin from the ground as a circle of *camorristi* stabbed at it with their knives, resulting in several painful but not fatal wounds to the initiate's hand. A "ceremony of reception" was described in which the new member stood at a table where a dagger, a pistol, and a glass of poisoned wine were placed. The *picciotto di sgarro* stabbed the dagger into the table, cocked the hammer on the pistol, and made as if to drink the poisoned wine.

In 1911 a mega-trial was held for 42 Camorra leaders in Viterbo, an old papal town 50 miles from Rome, after the body of Gennaro Cuocolo, a *camorrista* who had cooperated with police, was found on a beach. He had suffered "47 characteristic stabs and slashes of the Camorra." His wife was found dead—butchered in the family's home in Naples. After a casual police investigation in which Camorra members were arrested and later released, an inquiry was called and several *camorristi* were identified and charged. Security was tight; a local prison was refurbished and made more secure to hold the accused, and apartments were set up inside the prison so that the two judges presiding over the case, the investigators, and the prosecutors would be safe from assassination during the trial. Troops were brought into the area and the prison staff was doubled. To keep Camorra members away, certificates of good conduct were issued and anyone from Naples who appeared in the area without one was arrested.

Getting a jury was almost impossible. Anyone standing in judgment of the *camorristi* would be, in effect, signing his own death warrant. When a panel was finally convened, the accused in the case—including a priest—were kept in a steel cage in the courtroom during the trial.

The Italian government's aim in trying the *camorristi* was not so much to solve and dispose of the double murder as to strike a telling blow against the organization. It was thought that by sending the main leaders to prison, the Camorra would crumble. In what was Italy's longest criminal trial to date, the prosecutors not only pursued the murderers but brought in evidence of dozens upon dozens of other crimes they could tie to the suspects. It could be said that the Viterbo trial was the first anti-gang indictment—all crimes were committed under the auspices of the Camorra and the profits or benefits flowed to everyone in the organization.

The trial itself was chaotic. Since under Italian law the accused were able to cross-examine the witnesses for the prosecution, screams and threats flew out of the steel cage. Somehow the judge maintained control of the proceedings and, in July 1912, the verdicts came in. Nine *camorristi* were declared guilty of the Cuocolo murders and the rest were convicted of belonging to a criminal association. Three of the 42 indicted men vanished and were never brought to justice; three died during the trial. Twenty others were immediately freed, having already spent their sentences in custody awaiting trial.

The success of the Viterbo trial led to a retreat in the Camorra's public activities, but as it had throughout its history, the Camorra merely went underground until the government heat was off. Meanwhile, ironically, international press coverage generated by the trial spread the name of the Camorra and its bloody practices and secret rites.

∗　∗　∗

As immigrant laborers were brought to North America to work the mines, mills, and factories, secret societies emerged in the Italian colonies of Canada and the U.S. Among the migrants were criminals wanted in Naples, Sicily, and Calabria; they applied a strong Italian work ethic to their ruthlessness and predatory practices. And as problems in the Italian communities arose, many were blamed on the Black Hand or the Camorra. These terms, along with "Society" and "Mafia," became interchangeable. Media reports on the bombings, murders, extortions, beatings, and kidnappings kept an almost racist frenzy going, much of it aimed at readily visible, law-abiding Italians. Although the emerging American mafia gangs also garnered attention, it was the stories of the Camorra that were most widespread in the the first two decades of the 1900s. For the Camorra, though, the coverage generated widespread fear and enhanced its power.

In 1926 reports were published about the horrors of the criminals from Naples. Benito Mussolini's crackdown on the Camorra and the Mafia in Sicily, it was feared, would lead to new waves of criminals fleeing the country. According to one newspaper report,

> *This news [of the immigration of criminals fleeing the Fascists] was not regarded with joy by the several thousand Italian families in America who had come to this country during the last decade or more precisely because they had been marked for vengeance by the Mafia in Italy and hoped to be safer here. Some of the ringleaders had undoubtedly escaped, and Italians here felt that they would filter into America through the Canadian and Mexican borders. ...*

This reasonable interpretation of events quickly degenerated into yellow journalism. A drawing of a man who was obviously of Mediterranean descent, his body covered with tattoos, was accompanied by a cutline reading: "Warning of the 'Sfregio' or Death of a Thousand Slashes …" The act of "Sfregio" was described in detail:

> The victim is locked up in a big room with fifty or more members of the band. Each has a stiletto and each takes part in the punishment. On the first day they begin by cutting tiny gashes in the victim's face and shoulders. On the second day, they cut criss-cross gashes in his palms and on the soles of his feet, and on the third day they cut him slowly to pieces. …

The article also detailed how "an American girl, Miss Estelle Reid, of Haverstraw, N.Y. fell into the Black Hand clutches while on a visit in Naples and suffered a dreadful fate …"

> The Camorra kidnapped Miss Reid so they could extort from her certain information which they needed. In order to make her talk, they subjected her to an infernal torture called the "vigilio," or "long-walking." She was made to kneel in the center of a wrought-iron frame with a circle of razor-sharp steel spikes, pointing inward, which encircled her waist. If she moved, in an effort to rise, or to sink down, the spokes would plunge into her flesh. They tortured her in this way for two days and nights, and then drowned her in the Bay of Naples.

A meticulous drawing of the victim in the "infernal contraption" accompanied the story; in the background were several men, one with a whip, and all had leering looks on their faces. (It later emerged that the hapless Ms. Reid was a depressed person and had likely committed suicide; ultimately no Camorra connection was found.)

This stereotypical reporting led to the fear that the Camorra—the name was so widespread that even the Sicilian Mafia became known as the "Palermo Camorra"—took on a power that was mostly based on hysteria and falsehood.

In truth, except for the use of its name, the Camorra never really gained a foothold in North America—although some members of the American LCN were of Neapolitan descent, notably Al Capone and John Gotti. The primary immigrants to both the U.S. and Canada were of Calabrian or Sicilian descent, and criminals among them formed sects, mafias, or Societies of their own.

In Italy the Camorra continued to expand and retreat depending on the attention it received from the Italian government. After World War II, Camorra groups began to emerge in the black markets of Europe. They accrued massive profits and got into the post-war reconstruction of the Naples area, controlling construction and plowing their profits into a host of traditional criminal activities, including cigarette smuggling. In the 1950s the organization was still a loosely knit confederation of independent or semi-independent groups of varying degrees of power. But over the next 20 years *camorristi* took advantage of opportunities in several business arenas of Naples, primarily the building sector, becoming, in effect, super-ruthless capitalists.

After decades of change and the maturing of members—and the recruitment of young members—the Camorra by the 1970s seemed to be split into two levels. One became an "economic" mafia involved in quasi-legitimate endeavors, mostly by co-opting politicians and rigging public tender contracts; the other became a "criminal" mafia that formed links with other Italian crime groups, chiefly the Sicilian Mafia. In the 1970s this split led to a war between the two factions.

When the Sicilian Mafia convinced the "criminal" Camorra to allow them to use their cigarette-smuggling routes to move heroin out of Europe, a war ensued during which more than 400 *camorristi* were killed. Those Camorra who supported the Sicilians' drug-trafficking initiative won, and those opposed to drugs fell back on traditional criminal activities.

Despite their involvement in the globalized narcotics industry, most Camorra members prefer to remain close to home. Several, who have become millionaires many times over from the extortion, drug trafficking, and counterfeit products trades, still live in their family homes in rundown sections of Naples. Some members have formed ongoing criminal enterprises with other Italian crime groups and have even entered into joint ventures with Canadian, American, Baltic, and Eastern European organizations.

The Camorra has recently been engaged in a vicious gang war that has left hundreds of people dead. The crime-infested Naples neighborhoods of Secondigliano and Scampia resemble war zones as gangs battle for control of the area. The source of this homicidal strife is believed to be one of succession: when Paolo di Lauro, known as "Ciruzzo the Millionaire," went into hiding to avoid police in 2002, he left his 25-year-old son, Cosimo, in charge of his organization, the Alleanza di Secondigliano Cartel. Other gang leaders, unimpressed with Cosimo's leadership, broke away from the Secondigliano and formed a group loosely called the Secessionists. At stake was a drug trade that reportedly brought in more than $650,000 a day.

The conflict flared into a three-year wave of arson, bombings, murders, and disappearances. In one orgy of gunfire, six people died in less than a day and a half. Victims were shot as they ate in restaurants, as they walked on the streets, as they drove their cars and rode their scooters and motorcycles. The killings had a wide-reaching impact; several victims' family members swore out vendettas and thus perpetuated the cycle of violence.

As it had in the past, the Italian government moved to suppress the violence, flooding Naples with thousands of troops and police officers. But the heavy law-enforcement presence, the number of arrests, and the public outrage at the deaths of innocents, including children, have had little effect. The government recently moved to ban motor scooters as a way to limit gunmen's mobility.

The *Camorra*, even in the midst of bloody battles, continues to run their usual criminal operations. Several members have moved overseas, not only to avoid police and gang violence but also to generate a steady flow of funds back into the neighborhoods.

Canadian police investigating the sale of counterfeit Versace leather coats discovered that the organizer of the scam was Giovanni Bandolo, a 64-year-old member of the Secondigliano group. Bandolo had imported thousands of cheap plastic jackets, worth between $20 and $30, with counterfeit logos and tags from the Versace design house. They were exhibited on fancy hangers or put in designer boxes and shipped to criminal associates across Canada, where they were sold to gullible victims who were convinced the coats were worth hundreds of dollars. "You wouldn't think you could make a lot of money as an organized crime group by selling fake jackets in parking lots," Peel Regional Police Detective Rod Jones said in an interview with Adrian Humphreys of the *National Post*, who covered the investigation into Bandolo's activities. "But if every week there are 20 salesmen in cities all over Canada, in the States and Australia, you multiply it out and it is really good coin."

Police traced the scheme's profits back to Italy, where they were being used to fund the Secondigliano group. During their investigation police found that Bandolo was named in warrants taken out during the Italian government crackdown on the Camorra. He was deported under police guard to Italy.

As this book goes to press, the Naples wars continue. Observers of the Neapolitan underworld believe the slaughter will stop, not when the government increases its crackdowns, but when one group gains supremacy.

Sacra Corona Unita

Sacra Corona Unita—United Sacred Crown—is known as the Fourth Mafia, after the Cosa Nostra, the *'ndrangheta*, and the Camorra. Unlike these better-known groups, SCU's history can be traced back to the exact date and location of its origin. Also, unlike the other Italian Mafia groups, SCU wasn't founded in the cultural heritage of community aid, but rather as a criminal enterprise driven purely by profit. Members of the SCU get "baptized" into the organization and follow its code.

The origin of the name, according to informer Cosimo Capodieci, is simple: "The organization is sacred (*Sacra*). ... The Crown (*Corona*) because it resembles a crown, meaning the rosary typically used in Church in order to carry out the functions of Jesus Christ and the cross ... United (*Unita*) because it was necessary to be connected to one another, similar to the rings of a chain."

Based in Apulia province on the east coast of Italy, SCU uses elements of the Neapolitan Camorra and the Calabrian *'ndrangheta*. From *'ndrangheta* the early SCU copied kidnapping operations and from the Camorra adopted elements of involved religious mysticism.

The boss of a group is called *crimine*; under him are *trequartino*, *evangelisti*, and *santisti*; the bottom layer is composed of *sgarristi*, or enforcers. Giuseppe Rogoli, who was serving a life sentence for murder, developed the concept and organization of the SCU in a prison cell in Lecce, in Apulia, on Christmas night, 1983. Rogoli, who'd been initiated in the underworld by an *'ndranghetista* serving a sentence in the same jail, meticulously set up a criminal structure that would grow to dozens of clans or cells and include more than 1,500 members. Over the years links were formed with Balkan criminal groups—primarily weapons, cigarette, and migrant smuggling organizations—as well as with the Sicilian, Calabrian, and Neapolitan mafias.

Police also monitored meetings between SCU members and traffickers from the Colombian cocaine cartels, and by the early 1990s surveillance reports showed similar meetings with Asian and Eastern European criminals. In October 1994, an SCU migrant smuggling operation carrying thousands of Albanians into Italy was uncovered; the SCU was making $3.2 million a month from the scheme. Like the Chinese "snakehead gangs" that ship migrants from eastern China to the U.S., Canada, the U.K., and Australia, the SCU further capitalized on their human cargo by forcing the women into prostitution and men into a workforce rented out to do menial labor. And, according to a report by the Italian Ministry of the Interior, the SCU got value added by using the ships carrying the migrants to smuggle drugs into Italy and then throughout Europe. These Albanians, the report says, are "illegal immigrants who, like in the past, are forced to disembark heavy bags full of cannabis, but have more and more often to perform the role of heroin and cocaine couriers." By 2002, Italian authorities were investigating the SCU for massive money laundering, widespread extortion, currency counterfeiting, the exploitation of government contracts, and increased drug and migrant smuggling.

The constant flow of Baltic criminals into Italy has led to several cooperative operations, mostly involving heroin smuggling and the movement of migrants from several Central European countries. Italian police have also reported a flood of heavy weaponry, and have made several seizures of military-quality firearms in Italy's eastern provinces.

The SCU, which 10 years ago was given a relatively short life expectancy as a result of police crackdowns, turf warfare with other organized crime groups, and the seemingly endless stream of informants, has proven itself to be resilient and adaptable.

Endnotes
'Ndrangheta

1. Information from informant Romeo Annunziato, May 16, 1996. He also said that all the *'ndrangheta* families in Platì answer to the Barbaro clan. Perre is the original form of the name for many people who have emigrated from Platì. A *carabinieri* report also notes the families of Sergi, Papalia, and Trichilo. Barbaro and Sergi are the most powerful of the top six clans in the Platì federation.

2. San Luca—and specifically the nearby *Santuario della Madonna di Polsi* (Sanctuary of Our Lady of Polsi)—is the very heart of the *'ndrangheta*. Italian authorities were told by *pentiti*, cooperating informants, that virtually every male in the town is a member of *'ndrangheta* and that the San Luca clan still receives a small percentage of profits from mafia activities in Calabria. The *Santuario* has for generations been the location for formal *'ndrangheta* events, as well as for meetings of leaders from around the world. The meetings are held annually and, as a result, have suffered from police raids. The meetings occur during the September Feast. According to Cesare Polifroni, who gave information to police, "All the villages are called one after the other ... and every *capo società* must give accounts of all the activities carried out during the year and of all the most important facts taking place in his territory such as kidnappings, homicides, etc. He must also communicate the number of new affiliates and the eventual punishment given to transgressors." Senior *'ndranghetista* from Canada and Australia—the two most powerful and entrenched overseas countries with Calabrian organizations—as well as from the U.S., across Europe, and South America, regularly attend the September Feast meetings. After police attention caused problems for the clans—one meeting was held by the long-hunted fugitive Giuseppe Morabito—similar conclaves were carried out at Africo.

3. The three knights are part of every form of *'ndrangheta* oath and are a constant among *cosche* throughout Calabria. Several handwritten copies of the code have been found over the past century, and all refer to the knights and their voyages. Typically: "In the name of the organized and sacred society, I consecrate this place in the same way our ancestors Osso, Mastrosso, and Carcagnosso consecrated it, through irons and chains. ... Arm ourselves dear comrades of knife and misfortune

in the same way our ancestors did, they who fought in Calabria and in Sicily and in the whole State of Naples. ..."

4. A finely detailed and contextual essay on the events in Hillsville, Pennsylvania, can be found in *The Hunter's Game: Poachers and Conservationists in Twentieth-Century America* by Louis S. Warren, Yale University Press. Warren has examined the prevailing game laws of the time as well as the situation of Italian migrants in a foreign colony; his reportage provides a prime source of research in the origins of Italian criminal organizations in America. His analysis of Pinkerton reports and the Society rivals much of today's research into the activities of the *'ndrangheta*. Warren points out that the Pinkerton agent didn't inflate or sensationalize his findings by using the popular term "Black Hand"; instead, he used the term "Society." As a tool for researchers of Southern Italian criminal organizations, *The Hunter's Game* is invaluable.

5. This punishment is traditional *'ndrangheta* "mid-level" penalty for violations of the code. Generally the most minor violation—as long as it doesn't involve an actual danger to existence of the Society—is punished by a fine paid into the clan's coffers. Next is *zaccagnata*, in which the violator is slashed repeatedly with a knife on the torso; often this is ceremonial and done by *puntaiolo*, relatively lower-status members of the Society. (Although there have been reports, mostly in Toronto, Canada, of members being seen with "*zacca*" marks on their cheeks, this may involve violations in which someone's personal respect has been damaged.) More serious penalties include being suspended temporarily from a position of power and reduced to a lower status. Next is the fate of Nick Ciurelo: in this punishment ceremony the violator is stripped naked and his entire body is brushed with human excrement; the practice is described by *pentiti* as being humiliating almost beyond endurance. More serious violations are punished with being "neglected"—ignored and in essence exiled within the group or expelled from the Society. Almost always expulsion is quickly followed by assassination. It's interesting to note that the Pinkerton agent noted Ciurelo's punishment more than a hundred years ago, long before anyone in America—and many in Italy—were aware of this practice.

6. Calabrian immigrants with the first name of Vincenzo tend to take the Anglicized name "Jimmy"; Sicilians who emigrate shorten Vincenzo to "Enzo." "Vince" in also used. It's intriguing that a "Dommick Murdoc" turned up in the Fort Frances list of Society members at around the same time as the Pennsylvania Society was in operation.

7. Names of individuals mentioned throughout this section vary wildly. The spelling of Italian names was beyond most officials; while "Tino" has been consistent in several reports (except that through media or court errors it appeared as Tine in a July 1909 American media report), Muro appears as Mauro. Adding

to the confusion is the fact that the surname "Tino" was also used as an alias for Cosentino in at least one U.S. criminal case.

8. Exactly which murder remains unrecorded. However, a review of several archives indicates that there appears to have been a wave of killings of Italian migrants in 1904 and 1905 across Northern Ontario. Some—such as an axe murder carried out in a rooming house after a simple Italian verbal game—were clearly tied to the near-insanity some migrants were driven to, being far from home, at loose ends, and constantly preyed upon. Others appear to be related to mafia-like activities. Surnames of some people involved are the same as or similar to names of men who emerged in the 1930s and 1940s as organized crime figures in Canada.

9. Rocco Zito was born in Fiumara, Italy, in 1928. He comes from a long line of 'ndrangheta members. Since his arrival in Canada his name has come up in several homicide investigations—his father was a leader of the Crupi 'ndrangehta clan. In the 1980s Zito was charged in the murder of a photographer who'd borrowed money from him at extortionist rates. Zito beat the man with a liqueur bottle and then shot him through the head. Zito was convicted in October 1986 of manslaughter after he pleaded self-defense.

Zito has long ties to the 'ndrangheta families across Canada, as well as American La Cosa Nostra groups and Sicilian Mafia in both Canada and in Sicily. He was investigated—but not charged—for providing false documents to Mafiosi fleeing Sicily during a government crackdown in the 1980s. In 1975 Zito's brother, Giuseppe, was slain during a gang war in Calabria. His father, Domenico, was denied landed immigrant status in Canada because of his long history as a powerful 'ndranghetista.

In September 1991, according to Italian authorities, "a certain Rocco Zito of North America" was among prominent 'ndranghetisti from France, Australia, and Canada who attended a summit of the Honored Society at the *Santuario della Madonna di Polsi* (Sanctuary of St. Maria of Polsi) in the Aspromonte Mountains near San Luca. San Luca is mafia-ridden town in Calabria, the site of many 'ndrangheta meetings and ceremonies—in 1969 a police raid found more than a hundred 'ndranghetisti. In attendance with "a certain Rocco Zito" at the 1991 conclave was a European businessman, a so-called *colletto bianco* or "white collar," one of several covert 'ndrangheta members whose identities are kept secret because of their prominence in international business communities.

Rocco Zito lives near Toronto and is alleged by police to be the elder statesman of the 'ndrangheta in Canada.

10. Kidnappings fell out of favor in 1991 when the Italian government, in a desperate move to calm the public and put a stop to the increasing outrage, make it illegal to pay kidnap ransoms. It was also illegal to hire intermediaries to

negotiate with kidnappers. Bank accounts of victims' families were frozen to keep funds from being paid out. It didn't put an end to the racket, but the instances of kidnapping—of those reported, anyway—decreased by 80 percent. In 1999 a scandal broke out when a magistrate was accused of violating the anti-kidnapping legislation by dealing directly with the 'ndrangheta to secure the release of a Milan businesswoman who was held hostage in a cave in the Aspromonte Mountains for 267 days. The magistrate dealt directly with a jailed 'ndrangheta boss to successfully effect the woman's release, offering to reduce his sentence and to ease police pressure on Platì.

11. The only Sicilian Mafia families that have prospered over the past 10 years of strife are the ones located in Canada, Venezuela, and the U.S. The Rizzuto and Caruana-Cuntreras effectively removed themselves from Sicily decades ago and positioned themselves in the international drug trade. Sicilian Mafiosi—primarily in New York City and environs—also continue drug trafficking, increasingly with fewer and fewer ties to Sicily. Police believe that an arm's-length relationship is maintained, but the Families in Sicily fear jeopardizing the profits that flow back to them. In Venezuela the Caruana-Cuntreras, along with several expatriate Mafia groups, keep to themselves. Recently, however, police in North America are seeing a resurgence of previously convicted traffickers; they fear the Families in Sicily are replanting themselves in the U.S. and Canada.

Sicilian Mafia

12. In our 1995 book *Global Mafia: The New World Order of Organized Crime*, we identified a criminal organization, *Stidda*, or the Star. We described *Stidda* as a purely criminal organization that emerged to challenge the bloodthirsty dictatorship of Salvatore "Toto" Rina. Many **stiddari** challenged this Sicilian Mafia outright for both criminal operations and territory. While it initially appeared that Stidda might replace the at times badly damaged Sicilian Mafia, it has in effect been wiped out—by arrests, defections of its founders, and a brief but savage wave of violence by the traditional Cosa Nostra.

13. Calogero Vizzini (1877–1954) may have appeared to be a peasant, but his power during his life was almost unparalleled. When he was 17, he showed his "manliness" by severely beating a rival for a girl both men liked; when he was 18 he was among a gang of bandits that, on horseback, engaged in a campaign of robbery, rape, and murder throughout the isolated villages of western Sicily. In early 1900 he became a member of the local *cosca*, or family, of the Honored Society—this was in the days before the name "Cosa Nostra" was commonly used—and gained much respect from other members. Ultimately he became the

most powerful leader in the province of Agrigento. After World War II, when the Americans liberated Sicily, Vizzini was named mayor of Villalba, one of many Mafia bosses put into a position of power by the U.S. government.

14. This may have been true a century ago, as a method to bind the initiate to the group or organization and to keep police from infiltrating. More recently, though, with the amount of money being made from the drug trade, this requirement has fallen by the wayside. An "earner" in the American Cosa Nostra might be required to participate in a murder by being a driver, lookout, or planner, but his main requirement is that he "earns"—provides a steady stream of money to the group. In Sicily and Calabria members are no longer required to have killed someone on behalf of the group, but reports say that most of the most prominent 'ndrangheta members have committed a slaying, although often for honor reasons or to maintain their self-respect in a social situation. More than a reflection of their devotion to the organization, personal murders show a willingness to be ruthless and "manly."

15. The Apalachin meeting was the first indication the American public had of the breadth and power of the American Cosa Nostra. The meeting was supposedly held to issue orders that LCN members must not engage in the drug trade upon pain of death. This interpretation came from several sources, including informants who'd heard rumors, media outlets who played them up, and police who believed them. Subsequently, many murders were carried out in the U.S. against those who violated the LCN rule against drugs. But the meeting had in fact been held to bring American LCN members up to date on the Sicilian negotiations and to provide guidelines under which both sides would conduct the heroin trade.

16. Bernardo Provenzano has taken on the aspect of a ghostly legend in the underworld. After the capture of Salvatore "Toto" Riina in 1993, Provenzano took over leadership of the Corleone Family. He has been Italy's number-one Sicilian Mafia target since vanishing more than 40 years ago. Now 72 years old, Provenzano has eluded several dragnets. Periodically rumors or sightings arise. He reportedly received prostrate treatment in France; he appeared at a Cosa Nostra summit dressed in a bishop's purple vestments. Constantly on the move, Provenzano has narrowly escaped capture: in one raid police missed him by mere hours. However, police are continually rounding up Mafia members who are helping him operate. Provenzano communicates his instructions to Mafia members using brief handwritten notes that follow a tortuous route before reaching their intended recepient. With only a decades-old photograph to work from, police admit the fugitive could be living in plain sight, likely in Palermo.

La Cosa Nostra

17. Paolo Violi has been practically nominated for sainthood by several organized crime writers, filmmakers, and observers for his patriotic stance against American control of Canadian organized crime. But more accurately, Violi's problems were never with the Americans, but with the Sicilians, specifically the Caruana-Cuntrera-Rizzuto clans who wanted to operate freely in Montreal as part of the heroin pipeline that later became known as the Pizza Connection. A large measure of romanticism has arisen around Violi: that he was a nationalist criminal who wanted neither the Americans nor the Sicilians dictating the activities of the Montreal Mafia and was willing to die for his beliefs; and that he willingly went to a meeting in a café and, knowing that a Sicilian wielding a shotgun was behind him, allowed himself to be assassinated because of his belief in the "code." In reality, according to recent interviews with underworld sources, Violi had no idea he was being drawn into a trap by the Rizzuto Family the day he died. He believed a meeting was being arranged for the following week that would accommodate the use of Montreal as a heroin pipeline into the U.S.; the arrangement, he was told, would leave him in control of the day-to-day organized crime activities of the Quebec underworld. Rather than a Canadian ultra-nationalist of deep thought and foresight, Violi was a relatively unintelligent thug and provincial thinker who had an inflated view of his own power. He grossly underestimated the global power of the Sicilian Mafia clans who were, in the mid-to-late 1970s, creating a transcontinental drug pipeline that would yield hundreds of millions in profits.

18. Organized crime figures prefer to be caught in Canada, rather than the U.S. Sentencing in Canada is lenient in the extreme and parole guidelines are laughably lax. Alfonso Caruana, dubbed one of the most wanted Sicilian Mafia drug traffickers in the world, was finally caught in Canada in 1998 after an investigation into multimillion-dollar cocaine trafficking. He pleaded guilty and received an 18-year sentence. He became eligible for parole after six years and would have been released had he not been immediately rearrested on an Italian criminal warrant. Caruana's organization trafficked in thousand-kilo loads of cocaine and made millions of dollars. However, he was able to negotiate with the Canadian government and only had a small fraction of his assets seized. During the Caruana investigation, several attempts were made to convince him to cross into the U.S. to conduct business, but Caruana said he "felt safe" in Canada.

19. Gerlando Sciascia has long been underrated, both in the U.S. and Canada. A member of the Mafia in the Sicilian province of Agrigento, Sciascia was a key point man between the Sicilian heroin traffickers and American and Canadian organized crime groups. Interviews conducted by the authors in Sicily showed that residents there believe Sciascia was one of the most powerful Cattolica Eraclea organized crime figures to be sent overseas.

20. The Gagliano allegations were covered in detail in the authors' 2001 book *Bloodlines: The Rise and Fall of the Mafia's Royal Family*. Mr. Gagliano, in the wake of allegations of connections to organized crime in Montreal, was investigated each time—by the RCMP and the federal ethics commissioner—and was cleared on every occasion. In an unrelated development, he was dismissed from the posting as Ambassador to Denmark in the midst of a political corruption scandal. He has filed suit against the Government of Canada.

21. Debriefing of Oreste Pagano; September 21, 1999, and November 18, 1999; by Constable Regina Marini, RCMP Proceeds of Crime Section; at Markham, Ontario, Canada.

PART TWO
Asian Organized Crime

Structure

Asian Organized Crime (AOC) ranges from the Chinese Triads with bases in China, Taiwan, and Hong Kong to street gangs confined to small areas of Chinatowns and Asian areas of cities and towns in Canada, the U.S., Australia, the U.K., South America, and even South Africa.

Triads—hundred-million-dollar criminal dynasties with a global reach in heroin-smuggling operations—sit atop the loose structure of AOC. Equally powerful, but without the Triads' traditional trappings and titles, are the syndicates, primarily the Big Circle Boys (BCB), a loose confederation of crime groups based in and around the Guangzhou, formerly Canton, area of China.

At the bottom are street gangs with local turf, often as small as a few blocks of a neighborhood. Within their area the gangs are able to eke out a living, but always with an eye to linking up with a larger, more powerful criminal leader. Most of the public violence occurs on street level, as small gangs try to encroach on another's turf or a struggle breaks out over small matters, even who gets to extort a particular shopkeeper. For street-level gangs, any excuse for violence is a good excuse; it gets them noticed and builds their reputation.

In the middle are the Tongs, self-declared benevolent associations arranged on the basis of family clans, business or social fraternities, or political lines.

Triads

The most secretive and longest operating Chinese organized crime groups are the Triads. Throughout the history of China there seem to have always been Triad organizations or similar groups. They were formed as secret societies and lodges in response to outside invaders, corrupt government, or as political movements. Research indicates that the forerunners of modern-day Triads came into existence in Fujian province in eastern China in the second half of the 17th century. At that time, a fierce warrior class called the Manchu occupied China, forcing the ruling class, the Ming dynasty, to collapse. The Manchu set up their own dynasty, the Ch'ing, where for 40 years they controlled the northern half of China. In the south, they came up against fierce resistance and rebellion. In

Foochow, in Fujian province, 128 monks began organizing citizens in their monastery against the Manchu. The monastery became a center for the resistance movement, with the monks training themselves in kung fu and other fighting arts. The Manchu sent troops to Foochow to root out the monks and their followers, and for three weeks the temple was besieged. The monks managed to resist their attackers; however, one of the monks betrayed the cause and allowed northern troops into the monastery through a network of secret tunnels. They set the monastery ablaze, and in the fighting that ensued only five monks managed to escape. It was they who set up the first Triad society, binding themselves together with secret oaths and rituals based on a blend of the teachings of Taoism, Confucianism and Buddhism, and Chinese mythology.

Soon other secret societies formed along the same lines as the monks' and, over the following century, dozens, if not hundreds, of similar societies spread across China. People who were dispossessed, who felt oppressed, or who fell in love with the popular romance of the societies flocked to join. Of varying sizes and influence, the societies became unofficial governments, drawing membership from across the country's classes. And the Triads were not without a benevolent aspect: they settled disputes, organized labor, and served as outlets for political frustration.

In the mid-1800s the Manchu increased their crackdown on Triads, sending members on the run to Hong Kong and as far away as North America. Far-flung connections emerged and, to fund their battle against the Manchu, the Triads turned to crime, mostly smuggling, extortion under the guise of political donations, and piracy. The Triads found that their rigid structure, obsessive secrecy, romanticized rituals, and gathering wealth and power were the essential ingredients in maintaining a criminal group and in committing criminal acts. While many Triads still kept to some of their social and political aims, the early 1900s saw an increasing shift into purely underworld activities.

By the late 1950s Triads were prolific throughout Asia. Hong Kong alone was home to dozens of varying sizes and persuasions. The Ching Nin Kwok Ki Sh'e, for example, was a small group with pre–World War II roots; membership was limited to low-wage workers who trained at the Boxing (kung fu) Club of the Sanitary Department Employees Association. The Ching Wah was a tiny society made up of members of the fire department. The Chuen Yau Chi was an association of pickpockets. The Chui Tung Wo began as an employment agency. Some weren't true Triads but rather sub-branches of some of the larger societies. Some stood alone. Accurate numbers have always been difficult to determine, but membership in the various Triad or Triad-related societies has numbered in the hundreds of thousands.

On the international stage, the Triads' primary activity is heroin smuggling. After the communist victory in the 1950s many Chinese bandits and Triad members fled through Southern China into Burma and Thailand, where poppy fields were rife. The first group to penetrate the already active heroin trade were the Chiu Chau Triads, expatriate Chinese who had, through diaspora, spread throughout the world. In Thailand the Chiu Chau have long been part of the makeup of the country's Chinese population; they are similarly prolific in Vietnam, Malaysia, and Indonesia. The history of Chiu Chau people in the opium industry dates back to the mid-1800s, when they were effectively a "mafia" with a large measure of control over the trade. Over the generations they've become the number-one Asian criminal law enforcement target, but have proved increasingly difficult to penetrate or investigate. Chiu Chau members are, today, owners or part-owners of banks, casinos, construction companies, shipping lines, pharmaceutical companies, brokerages, and import-export firms; they're also either hidden or public owners in a host of international conglomerates. They are established in the world's leading cities, from Hong Kong to Toronto, New York City to Sao Paulo.

The Chiu Chau continue to dominate segments of the Asian underworld and several cultural, financial, and social associations. While many members, especially those of the later generations, have evolved into outwardly legitimate and wealthy businesspeople, small Triads continue to be brought under the Chiu Chau umbrella. This provides a firm base and a wider geographical workforce to draw upon.

Triad groups number in the hundreds, but there are four that dominate: the Chiu Chau, the 14K, the Wo Group, and the Big Four. Within the network of these major Triads are lesser, smaller groups of varying sizes, as well as groups that operate independently or semi-independently in Taiwan, Burma, Malaysia, and Singapore. Of special note are the Taiwanese Triads that have, over the past decade, increased their wealth and power through the international migrant smuggling trade, profits from which are said to rival those of the heroin business.

Emerging Triads periodically appear, sometimes with no firm links to any of the four major groups. In Canada, the Kung Lok, set up by Hong Kong businessman Lau Wing Kui, came on the scene very quickly and established itself in several Canadian centers, most prominently Toronto and Ottawa. A well-connected criminal in his own right, Lau Wing Kui's modus operandi: was to add local components to his organization and then move ruthlessly through Canadian Chinatowns; at the same time, he used his overseas connections for a foray into the international heroin trade. Although Lau Wing Kui has long since left Canada, the senior members of his group remain in Toronto, Ottawa, and Montreal, where they've constructed fronts as businessmen while continuing criminal activities that range from heroin trafficking to prostitution and migrant smuggling.

In an interview with one of the authors, one of the men, who owns a restaurant in downtown Toronto and is involved in outwardly legitimate cultural exchanges with China, fondly remembers the Lau Wing Kui days:

> We were bad boys, then, but no more. We tried to help each other, to make a good way for especially the new ones who came. Our community had problems, and we stood up to fix those things. Maybe we broke a law, sometimes, but not anymore. You ask anyone about me and they say, [I'm a] good man now. Once I made mistakes but now, no more.

Intelligence reports in Canada and the U.S., however, paint a different picture: the restaurateur, a U.S. Asian crime intelligence report states,

> regularly visits New York City where he meets known o/c members and associates on East Broadway. ... Operating with the remnant [sic] of the Kung Lok he has interests in the massage business, funnelling sex workers through Toronto, across the border, and into Manhattan and New Jersey. ... According to sources he has

been elevated to the Number 2 position in the Kung Lok due to a homicide that occurred in the Toronto area.

In Toronto's Chinese community, he is widely believed to be protected by the Canadian Security Intelligence Service, providing information on political and criminal activities. His name was mentioned in a secret CSIS/RCMP report into the activities of Chinese government agents in Canada's business community.

Other members of the Kung Lok also continue to be active in both community events and criminal activities, including extortion, money laundering, migrant smuggling, loan sharking, gaming, and real estate fraud. Some members operate kung fu clubs that are little more than hangouts for gang members, where young toughs train for duty on the streets. Others have attached themselves to community associations whose membership dues are thinly veiled extortions.

But of all the interconnected and independent players in the Chinese underworld, the most active is the Big Circle Boys (BCB), or Dai Huen Jai. The term "Big Circle" is from the prisons around the city of Guangzhou, formerly Canton, which are often delineated by a large circle on maps.

With its roots in the early 1960s purges in mainland China, the children of the original BCBs are at the forefront of many of today's major criminal initiatives. Originally members of the Red Guard, the BCB were swept up by the purges of the People's Liberation Army and sent to detention camps. After several years in custody, the original BCB members were released from prison; some escaped, others bought their way to freedom. By the hundreds the former Red Guards fled to Hong Kong. An estimated 25 leaders emerged in the group and, using their military training and the toughness they developed while in Chinese prisons, they began a reign of terror, specializing in lightning-fast violent robberies carried out with a high degree of precision. Jewelry firms, casinos, cash-transit companies, and payroll offices were their primary targets. In individual initiatives, members of the BCB offered themselves to established Triads and drug trafficking and gambling syndicates as bodyguards.

There is no known ceremony of membership in the Big Circle, although in the past some members may have undergone formal initiation rites in mainland Chinese Triads. Rather than a Triad-style group, the BCB is a syndicate, or a confederation of syndicates. Leadership is non-elected and fluid; there are certainly powerful operators of the groups but no top-down issuing of marching orders. And while some mediation role is played by the powerful leaders of BCB syndicates, no known rules of behavior exist beyond the informal expectations of any criminal group: not to cooperate with police, not to poach on one another's turf, not to cheat each other. But this is just good underworld governance.

The main thrust of the BCB is profit, preferably but not necessarily profit for all. By the mid-1980s the BCB had spread beyond Asia into North America using the services of "snakeheads," operators of migrant smuggling rings. They brutally muscled their way into Chinatowns, dislodging the traditional Asian gangs and committing kidnappings, high-dollar robberies and extortions, and home invasions. Within a few years the BCBs again branched out, this time into the counterfeiting of Canadian and American cigarettes credit-card fraud operations, and heroin importation.

Today they're considered the most powerful and active Asian crime threat both locally and internationally. Their operations are truly global, and they've formed alliances with Triads and other syndicates in the migrant smuggling trade, the credit-card counterfeiting industry, heroin importation, counterfeit goods manufacture, hydroponic marijuana and Ecstasy production and trafficking, and the organized global sex trade.

Tongs

Tongs—or benevolent family or business associations—were long considered necessary components in the financial and cultural life of the world's Chinatowns. New immigrants could go to a Tong—either a family name society, for instance the "Lee" or the "Wong," or a Tong connected to their birthplace—and receive help in adjusting to their new life overseas. Small loans were made, accommodations were arranged, jobs were set up. As well, the Tong arranged the new immigrant's social life: dances, fundraisers, parades, old folks' homes, cultural clubs. But the Tongs were also involved in gambling and prostitution for the mostly male new immigrants. Little law enforcement was expended on policing the vices of Chinatown; as long as things remained quiet, almost no effort was made to go after the Tongs. It was crime, to be sure, but it was private crime. When some public disturbance—a shooting, for example—drew the attention of the outside authorities, raids and a brief crackdown would ensue, but soon things would return to normal. Increasingly, as Asian populations grew, politicians had a vote to woo, and too much pressure on Chinatown's profit margins could mean the withholding of that vote or its transfer to an opposing party.

The Tongs were happy with this arrangement, and so were police. But all that would change. In the 1980s an FBI report on Asian organized crime revealed that although many Tong leaders were legitimate businessmen, others had come under the influence of Triads and criminal syndicates. Then in 1990, when the FBI targeted the On Leong Tong for investigation, it all proved to be true. The probe resulted in racketeering, gambling, and tax violation charges, and demonstrated that, as more and more young migrants flooded North America's Chinatowns, the Tongs had hired street gangs to protect their illegal interests from robbers and extortionists. In the On Leong Tong case their "protectors" were the Ghost Shadows, a wildly violent group of young men that had terrorized New York's Chinatowns for several years.

More recently, police in the U.S. and Canada have found other cases where criminal elements have either set up their own Tong-like associations or have infiltrated and taken over existing Tongs. And with the influx of smuggled Chinese migrants into North America, several Fujianese social and cultural Tongs have evolved into almost purely criminal structures. One Tong-like association in New York City accepted a series of donations by Fujianese snakeheads—people traffickers—and ended up thoroughly riddled with criminals who used the Tong's reputation and power in the community to further their illegal activities.

In Canada, several members of the Fujianese community told the authors that in the past five years a Canadian Fujianese Tong-like association has stepped in with lawyers and other immigration assistance to help captured illegal migrants fight deportation back to China. But instead of getting the migrants bailed out of custody, the lawyers quickly handed them over to the snakeheads who'd smuggled them into Canada in the first place. The migrants were then pressured, even tortured, some said, to pay the remaining fees owed for the transit from Fujian province. Several women said they were put to work in brothel/massage parlors where they were forced to service a specific number of clients a week. One woman said she was told the brothel she worked in was jointly owned by a Chinese-Canadian lawyer, a lawyer in a large Canadian law firm, and the treasurer of the cultural association that had provided her lawyer's fees. The brothel, she said, was guarded by young men, some of whom she recognized as passengers on the boat that had brought her to Canada. They were paying off their passage by working as bodyguards and protectors of brothels and gambling clubs.

* * *

The lowest level of Asian crime activity is the street gang. Each ethnic group, when it first transits from its home country, has a small proportion of children and teenagers who band together, almost as a second family. These groupings can range from three or four youths to dozens as their activities progress. The fledgling street gangs are essentially a mutual support structure for protection and societal benefits. In most North American and European cities, there's often an existing gang that's amenable to accepting new members. Strength in numbers is one of the measurements of street gangs, and is more important even than connections to more senior criminal groups.

With migration from Vietnam in the 1970s and 1980s came a host of youth that banded together into violent gangs, concentrating their activities in New York and the eastern seaboard of the U.S., California, and Texas. In Canada they built bases in Toronto, Ottawa, Montreal, Calgary and Edmonton. Many had known each other in refugee camps, which made for a built-in intercity network. For several years these gangs struggled to find their place in the Asian underworld, kidnapping and extorting citizens, robbing jewelry stores, raiding gaming houses and brothels, trafficking drugs, and organizing prostitution rings. Entrenched Chinese criminals, recognizing that everyone needed a "bowl of rice," began hiring the Vietnamese youths to protect their establishments.

"We came with nothing and had to fight the white boys," remembers a man who says he was a former member of the Kung Lok group.

> *Then came the ones from Vietnam. They needed a bowl of rice and if they couldn't get it, they took. It was very bad in those days for everybody. Business was poor, the police were everywhere, interfering and breaking houses [doors of gaming houses]. We helped the police, but the young [Vietnamese] men were difficult. They were offered jobs. Some took, some would not. The ones who took do well now. The others? Prisons. Death.*

Today the young Vietnamese gang members are involved in the usual array of crimes, but at a slightly higher level. One, who was notorious in the 1980s for raiding massage parlors and holding them under control while he robbed customers as they arrived, now operates his own string of hairdressing salons that front for brothels. Another former street-gang member is married to a real estate broker; she identifies houses that are ideal for hydroponic marijuana cultivation and he, through his mortgage firm, finances leases for drug traffickers. A former gang member owns a popular Vietnamese restaurant; in partnership with an older "old Chinatown" businessman he loans money and together they operate a loan-sharking franchise at one of Ontario's casinos.

Entrenched Vietnamese gangsters often show up in conjunction with other Asian crime figures, and even mafia groups. In the migrant smuggling trade, for example, Vietnamese criminals are often used by Chinese syndicates to transit migrants en route from Asia to the U.S. via Canada. Investigations in the Toronto area indicated a Vietnamese connection to firearms being sold to members of the mafia in Hamilton. Police believe that many of the connections between groups are made while members are serving time in prison.

But as the Vietnamese rose from the streets and the public crimes that brought so much attention, new migrants from Mainland China quickly took their place. The influx of Fujianese migrants, who entered the U.S. either through Mexico or Canada, brought with it several young men who quickly carved themselves a piece of the underworld in New York, New Jersey, Boston, Toronto, and Vancouver. Some were criminals before coming to North America; others found themselves carrying out activities on behalf of already-entrenched Fujianese Triad-like organizations in order to make money and to pay off the balance of their transit fee from China.

As with earlier gangs, particularly the Vietnamese, the Fujianese had their turn as the current threat in the popular crime culture. Using terms like "ruthless," "murderous," and "stone killers," law enforcement dubbed the Fujianese—Fuk Ching, or Fujianese Youth—as a threat that surpassed even the existing street gangs. But in essence, it was merely the turn of the Fujianese. Initially lacking in structure and having no time for subtlety, their activities were often quite public and garnered both headlines and the dire law enforcement warnings that quickly followed. There were small gang wars in major cities where the Fuk Ching had set up; and there were battles over turf, determining which street or set of blocks could be safely preyed upon by extortionists. It was, taking a long view, criminal history repeating itself.

But in the 1980s and 1990s the Fuk Ching gangs were quickly absorbed by the Fujianese-based Triads that were already deeply involved in international heroin trafficking, credit-card fraud and, in particular, migrant smuggling. The Fujianese associations were quick to offer *kong so*, or mediation services, to bring the often Wild West methods of the gang into control.

The head of the Big Sister Ping organization—the most notorious of the international smuggling trade—was herself the victim of a young Fujianese gangster. As with the Cantonese criminals who were confronted by a new wave of migrants poaching on their territory, Cheng Chui Ping easily absorbed the young upstarts, using them as part of her rapidly growing organization by assigning them to meet ships off the U.S. coast and ferry hundreds of migrants to shore. Once the human cargo was on American soil, the Fuk Ching held them hostage until families in New York or Fuzhou remitted the transfer fee.

Today, those who were once dismissed as Fujianese youth are powerful middle-aged men involved in the international heroin trade, the migrant smuggling syndicates, and money laundering.

✳ ✳ ✳

As time passes and simple things like ESL (English as a second language) courses take root, the commonality of language—in schools, but in detention centers and prisons, too—has changed the makeup of street gangs. One gang identified by the authors as operating in east Toronto consists of a Malaysian-Chinese immigrant, a Caucasian female, a Caucasian male, three Hong Kong visa students, a Laotian male, and a mulatto male. Their connection? All belong to the same Chinese boxing club long operated by a retired Hong Kong gangster now living near Toronto. The gang practices extortion on primarily Asian students, but has also forayed into street-level drug trafficking. It has no name or headquarters beyond the schoolyard and some restaurants.

Police believe this is the newest threat from Asian-based street gangs: that their assimilation into Western society will lead to a co-joining of criminal activities. Violent and criminal youth are meeting in youth detention centers and at social dances, schools, and sports clubs. They're able to communicate in a common language and have the same interests in music, clothes, and movies.

An undercover Canadian police officer who investigated a theft ring involving a diverse group of youths noted that they all make a point of saying they're not a gang.

> *They say they just hang together. You can't really get a handle on them as you can with other criminal groups. You have to start with a crime, and in some segments of the community that's hard to get information on. With a Triad-type investigation, or a hard-wired Vietnamese group, you can set up on the organization and the players will take you to what they're up to, and you can move on them. These kids? They look like everybody else. No tattoos, no club jackets, no hangout.*

Operation Candy Box

With traditional organized crime groups coming under attack by increasingly sophisticated law enforcement techniques, through the 1990s and into the 2000s the groups began to move away from their rigid, hierarchical structures. Rules and regulations that had formed the skeleton of the criminal body also made the group slow and unwieldy; anyone appearing in a position of power within, for example, a Cosa

Nostra group would almost instantly attract the full attention of the U.S. government. With a fixed target at the top and without the traditional loyalty of mid-level members that once protected and insulated the leaders, America-based mafia organizations could be identified and deconstructed by police agencies and an often-successful plan of attack could be formulated. A perfect example of this fixed-target method of investigation are the continual successes against the LCN, particularly the Bonanno/Massino Family. The FBI's Operation Buttondown—a coordinated assault on the LCN—was so intense that even the boss of the Bonanno group ended up caving in to become a government informant. In short, the very solid structure of this traditional organized crime group—once its strength—made it vulnerable.

Asian organized crime, particularly those groups based on Triad structures, has long had dual structures. There continue to be ritualized initiation, a rigid hierarchy, and secret codes and signals, but also a system of ascension within the Triad itself, permitting emerging leaders to create their own "family" grouping while strictly following a basic set of requirements. The new grouping is an outgrowth of the main Triad and ultimately seeks to insert itself into the main body.

But the past few decades has seen the emergence of a syndicated criminal organization method. Many of the syndicates—most popularly the Big Circle Boys—have varying degrees of attachments to Triads but essentially stand alone. And many are fluid and able to engage in diverse criminal activities at different times in different places. The makeup of the organization changes often, with new participants entering a particular conspiracy for sometimes brief periods of time, then branching off into another enterprise. Sometimes the syndicate itself shifts entirely out of one activity and into another, retaining the same core leaders but drawing an entirely new set of players.

In the absence of a visible target and a rigid criminal structure, then, in order for law enforcement to successfully attack a syndicate they need to begin their investigation with a particular crime to solve. Only then do they have a chance of taking them down.

* * *

The Wong Ze Wai syndicate began in Canada, but in just a few years what was a relatively minor credit-card fraud group emerged as an international drug organization operating in several countries and with financial channels stretching to China and Vietnam. And as with most Canadian-based syndicates, the main target of the enterprise was the United States, the world's largest illegal narcotics market.

The product of the Wong Ze Wai syndicate was Ecstasy, the street name for MDMA, or N-methyl-3-4-methylenedioxyamphetamine, a designated illegal substance. Ecstasy is primarily sold in tablet form and is produced solely by illegal means, unlike legal drugs manufactured by pharmaceutical companies that have a legal but regulated market. Buying Ecstasy, therefore, has built-in dangers: the conditions under which it's produced, the strength of a dose, and the uncertainty about the ingredients' quality. Even the production of the drug is fraught with danger, with hazardous ingredients being prepared and mixed in unsafe conditions. And many Ecstasy labs are located in residential areas, making neighborhoods unsafe for their residents.

Ecstasy is in great demand as a party drug and is used across classes, which makes for an enormous marketplace. Costing literally pennies to produce, Ecstasy tablets can sell for up to $25.

For criminal syndicates, Ecstasy has become what heroin was for traditional Triads: a high-profit illegal product generating tens of millions of dollars from a relatively small investment. And having access to a market and a supply of product is at the heart of any successful criminal operation.

Operating from Canada gave the Wong Ze Wai organization the best of all possible criminal situations: a location easy to enter either as a refugee or landed immigrant; a long, largely unprotected border with the U.S., even post-9/11; and a huge Asian population with criminal support systems throughout the country. Relatively easy access to the core ingredients that make up Ecstasy was a further factor. Historically, most of the Ecstasy found in Canada was imported from Europe or Israel and destined for the U.S. But in the past several years, Canadian police have uncovered several laboratories, mostly in the Toronto area, that churned out tens of thousands of pills; that many of the operators were also involved in the hydroponic marijuana trade and had their own routes into the U.S. made for an even more lucrative situation.

For Wong Ze Wai in Canada, the American Ecstasy market would lead to what Karen Tandy, the administrator of the U.S. Drug Enforcement Administration, called "a full-blown criminal machine" that supplied an astounding 15 percent of the American market.

And Wong Ze Wai wasn't even supposed to *be* in Canada.

He first came to the attention of Toronto police in 1993 during investigations into high-tech credit-card fraud. The police discovered two criminal organizations—both linked to the Big Circle Boys syndicates—operating in the city; together they were estimated to have turned out one-fifth of the world's phony credit cards. It was also estimated that the organizations had cost Canadian consumers tens of millions of dollars through credit fraud. Detectives also discerned a typical Big Circle Boys' trait: while the credit-card scam was generating huge profits, members were also engaged in several other operations, including the smuggling of stolen cars from North America to Vietnam via Singapore, telephone fraud, and the production of counterfeit documents. The fraud investigation led police across the globe to China and Hong Kong.

An undercover agent who penetrated one of the gangs as a buyer of illegal credit cards identified one of the participants as Wong Ze Wai, a grade-nine-educated immigrant from Guangzhou, China. In April 1994, after a six-month investigation, police carried out several raids and seized computers, encoding equipment, blank credit cards, and other devices and materials used to create bogus cards. Holograms, then touted as the latest initiative to thwart fraud artists, were also seized, leading RCMP Corporal Gord Jamieson to observe that the gangs were always one step ahead of whatever security efforts were put into place. Wong Ze Wai was among the 18 people arrested. When police raided the home of co-conspirator Kwok Yung Chan, they found an imprinter and a laminating machine. Wong, who was present in his home in Scarborough, a suburb of Toronto, had 25 forged credit cards. Police also found devices that indicated he was turning out drivers' licenses and phony immigration documents.

In April 1993, in custody awaiting trial, Wong was granted permanent residency status in Canada; three months later he was convicted and sentenced to 18 months in jail. He served six months and, upon release on parole in January 1997, promptly became involved in another huge credit-card fraud operation, this one stretching from Canada to the U.S. and on to Latin America. One of the locations raided by police was a house that had been rented by Wong; detectives discovered an embosser, stacks of blank plastic cards, and holographic images.

Wong wasn't at his residence when police arrived; and when he returned home and found the door broken down he fled, moving between Ontario, Quebec, and New York State as he continued committing frauds. Eventually he returned to Toronto and surrendered, ultimately pleading guilty to parole violation charges, conspiracy to commit fraud, and possession of forgery instruments. He was returned to prison.

In October 1997 Wong appeared before an immigration hearing to appeal an order to remove him from Canada. While law-enforcement, prison, and immigration files all showed him to be a member of a sophisticated criminal organization, his lawyer described him as a married man, with two Canadian-born children, who worked at low-level employment and looked after the children while his wife worked long days in a restaurant. Wong, lawyer Peter Boushy argued, had been overpowered by a gambling addiction that forced him into crime. And, Boushy said, Wong wasn't a violent offender and had a low likelihood of re-offending.

Wong Ze Wai was still operating five years later when the United States was in the midst of an Ecstasy epidemic. And, the FBI quickly determined, he was at the center of the operation that spanned 16 American cities, three Canadian cities, and in at least four other countries. Wong, who had become what the Drug Enforcement Administration called a "Priority Target," was named as the prime focus of the operation.

In May 2001, acting on intelligence gleaned during an unrelated investigation, American authorities notified police in Toronto that huge quantities of Ecstasy were being shipped into the United States. Authorities determined that Wong had created a huge criminal network with profits so immense that the group had quickly developed financial channels for the laundering of tens of millions of dollars.

Among his "crew," according to indictments filed in several jurisdictions, including New York City, Houston, and California, were a host of mostly mainland Chinese players: his wife, Wu Kay, aka "Maggie," was named in U.S. indictments; as well as "Ah Kit," "Big Boobs," "Big Sister," "Lau Bau," "Sloppy," "Ah Teet," and "The Principal," to name a few others. Each player had a specific role to play in the sales and distribution network. The indictments identified Ha Duc Kiet, aka Ah Kit, as the U.S. broker for Wong's product; Le Thi Phoung Main, aka Big Boobs, of Ottawa coordinated the movement and laundering of the profits; and Tse Wei Kuen, aka Big Sister, was a financial investor who worked with Wong in the collection of debt. The indictments said Toronto laboratories were supervised by Wong Yuan Chang, aka Sloppy, who made certain that enough product was on hand for the distribution lines. Acquiring the raw materials needed to produce the Ecstasy was the chore of Wan Tak Chi and Wu Shu Yu. There were also co-conspirators with distribution and collection roles in several states including Texas, Iowa, Georgia, Tennessee, and Louisiana.

Throughout the summer of 2001 American agents monitored the players' conversations and movements and discovered that the Wong Ze Wai Organization was manufacturing massive quantities of Ecstasy pills in rundown "laboratories" in Canada, smuggling them into the U.S., and marketing them in several states from New York City to California. These ad hoc laboratories were mostly in the Toronto area, and while the word "laboratory" conjures up a sterile, well-lit environment, Ecstasy labs were often set up in dirty warehouses or basements with equipment consisting of buckets and pieces of tubing. To identify their product, the Wong Organization stamped logos on each one, including two hands in a handshake, a blue dolphin, and an anchor. Once in the U.S., the pills were sold through a series of distributors for resale on the streets or in nightclubs, where they were in great demand.

The organization communicated through prepaid cellphones, which could be purchased without showing identification. By January 2002 the Americans had managed to insert an undercover officer on the edges of the operation, and he spoke with Wong on the phone and arranged a small sale of 800 pills. Wu Kay, aka Maggie, Wong's wife, met with the undercover agent in Toronto and turned over the Ecstasy. In November of the same year the undercover agent made another purchase, this time of 1,000 pills.

For a year investigators continued to make small purchases to monitor the organizations' communications. By April 2003, Toronto laboratories were found containing massive amounts of product either ready for market or in production. Raiding parties of police and Health and Welfare Canada officials dismantled labs set up in residential areas of Scarborough, in east Toronto. Seized were several kilograms of Ecstasy powder, 55,000 pills, 147 Ecstasy stamps, and two compression presses used to stamp out the pills. At another Scarborough location, authorities discovered 80 kilograms of powder, 330,000 pills, 70 stamps, and two more pill presses.

In the wake of the raids police monitored phone calls regarding debt-collection problems. Several shipments hadn't been paid for and, three months earlier, Wang Zong Xiao, a California-based heroin and Ecstasy trafficker who was behind in his debt, was murdered in New York by two Asian youths armed with meat cleavers.[1] Another man, "Tony," hadn't paid his debt, police heard, and had to be taught "a lesson."

There were also conversations about the distributors and their clients' preferences: some favored specific logos, others specific colors, often red or blue. Price—ranging from $1.35 to $4 for a single pill in the U.S.—was often discussed, as was the granting of credit to customers. Police heard "Big Boobs" discussing how to launder the $30,000 a week being collected in New Orleans. Clearly the organization was becoming unwieldy, given the debt-collection problems and the sheer amount of money that had to be moved out of America.

By July 2003 Canadian police determined that yet another laboratory was in action. This time they raided the location—also in Scarborough— and seized 100 kilograms of powder, 93,000 pills, stamps, and presses.

Information continued to come in about the day-to-day inner workings of the organization. One man was granted distributorship of Ecstasy in Louisiana; samples and full shipments were arranged to several American cities; a conspirator was stopped by police but they failed to find the drugs; a courier carrying drug profits was in a traffic accident and needed a tow truck; prices were too high, quantities were too small; new laboratories had to be set up. Hundreds of thousands of pills worth millions of dollars were moved, with profits picked up from across the U.S. There were discussions about whether to fly bags of money from city to city or to drive: was it worth the 13-hour drive to move profits from Seattle, Washington, to Oakland, California? Drugs were seized in raids and money was seized in seemingly random searches. One shipment of $133,000 was seized in August 2003 in Bellevue, Washington; the courier said it was to be used to buy jewelry, and then he said it was to buy construction equipment. Plans were made to create a legitimate source for the seized money.

Financial channels involved Western Union, the Wells Fargo Bank, the Royal Bank of Canada, travel agencies, and mortgage companies. Funds were tracked and several safety deposit boxes were found packed with cash. Gas tanks of vehicles were stuffed with heat-sealed packages of currency and run through the U.S.–Canada border. Some profits were sent overseas to Vietnam and China for laundering.

By the end of March 2004, police in the U.S. and Canada had enough evidence to take down the Wong Ze Wai Organization. In a series of coordinated raids police teams across North America began serving warrants. More than 100 indicted suspects were arrested in 16 cities in New York State, California, Florida, Louisiana, Alabama, Massachusetts, Georgia, Virginia, Indiana, Utah, and Minnesota. Canadian police executed 50 arrest warrants in Toronto, Ottawa, and Montreal.

Wong and seven of his associates were rounded up in Toronto; three others were named in warrants but weren't picked up in the initial raids. And in southwest Ottawa, 36-year-old Vietnamese-Canadian Thi Phoung Mai Le, aka "Big Boobs" or "The Queen," was arrested at her home. She was described as the operator of several small businesses. Several relatives were also picked up, and police discovered eight busy marijuana grow operations.

Wong, who faced 39 charges, was described by RCMP Chief Superintendent Ben Soave, commander of the Combined Forces Special Enforcement Unit, as the "chief operating officer" of the organization; Mai Le was called the chief financial officer. "We have arrested the finance department, the rest of middle management, and the sales force," Chief Superintendent Soave said. "This organization operated in a manner similar to a large corporation."

American authorities found it difficult to overstate the breadth and power of the Wong Organization: "We accomplished what is believed to be the largest single United States–Canadian enforcement action ever taken against Ecstasy traffickers," DEA administrator Karen Tandy said. "We, together, decimated a major Ecstasy and marijuana cartel believed responsible for supplying as much as 15 percent of the Ecstasy consumed in the United States."

The fallout in the criminal marketplace was almost instant. The purity of Ecstasy decreased by almost 11 percent, reaching the lowest level since 1996. In one jurisdiction, Jacksonville, Florida, there were no Ecstasy-related deaths for six months after the Wong Organization was dismantled, whereas in the three months alone before the takedown, four related deaths had been reported. Prices shot up significantly, increasing in the Miami area by 110 percent, or from an average price per tablet of $5.52 to $11.62. In New Orleans the price went up 66 percent, and in Los Angeles the increase was a stunning 147 percent. Each of these cities was a significant marketplace for the Wong Organization.

A list of seizures by U.S. authorities during the two-year probe indicates that the organization generated a financial cycle of as much as US$5 million a week. In other words, despite the seizure of $8.7 million in cash, 46 weapons, 35 vehicles, almost a half-million Ecstasy pills, and 1,370 pounds of marijuana, the Wong Ze Wai Organization was continuing to grow even as the arrests were made.

Wanting the ringleader of the organization before their courts, U.S. authorities filed to have Wong extradited to face charges in America, where punishment is significantly harsher. Observers of the case forecast a long, bitter battle by Wong to avoid that fate. But the stubborn man who had long fought Canadian government attempts to kick him out of the country suddenly pleaded guilty to a single drug charge in a Toronto courtroom and was sentenced to time served. The following day he waived his rights and agreed to go before the U.S. courts. His wife, also picked up in the raids, agreed to plead guilty to a single charge and was given a conditional sentence, which meant she wouldn't have to serve any time in jail.

Adrian Humphreys, the national crime reporter for the *National Post* who uncovered the unusual and secret negotiations, said that Wong agreed to go to the U.S. in order to save his wife from going to jail herself and thus losing custody of their two children. "The deal was that he'd go if they dropped charges in the U.S. against his wife," Humphreys said. He added that police teams carrying out close surveillance on Wong, who himself had been given up for adoption in China, often saw him lovingly spending his days with his children in a local park.

"A sordid crime chronicle," Humphreys said, "turned into a hard-luck love story."

* * *

The Big Circle Boys and related satellite groups like the Wong Organization aren't the only stand-alone, profit-motivated criminal organizations with fluidity, mobility, and an invisible, changing structure. In November 2004 American federal agents announced that, in just one-and-a-half years, they had identified, investigated, and broken up three gangs based in New York City. Indictments filed in the case showed more than 50 men and women, described as "Chinese organized crime figures and associates," were taken down in a coordinated series of raids. The Lim Shang, the Wang Shao Feng, and the Bi Juan Wu—unlike other groups such as the Ghost Shadows or the Fuk Ching—had no official names. Each conducted a wave of terror in the city's Chinatowns, murdering, extorting, beating, and terrorizing residents, U.S. indictments said.

"It was reminiscent of the early days of the Mafia," an undercover agent said. "They identified their turf, picked their game, and went to work. These aren't Tongs or Triads or even Big Circle; they're groups who came together and found they had a common goal." The name of the game, he said, was "survival and connections. ... If they were able to keep their activities going successfully and were able to connect, even in an informal way, with larger, more stable groups, their futures were assured," he noted.

The new groups were full-service criminals, and although they moved easily from extortion to robbery, their main activities were counterfeit goods and migrant smuggling. And like many of North America's most recent criminal gangs, many were from China's Fujian province. "There was no effort to control an entire activity," the agent said. "They just went for the money." Recent successes against more entrenched gangs, he went on, had created an opportunity for these new and aggressive groups. "Crime abhors a vacuum."

The New York indictments outline the allegations against the accused. Lim Shang—also known as Ah Ho, Bo Ban, and Lin He—was the leader of the Lim group. An immigrant from China, he was described as a man with a powerful personality who had a personal security force of a dozen thugs. The main businesses of the Lim group were extortion, counterfeiting goods, gambling, and debt collection. To back up their activities, the group was notoriously violent, not stopping short of murder. The Wang group was run by Wang Shao Feng, aka Yi Fen Ah Fung and Yan Xie. Like the Lim group, the Wang organization had a penchant for sudden and severe violence. Their activities—extortion, beatings, and murder—were carried out in a similar fashion to the Lim group; the Wangs were also involved in smuggling illegal migrants to the U.S. from China. The Bi Juan Wu group, cited in another probe, was named after the primary member of the small crime cell made up of members from both groups. They were engaged in the smuggling of illegal migrants from China; there were also reports of hostage takings and money laundering, with the funds being repatriated to China.

While successful initiatives against emerging groups within North America's Chinatowns don't have the same media pull as a major probe into Triads and other notorious organizations, the targeting of low-profile gangs can prevent the growth of major national and even international criminal organizations.

The Big Sister Ping Organization, for example, was largely ignored when it began operating. From a small mom-and-pop migrant smuggling group of less than a half-dozen core members, it evolved into a sprawling syndicate operating across the U.S. and Canada and into South and Central America, Mexico, Thailand, Hong Kong, and China. The Ping Organization, named after its main player, Cheng Chui Ping, herself an illegal migrant from Fujian province in eastern China, began operating in the mid-1980s. Ping, based in Toronto and New York City, at first brought a few migrants at a time from China to Canada, funneling them through the U.S. border. The core of the group consisted of Ping and a few relatives and associates. The migrants, who'd each paid a small deposit before leaving China, were settled with their relatives in New York City and were expected to pay the rest of the transit fee. With only a few clients to deal with, the Ping group was able to collect their money and invest it into small businesses along East Broadway in Manhattan.

But with success came problems: as more and more Fujianese wanted to get to New York, Ping's success became legendary and she was swamped with applicants willing to pay tens of thousands of dollars to make the trip. Soon the little network became unwieldy and Ping had to use local members of the Fuk Ching gang to meet boatloads of migrants, ferry them to shore, and warehouse them until the rest of the payment was made. There were beatings and tortures, rapes and murders. And even after the payments were collected—and the Fuk Ching collected their percentage—anarchy prevailed and many migrants were tracked down and extorted of whatever money they were earning at day labor or at menial jobs in restaurants. The Fuk Ching became partners in some of Ping's operations, and eventually they carried out their own migrant importation in conjunction with criminal organizations back in China.

As the Fuk Ching terrorized migrants, Ping's migrant smuggling business was pulling in tens of millions of dollars—and that required a money-laundering arm. Again, with success came problems: so successful was Ping that other criminal organizations began bringing her their profits to be sent out of America to Asia. These organizations, now aware of the massive money to be made in Ping's business, began arranging their own shipments, often in partnership with her.

By the mid-1990s migrant-smuggling had become a free-for-all, with shipments of hundreds of migrants at a time hitting the shores of the U.S. and Western Canada. Suddenly, established criminal organizations, previously involved in the drug trade, were growing rich and powerful, and newer, more immature groups were making themselves small fortunes and branching out into other criminal activities, from counterfeiting goods to credit-card fraud to heroin smuggling.

When the *Golden Venture*—a ship carrying some of Ping's clients— went aground in the waters off New York City in 1993 leaving 10 migrants dead, Ping fled. She was able to evade capture by leaving the U.S. and living in Fujian, her home province. In 2000 she was arrested while in Hong Kong and, four years later, was extradited to New York City, wherein June 2005 she was convicted on conspiracy and money laundering charges. She is awaiting sentencing.

But Ping's migrant-smuggling operations sparked similar schemes across the world, from the U.K. and Eastern Europe to Australia and

Canada's west coast. The number of deaths rose as ruthless Taiwanese and Chinese gangs with an eye on high profits stuffed ships and containers with hapless migrants. Fifty-eight died in a sealed truck in Dover, England, when the oxygen supply was shut off; three died on America's west coast when they ran out of food and water and drank their own urine. Some ships left Asia never to be seen again: it's believed the rickety boats, originally bought for scrap, went down at sea with hundreds of migrants aboard.

"Big Sister Ping started off as a small operation run out of a used clothing store in New York," former RCMP assistant commissioner Richard Dickins says. "In the typical fashion of organized crime, she identified a need and filled it, making profits, sure, but also creating around herself the aura of an angel of mercy who was only reuniting families, bringing hope to people trapped in China." But Dickins, who's written a forthcoming book about Big Sister Ping and the world of migrant smugglers,[2] said that the number of travelers was so huge and the profits so massive that it took organized crime methods and harsh action to keep things under control. "Then, the good times were over." Getting at gangs when they're relatively small and poor, he noted, is simply good police work. "With the Wang, Lim, and Wu indictments, the Americans may have stopped dangerous criminal organizations now, rather than having to deal with them later."

While criminal syndicates like the the Ping Organization, the Big Circle Boys and smaller, low-profile Asian groups are proliferating across the world, organizations with strong overseas ties continue to operate in the old Triad-connected style, particularly in the heroin-trafficking business. And although their operations are far-flung and involve massive quantities of the drug, their ties to corrupt officials overseas and their caution when doing business make them difficult to penetrate.

The 125 Organization

The investigation into the 125 Organization illustrates the depth and persistence of Triad-related operations around the world. Named after the body weight in kilograms of the main player, Kin Cheung Wong—also known as "Yeung Pak" and "125"—the successful investigation was hailed as a landmark in joint anti-crime initiatives involving the U.S., China, and Hong Kong.

The 125 Organization stretched from the Myanmar–Chinese border, where opium poppies are rife, through the Triad stronghold of Fujian province in eastern China and on to Canada and several U.S. states. In China the organization was dubbed "The Untouchables" owing to its members' ability to avoid capture. The Untouchables included such key players as Kin Cheung Wong, who controlled the operation from his haven in the People's Republic of China, and Rong Hua Chen, aka "Cuttlefish," Mei Qiu Zheng, aka "Mei Qiu Chen," and Jian Bao Zhang, aka "Kin Po Cheung."

The organization was a vast "farm to arm" heroin conglomerate, acquiring their opium supply from warlords at the farm gate in Myanmar. After processing the opium into heroin, it was taken by truck across the bottom of China to the home of the Fuk Ching Triads, the southeastern province of Fujian. Another segment of the network unloaded the trucks, put the heroin into shipping containers, and sent them on to North America. A distribution cell made up of several conspirators sold the heroin at several points across the U.S.—including New York, Florida, North Carolina—and in Canada. A laundering stream was organized whereby the profits could be repatriated back to Mr. 125 in Fouzou, the main city of Fujian province. During the known life of the conspiracy—between 2000 and mid-2003—more than $100 million in heroin was moved through the pipeline; much of the profit was sent back to China.

Kin-cheung Wong—Mr. 125—a Hong Kong resident who lived in Fuzhou, the Fujianese capital, was at the heart of the vast case. A high flyer in Fouzou, he owned the Huamei Entertainment Company, a successful gambling den where hundreds of thousands of dollars crossed the table each night and the prostitutes, rumored to be the best in China, were kept busy servicing businessmen, gangsters, and political figures. Among his friends were the vice-minister of police in Fujian and assorted Customs officials and powerful Triad leaders. In his mid-fifties, Mr. 125 relished his nickname, even though it was attributed to his 250-plus-pounds on a short frame. He had the number

125 stamped on many of his possessions, from his license plate to his phone number.

An experienced criminal with a long career in the drug trade, Mr. 125 had had huge successes and some minor losses. In 1988 a load of heroin was sent from Thailand to New York City hidden in bales of rubber. The shipment was discovered at a warehouse in Queens when rainwater penetrated the bales and a chemical reaction ensued. Mr. 125 was arrested and imprisoned the following year and in 1994 was deported to Hong Kong. That he quickly went back into the drug business was no surprise to those who knew him in those days.

Cheng Cheung, a former associate interviewed in Manhattan's East Broadway Chinatown, said that Mr. 125 was a charismatic man who elicited loyalty from his colleagues and workers. "Fat, big and fat, but he knew his nickname was also The Fat Man," Cheung said. "He'd say: 'I'm fat because I eat. I eat because I'm successful. So look on my fat with envy.'" Cheung laughed. "When he was fat, he said, everybody got fat." Being in Mr. 125's company, Cheung said, was exhilarating. "He loved life, everything about it. He is a man of appetites. Women, parties, gambling. He sleeps all day and all night it's parties and friends." He said that Mr. 125 was educated in Hong Kong but moved to mainland China for protection. "No Americans can touch him there; there's no send-back [extradition], so no problem." Cheung pointed out that Mr. 125 had carefully pored over government documents filed in his Thailand–New York City case, determining where he went wrong and how the American authorities operated. "He learns."

Within five years American authorities began hearing that he was back in circulation after an FBI source was given three-quarters of a pound of heroin in New York. The international reach of the emerging operation led American police, in September 2001, to request help from China's public security minister.

Getting Chinese help and cooperation would be key to a successful investigation, but relations between governments in both countries on criminal matters had been in tatters for several years since the debacle known as the Goldfish case. In that incident, a suspect had been arrested by Chinese security officers and tortured before being sent to testify in the U.S. When it came out that the man had been beaten and struck with a cattle prod, the suspect was freed and the U.S. courts refused to return him to China.

Surprisingly, the Chinese agreed to put the Goldfish case behind them, and a joint operation was set up. Within a month a confidential DEA informant met with Mr. 125 in Fouzou; Mr. 125 agreed to provide a three-quarter-pound packet of heroin to be delivered in New York City. In December 2001 the heroin was handed over at 53rd Street and 7th Avenue in Manhattan. Then for almost two years four more shipments were sent from overseas to locations in the U.S. as Mr. 125's organization was being investigated in the U.S., China, and Hong Kong. The suspects practiced the tradecraft of the underworld, often switching cars and speaking on code on telephones.

Chinese authorities set up a wide surveillance net on Mr. 125 and found that he was planning a massive shipment. As they unraveled his high-level contacts in police and government and put together the key components of his group, they discovered that Mr. 125 was extremely cautious. He conducted heroin- and criminal-related meetings in a steam bath; whomever he was meeting was required to be naked to ensure that no listening devices were in use. He bragged that he was far beyond the reach of the American government, particularly in light of the shambles of the Goldfish case. Plus, there was no extradition treaty between the U.S. and China.

Meanwhile, information on the 125 Organization was pouring into the American team. Conspirators nicknamed Cuttlefish, Four-eyes, Kitty, and Lazy Man began turning up. Connections in several countries began to appear. And with intelligence indicating that Mr. 125 was planning a huge heroin shipment, the team decided to take down the shipment and the mastermind at the same time. Shipping containers out of Fujian province were monitored and searched, but no heroin was found. In frustration, and believing they'd missed the big shipment, the Chinese decided that they needed to catch Mr. 125 committing a crime on Chinese soil, thereby creating a conspiracy case that would allow the Americans to arrest his partners in North America. To be used in American courts, though, it was necessary for American agents to collect the evidence themselves.

The 125 investigation looked like it might grind to a halt. But on May 16, 2003, Chinese security officials, using $180,000 in front money provided by the American government, were able to set up a sting operation—and to catch Mr. 125 with 77 pounds of high-grade heroin. With his arrest, police in the U.S., Canada, and India began taking down more than 30 suspects.

In India, where the DEA had identified the address of a clandestine drug laboratory, the country was shocked to learn that the 125 Organization's influence had reached into the ranks of anti-corruption crusaders. The laboratory was hidden in a home called "Dzonga Gods" and was owned by a prominent anti-corruption fighter, a former criminal investigations officer.[3] Indian investigators took five people into custody, two of them from mainland China and two from the opium-producing country of Myanmar. One of the arrested was identified as Mr. 125's son. Twenty-four kilograms of ephedrine hydrochloride, a controlled substance used to make amphetamine and methamphetamine, were seized. A previous shipment of 200 kilograms—the potential to make more than $35 million in illicit drugs—wasn't successfully delivered and was later seized at Calcutta airport. Police determined that Mr. 125 had set up a methamphetamine factory where he was producing 500 kilograms of product every month.

In Canada, members of the Combined Forces Special Enforcement Unit (CFSEU), an anti–organized crime police unit, arrested two people who were the Canadian end of the 125 Organization investigation. A third Canadian resident was picked up in New York City in possession of six kilograms of heroin. A CFSEU investigator said that the 125 case is typical of "99 percent" of international organized crime investigations:

Canada, Canada, Canada. This is a common component, especially when it involves Asian syndicates or Triads. Getting the product into Canada is a hundred times easier than directly into the United States. All the [Asian] criminal groups have cells in or around Greater Toronto, waiting to be activated when a shipment is ready to clear. If the Americans were smart they'd shut the border until we smarten up and start kicking these people out.

China's response to the takedown was swift and relentless. Focusing on the province of Fujian, where several international drug and migrant-smuggling rings are based, the Chinese government cracked down on the corruption that allowed the rings to thrive. In the months following the 125 investigation, Chen Kai, a member of the Chinese People's Consultative Congress, was accused of running a gambling ring. Investigators said that Chen Kai controlled more than 200 companies and had several serving and retired officials, or their children, on his payroll. He was charged with laundering the drug profits of the 125 Organization through real estate schemes. A senior communist party secretary in Fuzhou, who was responsible for law enforcement, was investigated, as well as the deputy chief of the Fujian province state security bureau and the son of a former police chief in the province. Several suspects, tipped off that the crackdown was coming, fled to the U.S. and Canada.

King Cheung Wong, aka "125" and "The Fat Man," faced execution in China after his conviction. Word of his fate has not been released by Chinese authorities.

Japanese/Korean Crime Groups

Within Japan, organized crime groups called Yakuza are involved in all areas of criminal activities. Internationally, their activities center on financial crimes, the trafficking of sex workers, and the sale of synthetic drugs, particularly Ice, a smokable form of methamphetamine. The Yakuza invest their profits globally, particularly in the western United States—Nevada, California, and Hawaii—and to a lesser extent on Canada's West Coast. Several high-class sushi establishments have ties to the Yakuza; these restaurants serve as fronts for prostitution and escort rings, as well as channels for the movement of indentured young Japanese women through North America. Corporate extortion—where Yakuza shakes down major companies for money in return for not fiddling with their stock or disrupting shareholders' meetings—is a profit-maker, as are obtaining fraudulent loans from Japan's powerful banks.

Korean groups too are involved in the international sale of synthetics, sex trafficking, and extortion. Community members interviewed point to where Korean crime groups are most active in Canada and the U.S.: money laundering through traditional Korean restaurants and grills, non-Japanese sushi outlets, and grocery stores, primarily small corner outlets often run by a single family. Korean communities are widely believed to have strong espionage ties to the Korean government; for several years, some Tae Kwon Do martial arts studio chains were linked to Korean government intelligence agencies. And like many modern organized crime groups, the Koreans have suddenly emerged in the trafficking of illegal migrants out of Canada into the United States. It's rare for law enforcement agencies to penetrate the tightly knit communities.

Interdependencies and joint ventures involve members of both Japanese and Korean organized crime groups; both also work with the Triads, particularly in the sex trade and the pharmaceutical underground, as well as firearms trafficking.

Yakuza

With more than 150,000 members, the Yakuza is the largest active criminal organization in the world. It is believed to have descended from *machi-yokko*, common folk who in the 1600s took up arms to protect their villages from the *kabuki-mono*, violent groups of plundering *samurai* who'd been displaced and unemployed during a period of peace. The *machi-yokko* were everyday people: tradesmen, shopkeepers, hostelers, and even a few former *samurai* who sought to live normal lives. Their exploits against the better-armed and better-trained *kabuki-mono* gave them a folk hero status as they defended the poor and victimized.

Common to the *machi-yokko* was gambling; *Yakuza* is a word for the lowest possible combination dealt in a three-card hand in the game of *hana-fuda*. Being dealt, for example, 8-9-3 (ya-ku-sa) equals 20, the worst score possible. In essence, they saw themselves as losers and outcasts, misfits and anti-social, hands of cards to be thrown away.

Over time the Yakuza began forming into "families" based on the father-son relationship known as *oyabun-kobun*. The *oyabun* was the father who gave advice, assistance, and protection to the *kobun*, or child. A ceremony was used to lock the two together: in return for the fatherly duties of the *oyabun*, the *kobun* swore undying loyalty, stronger even than that to his birth family. Similar relationships were initiated between members who became "brothers" to each other, or between members based on age—the respect given from the young to the old.

The two most famous facets of the Yakuza are the cutting off of one's own fingers—*yubitsume*—and tattooing. Finger-cutting, in which a single joint is severed, is done as an apology by a member who offended or dishonored himself before his *oyabun*. Tattooing began as a single band inked around a criminal's arm, with each ring indicating a crime committed. It was a permanent marking that displayed the adherent's permanent self-expulsion from society. Over time the tattooing, which was painful and required endurance and a strong will, would continue until the bodies of some members were covered entirely with markings.

Through the early 1900s, Yakuza were used by Japanese politicians to further their own ends, particularly those of an ultra-nationalistic bent. They suffered through a crackdown during World War II but sprang back in the post-war years when they took advantage of black-market opportunities and became a purely criminal network, much like the formation of Italian crime networks at the same time in parts of post-war Europe.

The template of the modern Yakuza was established in the 1950s with a wave of violence, extortion, and intimidation that the government was at a loss to control. Yakuza replaced their traditional samurai swords with firearms and, influenced by American gangster movies, took to wearing impenetrable sunglasses, conservative dark suits, snow-white shirts, and thin dark ties. They swaggered through the cities in groups, making no secret of their outsider and criminal status.

By the 1960s an estimated 185,000 Yakuza members were spread over more than 5,000 gangs throughout the country. After a long period of gang warfare, wherein the diverse groups fought over turf and criminal activities, a truce was reached and the underworld settled into relative peace. One of the surviving groups, the Yamaguchi-gumi, became the most powerful of the Yakuza organizations.

The Yamaguchi-gumi is a syndicate made up of hundreds of Yakuza groups. They live in plain sight, with a headquarters, business cards, and a fairly open face to the public. Periodically they turn up in press reports—even with their high position in the underworld, they still have battles with other syndicates and sometimes even within their own ranks. They control thousands of legitimate and semi-legitimate businesses in Japan, including loan-sharking operations disguised as mortgage companies, entertainment and sports facilities, restaurants, bars, shop stalls, and even some significant industries.

The Yakuza is active in the entire range of criminal activities, from gun smuggling to widespread narcotics trafficking and importation. Prostitution and gambling are constant providers of revenue streams. One of their initiatives is to buy a few shares in a publicly traded company then show up and disrupt the shareholders' meetings; the company often ends up paying them for peace. They're also at the heart of some of Japan's most severe banking crises, having received massive loans that they've never paid back. And yet the Yakuza take great pains to present a benevolent public face; after disasters occur, they're often in the forefront of relief efforts or the provision of assistance to charities.

On the international stage, the Yakuza is prominent in the methamphetamine trade, often in partnership with other criminal organizations. While not a major producer of the drug, Japan has one of the largest meth markets in Asia, with an estimated 600,000 hardcore users and more than two million casual users. This makes it feasible and profitable for Yakuza to create joint ventures with crime groups in China, Taiwan, and the Philippines, receiving multi-kilo shipments for distribution. Canada has emerged as a drug trans-shipment country into Japan; in one instance, two Vancouver residents were the architects of a shipment of 50,000 Ecstasy tablets from Seattle, Washington, to Japan. Canada also figures into the methamphetamine and marijuana market; in October 2004, for example, 45 kilograms and meth and 60 kilos of marijuana bound for Japan were seized on the West Coast. Most of the imported drugs fall into the hands of Yakuza syndicates and are distributed through myriad businesses and clubs in Japan's major cities.

Similarly, firearms are imported from America, where they're relatively inexpensive and available. In Japan, where there are few firearms, a single pistol can be marked up 600 percent. U.S. authorities have investigated links between American Cosa Nostra members and the Japanese firearms trade.

Japanese gangsters are prominent in the international trafficking of sex workers, with women being shipped around the globe to work in massage parlors and as indentured workers in restaurants. Upon arrival in cities across North America, the women are deprived of their travel documents and made to work off their fees and expenses. The trafficking goes the other way as well, as Yakuza-connected nightclubs and brothels in Japan advertise for Western women to work as hostesses or guides. Once in Japan, the women are made to work as prostitutes and professional escorts.

The Yakuza has also invested in America's casino industry and have long organized international junkets for gamblers from Asia. Loan sharks at the casino often lend money to the losers, who in turn believe their debt will be uncollectable once they return to Japan. But with the strong connections between La Cosa Nostra money lenders and the Yakuza, collections are quickly made and the money repatriated.

Korean Organized Crime

Like Yakuza, Korean organized crime is rooted in legend. When Korea began modernizing in the 1800s there were few job opportunities, so bands of young people with no prospects formed into street gangs. They found work in the lower levels of society as occasional construction workers, bar attendants, and guards for gaming houses and brothels. As they accumulated small savings, the *keondal*—delinquents, scamps, a little like the American Bowery Boys—expanded into minor-league criminal groups. Theirs was an informal code of the streets: loyalty, fraternity, and truthfulness with each other. They occasionally helped out the poor and seldom involved the general citizenry in their activities or internal conflicts. And given Korea's long tradition against an armed citizenry, the *keondal* were also proficient at martial arts.

In the 1960s the *keondal* were active and numbered in the thousands, having morphed into larger groupings with leadership and a chain of command. As modernization took root and opportunities grew, they became localized criminal groups with operations in Korea's entertainment industry. Politicians began employing them as bodyguards and as a force to use against their opponents. When police cracked down on the groups—more than 10,000 were rounded up—the public operations almost ceased, but within the prisons the members continued their activities and grew even stronger.

In the 1970s many members were freed, and as a result of the ensuing struggle for control they formed into "families" and became powerful and violent criminal organizations. Links were established between Korean organized crime groups and others in Japan, and to Korean residents in Canada and the United States. When in 1990 the Korean government conducted a crackdown on these mafia-like organizations, several high-ranking gangsters fled, some settling in North America. But they kept up their ties to their colleagues in Korea and increasingly in Japan. The leaders who didn't flee and were imprisoned were released in the late 1990s. They instantly picked up where they'd left off, and organized crime again flourished across Korea, with significant recruitment of young blood.

Today, the modern, grown-up version of *keondal*—with 12,000 members spread across 400 families—is involved in the international crime trade, including drug trafficking—primarily pharmaceuticals—and extortion, firearms trafficking, and loan sharking. During the past four years, Korean authorities have dismantled 10 separate organized crime groups involved in drug smuggling. The *Tongsongno-pa* organization specialized in methamphetamine, smuggling the drug into Korea from China. Also caught in the investigation were suspects on the West Coast of the U.S. and crime figures in Hong Kong. Meanwhile, the Korean crime syndicate *Shinsangsapa* has been involved in joint ventures with members of Yakuza, particularly in the smuggling of methamphetamines manufactured in North Korea. As well, 22 tons of permanganate, a raw material used in the production of cocaine, was smuggled from Korea to Colombia by a cartel member and a Korean businessman with links to organized crime.

In dealings with crime groups from Africa to America, the Korean crime families are carving out greater profits and higher levels of participation in the global crime industry. Korean organized crime figures have turned up in contract murder conspiracies in the U.S.; in the importation of smokable methamphetamine, Ice, in several countries; in counterfeit products ventures with Hong Kong Triads; in credit-card frauds with expatriate Koreans living in the U.S.; in the smuggling of Chinese from Canada into the U.S.; and in mutual-assistance projects with Russian criminal organizations. But the Korean mafia's activities focus primarily on illegal immigration, migrant labor, and the sex trade.

Women, not only from Korea itself but increasingly from Eastern Europe, mainland China, and Thailand, are commodities moved around the world by Korean brothel operators. In January 2000, for example, when a Seoul-based criminal conspiracy was broken up, investigators found that a group of Russian criminals had supplied 50 Russian women and received a "lease" payment for each of $1,000 a month from their Korean counterparts who operated an employment recruiting agency. Victims of the sex-trade syndicates are routinely drugged, beaten, and raped by brothel operators. They live in accommodations that are filthy and crowded. A fire at a South Korean brothel in 2000 killed five foreign sex trade workers; in 2002 a dozen women died in a nightclub fire because they were prevented from leaving.

The sex-trade gangs are particularly active in North America; women are brought from Korea and funneled into the U.S. through either Canada—primarily Vancouver and Toronto—or Mexico. The women, who are of many Asian nationalities, including Korean, Thai, Filipina, and Chinese, work the local circuits until arrangements are made to take them through the border to their ultimate destination. Many of the women are supplied with false Chinese travel documents; others enter Canada as tourists. There are even reports that American servicemen stationed in Korea are paid to marry women destined for the brothels of the U.S.; the servicemen are paid between $3,000 and $5,000 on delivery.

Once in the U.S.—or in Canada if the recipient brothel is located there—the women are deprived of their documentation and set to work at a predetermined turnover term and rate of pay. Some—particularly those in the Midwest where a Korean crime group "buys" the wives of American servicemen overseas—have no set buy-out target and are worked indefinitely.

The breadth of the Korean-based—or Korean-connected—massage/brothel circuit is stunning. Working from a stack of white file cards, an undercover officer who investigated one gang on the West Coast demonstrated the reach of a shipment of a single group. "Start off in Canada, in this case Vancouver, and away we go." Placing a card marked with the name of a Vancouver hotel, the investigator added cards for each person, city, and organization that had come up during his investigation. Very quickly he went through the two-inch stack of cards, covering a restaurant table. Included in his "single group circuit" were 77 individual names (although some of them, he said, might have been used by two or more people); 19 Canadian and American cities; 5 countries; and an astonishing 90 massage parlors, chiropractor clinics, or out-and-out brothels, a dozen of them in close proximity to American military bases. "The women, as you see, are in a very mobile business. The name of the game is to regularly provide each outlet with fresh faces. The operators sell them among each other, transferring their debt, sending them around the region with their documents carried by escorts." Paying off their transit debt—often as much as $15,000—means workdays of 17 or 18 hours and an endless stream of clients. "But first the traffickers deduct their own expenses," he noted. "This much for rent, this much for food, this much for condoms."

Some brothel workers, particularly in the western American states, enter the trade involuntarily, having been raped—"sexed-in"—by gang members; they believed they were to become members but instead were turned out as prostitutes. The brothel operators also use Korean youth and street gangs to maintain control and order as well as to ferry women around cities or between states.

The Korean Killers, the Korean Fuk Ching, the Green Dragons, and the Korean Power are the most prominent and active of the gangs. Some were founded in the late 1970s and early 1980s. Other groups are made up of Korean–American youths who banded together for protection against the established gangs after they were kidnapped or extorted. The gangs based in New York City were indicted as far back as 1986 after Korean businesses were extorted of more than $1 million; with subtlety, the extortionists forced their victims, who owned herbal shops, to buy decorations and herbs for their stores at vastly inflated prices. Home invasions—where Korean youth gangs direct Vietnamese bandits to the homes of prominent, wealthy members of the Korean community— have also been rampant, but largely unreported.

A member of Toronto's Korean community said that there were signs of the gangs in that city, but that very little is said about them. "There's talk sometimes that this one or that one is here," he said. "One or two came here after the Americans tried to arrest them. They took some money from a restaurant, but suddenly they were gone." A former investigator with the Toronto intelligence bureau, however, said that his force has documented the activities of Korean youths involved in gang activity with other Asian ethnic groups. And, he said, unreported extortion of businesses has long been a concern.

The North Korean Government

While organized crime traditionally attempts to penetrate governments, the North Korean government is often accused of trying to penetrate organized crime. But in the face of strong accusations by the United States and several other countries, the government of North Korea denies its involvement in international criminal enterprises. When North Koreans—almost always government or government-related individuals—are arrested in various parts of the world, the North Korean government is quick to distance itself from those arrested, claiming they're garden-variety criminals; they also blame the U.S. authorities, often accusing the arresting jurisdiction of being "pawns" of American foreign policy.

Kim Jong Il, the leader of the DPRK (Democratic People's Republic of Korea), rivals Ian Fleming's Doctor No in villainy. The diminutive dictator—at five-foot-two, he wears four-inch lifts in his shoes—is a vain, charismatic man who sees himself as an *artiste*. Often reclusive, Kim has a fascination with movies; his favorite is *The Godfather*. Before being named successor by his late father, Kim Il Sung, the "Dear Leader" of North Korea, young Kim was director of the Bureau of Propaganda and Agitation. Using his skills at manipulating facts and the truth, he's built around himself a cult of personality and turned North Korea into a fairy-tale paradise of workers' glory.

While hundreds of thousands of his citizens die of malnutrition and disease, Kim lives in a seven-story home where he indulges his bizarre taste for young women—he's said to prefer virgins culled from junior high schools for the pleasure of his closest cronies—and the world's most expensive cognacs. It's estimated that Kim spends 770 times the income of an average citizen every year on cognac. The paranoid leader of a paranoid regime, Kim also spends the bulk of the country's money on military and nuclear projects—almost three-quarters of his 1.2-million-member army is amassed on the country's borders.

Yet the people of North Korea seem to have an almost pathological reverence for the Kims both father and son—and the Kims have shown no qualms about exploiting it. In the early 1970s North Koreans were urged to donate to the government everything that could be sold for hard currency. And the people responded, handing over their savings, their gold and silver, their antiques, their few luxury items. When these were all gone, they went out in work parties and scavenged, gathering mushrooms, clams, wild ginger roots, and ginseng. They panned for gold in the rivers. Portions of their already minuscule salaries were "donated" to the North Korean government.

And when there was nothing left to donate, a vast criminal marketplace was generated for producing drugs, counterfeit goods, and counterfeit money for sale outside the country. Arable land was divided up to accommodate opium fields—and this in a time of extreme food shortages. Factories that previously produced legitimate goods were retooled and restocked to make synthetic drugs. North Korean embassies around the world were used as way stations for the movement of narcotics, becoming a global network of traffickers; some diplomats, protected by diplomatic immunity, smuggled drugs in diplomatic pouches.

Criminal activities linked to North Korea mostly involve heroin, synthetic drugs, or precursor chemicals. A fast-growing industry producing counterfeit consumer goods is estimated to bring about $100 million into the country. North Korean nationals, often government figures or employees, have been picked up across the world, notably in Thailand, Taiwan, and Australia. And with legitimate North Korean exports estimated at $650 million in 2003, estimates of country's narcotics trade alone fluctuate wildly between $500 million and $1 billion. Estimates suggest that as much as 40 tons of opium a year are produced from vast hidden poppy fields in the so-called Hermit Kingdom.

And in a country where power blackouts are commonplace and the average annual salary is $760 to $900—leading to widespread poverty and even starvation—North Korea spends a huge amount of its Gross

National Product on the military, particularly in the nuclear field. It's to keep the military powerful and well funded, as well as to pursue nuclear capabilities, that the regime has turned to organized crime. "When the Soviets were no more, the North Koreans had a revenue shortfall," said Tom Schieffer,[4] the American ambassador to Australia. "They seem to have decided that a mafia-like business model is the best way to replace that revenue." Schieffer also spoke of North Korean activities in pornography and trafficking in prohibited animal parts.

Fear of North Korea's criminal capabilities has led 11 countries, including America, Japan, the U.K., Australia, Germany, and France, to track the regime's activities. American intelligence officials have been gathering data on North Korea's possible activities involving a swap of its weaponry for Afghanistan opium. There have been several reports that North Korea uses pharmaceutical factories as processing plants to turn opium into heroin. The same facilities are believed to be used to make synthetic drugs; as proof, investigators traced the importation of 50 tons of ephedrine, a component of methamphetamine, into North Korea through front companies. Fifty tons is estimated to be 20 times as much as can be put to legitimate use.

Even more sinister is the possibility that North Korea will sell or trade some of its nuclear capabilities to the highest bidder, either criminal organizations or terrorists. It already sells missiles to many Middle Eastern countries; data used by Pakistan to produce a missile capable of reaching India was based on North Korean technology.

A U.K. investigator notes that its financial, diplomatic, and political entities across the world have provided North Korea with an "instant syndicate" whose criminal activities are masked by legitimate government travel. "They're all automatically red-flagged," she said, speaking on condition of anonymity. "It's all pretty obvious to us what's going on: they're operating networks." She added that one of the reasons for a recent spike in North Korean involvement in various criminal enterprises might be that embassies and consulates have had their funding cut off. "If you want to stay at an overseas posting, you'll have to pay for it yourself." North Korea has become a "massive bazaar," she went on, with everything and anything going on the block. But, as with many criminal conspiracies, drawing a line between activities on the ground and those of the higher-ups is difficult: "Any time you have the political, the espionage, and the criminal in a case, you're going to run into a lot of fear and few informants."

According to numerous intelligence reports in several countries, the hub of North Korean organized crime is the shadowy Central Committee Bureau 39, headquartered in a heavily guarded six-story concrete building in Pyongyang. Its mandate is to bring foreign currency into the country, initially by exports of legitimate products but more recently by any means at all. Bureau 39 has overseas subsidiaries of banks and trading companies in numerous countries. One defector, a senior official at one of Bureau 39's trading companies, was subtly moved from the "white" side of the Bureau—selling legitimate products outside the country—to the "black" side in which he was used as a drug trafficker operating in China and Japan. Other defectors told of huge opium fields where there was once farmland; the profits were funneled into North Korean bank accounts controlled by the government.

In the late 1990s, when poor growing conditions hit North Korea and the opium harvest was reduced, there was a shift to synthetic drugs. Trading companies made major purchases of precursor drugs from India and the precursors were used to produce methamphetamine. In one seizure in Thailand in 1998, authorities stopped a 2.5-ton shipment of ephredine en route from India to Pyongyang. They eventually allowed the shipment to continue on to North Korea.

That the North Korean government would use diplomats to traffic drugs came to light in the 1970s as seizures of counterfeit products and drugs were made in several countries. Over the next 15 years criminal charges were laid by 16 countries against Korean diplomats, mostly for narcotics offenses. The involvement of diplomats and political figures was confirmed by defector debriefings as well as by analysis of data from investigations in several countries. As an unnamed international crime analyst told the *U.S. News & World Report* in 1999, "If North Korea were not a nation, you could indict it as a continuing criminal enterprise." Said James Przystup, of the National Defense University in Washington, D.C.: "It's the mafia masquerading as a government."[5]

Probes into counterfeit U.S. currency, notably the $100 bill, have found North Korean involvement on several occasions. These high-quality "super notes" are produced by a machine valued at $10 million; it's similar to those used by the U.S. Bureau of Engraving and Printing. Factories producing counterfeit cigarettes have also been discovered, as have factories churning out counterfeit designer goods. These goods end up in street stands across the Middle East and Asia, and in New York City and other major cities where they're sold to distributors, particularly in Chinatowns. Operators of overseas counterfeit goods networks are often connected to the North Korean government, which maintains an espionage service mandated to monitor political activities of South Korean migrants and Korean local media.

Criminal investigations and seizures related to North Koreans—particularly diplomats—are rife around the world:

- In August 1994, a North Korean spy was arrested trying to broker heroin to a Russian organized crime group; the same year, North Korean trading company executives, carrying diplomatic passports, were arrested while depositing $250,000 in counterfeit American banknotes at a Macau bank; a further investigation traced $600,000 in counterfeit bills in Macau.
- In February 1995, two employees of the North Korean state logging company, one carrying a diplomatic passport, were arrested during the seizure of six kilograms of heroin; under questioning they said the six kilograms was a "quality sample" of a batch of 2.2 metric tons of heroin that were to follow.
- In August 1995, police in Macau arrested a North Korean trading-company official who was trying to import opium.
- In November 1996, a North Korean diplomat was arrested in eastern Russia; 22 kilograms of opium was seized.
- In April 1997, Japanese authorities found 130 pounds of methamphetamine hidden in 12 bulk cans of honey unloaded from a North Korean freighter.
- In January 1998, two North Korean diplomats were arrested with 35 kilograms of cocaine smuggled from Mexico; in the same month Egyptian police arrested two Syrian-based North Korean diplomats with a half-million "date-rape" tablets.
- In August 1998, 200 kilograms of North Korea-produced methamphetamines were seized by Japanese officials.

- In October 1998, German police arrested a diplomat and seized heroin produced in North Korea.
- In December 1998, a consulate worker was arrested in China with nine kilograms of opium.
- In May 1999, Taiwanese officials seized more than 150 kilograms of methamphetamine transported from North Korea.
- In February 2000, police in Japan seized 250 kilograms of North Korean-produced methamphetamines.
- In January 2002, Japanese authorities seized 151 kilograms of methamphetamine transferred at sea from North Korea.
- In January 2002, the crew of a North Korean gunboat were arrested while transferring 198 bricks of heroin onto a Taiwanese fishing boat.
- In June 2003, a South Korean Customs officer seized 50 kilograms of methamphetamine from a Chinese ship that had stopped at the North Korean port of Najin.
- In June 2004, two North Korean diplomats working at the North Korean Embassy in Egypt were arrested for attempting to deliver 150,000 tablets of synthetic drugs.
- In December 2004, two diplomats working at the embassy in Bulgaria were caught in a drug raid in Turkey with more than a half-million tablets of synthetic drugs.

In addition to the top two money-makers—drugs and counterfeiting—North Koreans tied to the government have been discovered in a host of criminal endeavors, including the sale of animal parts of endangered species and the smuggling of South African diamonds. Other activities range into the bizarre, such as the kidnapping of Japanese citizens so that Korean agents can learn Japanese and assume their identities.

North Korean drug traffickers, counterfeit products manufacturers, and other organized crime-type figures have been linked to Triads, Yakuza, Colombian and Mexican cocaine cartels, and Bulgarian and Baltic criminal organizations. In every case, the government of North Korea either distances itself from the accused, calling them renegades, or blames South Korea and the U.S. for malicious propaganda.

The most notorious incident involving North Koreans and drug smuggling came in April 2003 in Australia. For those who believe that the Kim Jong Il's government is deeply involved in global criminal activities, the *Pang Su* case was a perfect example. That a party secretary was on board the *Pang Su* pointed generally, but still not specifically, at the North Korean government.

There's no doubt that the *Pang Su*, a 106-meter-long, 4,000-ton North Korean freighter, was the mother ship for a drug-trafficking organization. Built in 1980, it had since been modified to accommodate extra fuel and supplies sufficient to cover vast distances without putting into port.

Registered in Tuvalua, the *Pang Su* left the North Korean port of Nampo. Exact records of its route are sketchy, but it traveled in the winter or spring of 2003 to China and Taiwan; it returned to Nampo briefly, then headed to Jakarta before moving on to the west coast of Australia. On March 25 it changed its North Korean flag to that of Tuvalua, a flag of convenience, a common ploy of smugglers that effectively concealed its identity. When it entered Australian waters, it didn't report its arrival. Empty of cargo, the *Pang Su* had no legitimate business in Australia. On board—and it was never determined exactly where it came aboard—were at least 125 kilos of heroin, believed to be from Southeast Asia. Among the crew was Ta Song Wong, 37, a Chinese national whose job it was to supervise the off-loading of the heroin. Also aboard was Choi Dong Song, a 59-year-old political secretary for the North Korean government.

The *Pang Su* sat offshore in a storm, waiting.

On shore the Australian Federal Police had three men under surveillance: two Malaysian Chinese and a Singaporean. All had arrived in March on separate flights from Beijing, all traveling on tourist visas. They'd raised the suspicions of Australian authorities—likely because the police had knowledge of their arrival. A listening device was put into the men's rental car and police heard coded conversations about the imminent arrival of a drug shipment.

Early on April 16, the surveillance team followed the men to the stormy beach at Lorne on the southwest coast. A dinghy was used to bring bricks of heroin from the *Pang Su* to the shore. In the heavy seas the dinghy flipped and the man drowned; 25 kilograms of heroin was lost. Two other conspirators buried the dead man in the sand. When police moved in they picked up two men on the beach; a third and fourth were arrested the following day in Victoria. Fifty kilograms of heroin was seized. (In May another load of packaged heroin was found hidden on a remote beach; the packaging was identical to that seized on the shore at Lorne.)

The mother ship, the *Pang Su*, headed out to sea. Ignoring orders to halt, the ship led the Royal Australian Navy and Customs boats on a four-day chase. It was finally intercepted by a Navy boat off Port Stephens, 90 nautical miles off Sydney on the New South Wales coast, whereupon special forces commandos slid down ropes from hovering helicopters and took control of the ship. The *Pang Su* was taken under escort to Sydney Harbor, where it was docked at a naval base and its captain and 29 crew were taken into custody. Crew members were found to have large quantities of U.S. currency.

North Korea, predictably, responded with belligerence, calling the *Pang Su* incident "part of Washington's moves to increase international pressure" on them. "The United States and Australia are now engrossed in the false propaganda that the Workers Party of Korea and the government of the Democratic People's Republic of Korea (DPRK) were involved in the drug smuggling. ..."

They called the *Pang Su* a "civilian trading ship," but the Australian government said that the *Pang Su* was in fact owned by North Korea and noted that there is no private enterprise in the country. "It's a totalitarian state," Foreign Minster Alexander Downer said, "so it is government-owned."

Coincident to the events in Australia, a South Korean media outlet reported that Kil-Jae-Gyong, described as the North Korean government official responsible for smuggling drugs and counterfeiting, had defected to the U.S. Kil-Jae-Gyong, who was believed to have been the architect of the *Pang Su* voyage, was reported to be giving the inside information on North Korea's involvement in criminal enterprises.[6]

For its part, the U.S. government couldn't have been happier with the huge seizure. North Korea's animosity, particularly toward everything

American or South Korean, had long raised fears in Washington that the Kim regime was using drug trafficking and state-sponsored criminal activities to fund part of its nuclear program.

With the *Pang Su* case emerging as a finger pointing in that direction, on July 24, 2003, representatives of the State department, the FBI, the DEA, the CIA, and the Secret Service went to Canberra, the Australian capital, to get a briefing on the case.

In the years since, the *Pang Su* case has been brought before several congressional hearings as an example of North Korea's evolution into a kleptocracy and a direct threat to the U.S. Not mentioned were the suspicions of a lead investigator that the entire case may have been related to a Macao-based Chinese organized crime figure who directed the operation from Malaysia to Australia. A number of factors, however—the presence of Choi Dong Song, a North Korean political secretary, on board; the ship's owners being essentially the North Korean government; the previous drug seizures connected to the North Korean government; and the testimony of several defectors about state-sponsored drug trafficking—point to the North Korean government itself as being in a position to profit.

* * *

The tragedy of the Hermit Kingdom is that while hundreds of millions— some say billions—of dollars flow into the country, most of it is used to fund an almost-paranoid military structure. Despite an estimated 300,000 deaths a year from famine, a male life expectancy of about 50 years, and 60 percent of children under seven suffering from malnutrition, the bulk of the inflow goes to the military and the country's nuclear program.

And while no smoking gun has been found to take the responsibility for the North Korean crime wave right to Kim Jong Il himself, the sheer accumulation of evidence over several decades indicates that the Hermit Kingdom could rival some of the most aggressive kleptocracies in the world.

Except this one has nuclear capabilities.

Myanmar

Nowhere is the line between government and organized crime more blurred than in Burma, now called Myanmar. It's a world of jungle laboratories, ex-spies, corruption, well-equipped private armies, and warlords who rule over fiefdoms that are more like 18th-century remote societies than 21st-century villages.

Few people outside law enforcement have ever heard of Wei Hsueh-kang.[7] And few people anywhere have heard of his base of operations—Mong Yawn—or his battalions of troops, the United Wa Army.

Wei Hsueh-kang was born in 1945 or 1952[8] into a prominent opium-trafficking family in China's southern province of Yunnan. His family—his parents and older brother, Wei Hsueh-long—gathered their wealth and fled China ahead of the communist victory in 1949, crossing the border into the Shan States of Burma. (This chronology of events gives weight to his true date of birth being 1945.) The family, supporters of the routed Kuomintang (KMT), settled in the hill town of Vingngun in the Wa State, where Wei's younger brother, Wei Hsueh-yin, was born.

For the next two decades the Weis worked with the Kuomintang and the Central Intelligence Agency organizing resistance against the communists in China. Wei's father operated an opium-growing business, donating much of his profit to the movement to take China back from the communists, and the three young Wei brothers attached themselves to CIA–KMT operations.

The three Wei brothers were prolific opium smugglers with strong connections to the major drug centers of the Golden Triangle. They had government contacts in several countries, not least with intelligence organizations, and their own experience with the CIA–KMT operations gave them a good understanding of the skills and secrecy needed to run an underground business. In the mid-1970s the brothers joined the Shan United Army, run by Khun Sa, one of the most prolific drug traffickers in Asia and one of America's prime law enforcement targets. Khun Sa, who was at war with the Burmese government, was in custody at the time, so the Weis worked for his chief-of-staff, a former KMT intelligence officer. Within the military structure of the Shan United Army, the Weis—with their knowledge of the opium trade, their willingness to work hard, and their already vast connections—steadily rose up through the organization.

When Khun Sa was released from jail in 1976 he immediately recognized the power and wealth accumulated by the Wei brothers; they had, in effect, created their own cadre of traffickers within the Shan United Army. Khun Sa had Wei Hsueh-kang arrested and imprisoned for smuggling, and Wei's brothers were stripped of their military rank and position. But Wei Hsueh-kang escaped from prison and the three brothers fled. They operated along the Thailand–Burma border, and, using their former contacts, organized a new opium network.

In the early 1980s they used their profits to bankroll an army of their own within the Wa National Army. This became key to the brothers' operations and safety as they worked their trade along the Thailand border. U.S. and Thai officials were aware of their activities but concentrated their efforts on getting Khun Sa, who had taken on almost mythic proportions. And so in the shadow of Khun Sa's notoriety the Wei Hsueh-kang organization continued to grow, protected by their own army as well as the corruption of local officials and Customs officers. Vast opium fields were farmed and ever-increasing shipments were smuggled into Thailand and then on to the United States.

The first public inkling of the Wei drug organization's operations came in October 20, 1987, when Thai authorities seized 680 kilograms of heroin from a fishing boat off the Chumphon coast. The drugs were traced back to Wei Hsueh-kang, and he was arrested on November 23, 1988, in Chiang Mai in northern Thailand. And while Wei was being held for trial in Thailand his brothers went about their now-vast opium business, always keeping a cautious eye on the activities of Khun Sa.

In 1989, with the breakdown of the Burmese Communist Party, Wei Hsueh-long—Wei's older brother—saw a great opportunity. He worked out a deal with the Burmese government whereby the Wei brothers would attract soldiers into the ranks of the United Wa State Army, one of several ethnic groups that had formed to help bring down Khun Sa and his organization. In return, the USWA—in effect the Wei brothers— would take over Khun Sa's opium fiefdom.

On September 17, 1990, Wei Hsueh-kang was found not guilty in the Chumphun heroin case. The prosecutors appealed, and Wei was granted bail. In 1993 the court's original finding of not guilty was reversed and Wei was sentenced to death. But he'd long since fled Thailand and returned to the safety of the remote Shan hills where, using Lashio and Pangsanh in the eastern states as his base, he went right back into the heroin trade. Wei and his two brothers are the prime suspects in a wave of drug-related murders of several competitors in north Thailand. Wei also led 1,000 of his Wa troops in battles against Khun Sa's Shan Revolutionary Army; most of Wei's troops were killed in the prolonged fighting. The Wei brother, however, while still producing heroin, continued a campaign against Khun Sa.

Wei's activities had become public and notorious: in New York City, where the 1993 indictment was gathering dust, prosecutors brought a huge indictment against him and his organization for their heroin conspiracies. The Wei brothers had become on of the most wanted Asian traffickers.

Then, in 1996, Khun Sa negotiated a surrender to Burmese authorities.[9] This essentially shifted power in the region to the United Wa State Army, and Wei was appointed a member of the standing committee of the United Wa State Party—the political arm of the Wa army. With brigades of troops at his disposal he became the most powerful opium warlord in Asia. Two of his heroin factories were turning out an estimated 140 kilograms of heroin a month, and the opium fields had expanded by more than 10 percent. Wisely, Wei didn't follow Khun Sa's high-visibility ways; instead he decentralized the drug operations, making them more difficult to penetrate. Mule and pony caravans were sent, packed with heroin, into China's Yunnan province or across the border into Thailand. The Wei brothers and other, smaller groups of traffickers were exporting as much as 75 percent of the opium leaving the Golden Triangle.

The primary victim of Wei's heroin trade was America—while he was running his army the purity of heroin in the U.S. shot from 30 to 80 percent. But with success came danger. The U.S. government put a $2 million bounty on his head, and on June 1, 2000, U.S. President Bill Clinton placed Wei's name on the "Foreign Kingpin Designation Act." Right above Wei's name was Chang Chi-Fu—the elusive Khun Sa, who was in loose protective custody in Burma.

Using diplomatic pressure and working through international back channels the U.S. urged the Thai government to aggressively pursue the Weis. In February 2001 Thai authorities seized $2.3 million of Wei's assets in Thailand, cutting off one of his money-laundering streams. In June one of his prime money-laundering officials was arrested in Cambodia and turned over to Thai authorities. Then, in December, Wei was accused by the UWSA leadership of recklessly ordering his troops into battle against Khun Sa; more than a thousand of Wei's men had been killed in a long-ago battle. The UWSA ordered Wei to leave their base in Mong Yawn or to pay $3.2 million. Some observers believe pressure was brought on the UWSA to sever the Weis from their operations and protection. In any case, it worked: rather than pay up, Wei took 2,000 of his loyal followers and left the UWSA stronghold, settling in a town near the Loatian border.

In 2003 the Thai military sent thousands of troops to the Burmese border in preparation for a strike on Wei. When the Burmese government protested, the troops were withdrawn. Meanwhile the American government made it illegal for any bank, company, or individual to do business with the UWSA or, specifically, Wei Hsueh-kang. Reports began circulating that he'd been arrested by Burmese officials. The Burmese quickly denied they had him in custody; in fact, they said, they had no idea where he was. Nor did they have any evidence that he was a key figure in the United Wa State Army's narcotics organization. He was, the government said, a leader of a group that assisted the Burmese in quelling rebel activity on the borders.

"They had him," a diplomat in Bangkok said.

No question about it. But they didn't get him for the Americans. They wanted to straighten him out about reducing narcotics coming out of his factories. The heroin, not the synthetics. They had him under loose house arrest. The Burms' problem is that a lot of Wei's heroin ends up in the U.S., and the U.S. is already making noises about the Wa being terrorists. The synthetics stay pretty much in Asia, so that's not America's problem. I think you'll see an even bigger shift from opiates to methamphetamine in the coming years.

Another diplomat said that the Burmese government wanted to "dress him down" over his reluctance to follow the government plan to make Burma drug-free by 2005. "Wei had been heard to say it would take longer," the diplomat said. "He wanted at least two more years." He said the result of the discussions wasn't known, but that Wei had been released and was back operating on the Burmese side of the border near Chiang Mai. If anything, his drug trafficking increased and he was seemingly immune to the pressures brought to bear by the U.S. government.

As heroin from Colombia and Mexico—as well as shipments from Afghanistan—began flowing into the U.S. in greater quantities, Wei predicted a sharp downtown in his fortunes and began constructing about 50 laboratories throughout the USWA-controlled territory around the Thai border. An estimated 500 million methamphetamine tablets—*ya ba* or "crazy medicine"—were churned out of the factories. The same routes that had been used to send heroin into Thailand were now used for the new product. Wei's factories were "taxed" by the Burmese government, which allowed him to operate freely and to continue his role as a local government leader, collecting taxes and building villages. As well as getting a piece of the profits, the Burmese government also got a standing army in the area to ward off rebels. And, with the reduction in opium fields, the Burmese government could point to their efforts in the war against drugs: speed factories are small and remote and don't show up on the satellite surveillance regularly carried out in the area.

Ya ba from Wei's busy factories flooded Thailand, India, Japan, and much of Asia. His caravans were huge and heavily armed, often confronting Thai military squads patrolling the border. By some estimates, Wei was making even more money from *ya ba* than he had from the heroin trade; the markup on each pill reached as much as 400 percent.

In 2005 Wei Hsueh-kang, his brothers, and five high-ranking members of the United Wa State Army were indicted by a federal grand jury in Brooklyn, New York. The charges rising from an international investigation called Operation Warlord, stated: "The UWSA, with approximately 16,000 armed forces under its control, purports to be an

independence movement seeking the creation of an ethnic Wa state. ...
[But] for decades it has been a powerful criminal syndicate and world-
wide narcotics trafficking organization."

Under the control of the Wei brothers, the UWSA grew to become
one of the largest heroin-producing and -trafficking groups in the
world. "Since 1985 the defendants ... have imported more than a ton
of heroin with a retail value of one billion dollars into the United States
alone... More recently the defendants and the UWSA began production
of methamphetamine for export to the United States and elsewhere."
Methamphetamine tablets, imprinted with the UWSA logo, had been
seized at several American postal facilities.

Operation Warlord found the full extent of the Wei/UWSA drug
network:

> [They] control all decision making relative to the cultivation,
> collection and transportation of opium. ... This includes the taxing
> of narcotics shipments and drug refineries and the collection of
> lucrative narcotics proceeds. ... [They] provide security for heroin
> and methamphetamine laboratories in Wa territory, as well as for
> drug caravans ... from Eastern Burma to Thailand, China, and
> Laos. ...

The Burmese government said it would go to the ends of the earth
to track down the eight suspects. The Thai government was skeptical:
it's long been accepted not only that the opium armies of Burma corrupt
local officials and customs officers, but also that their influence—and
profits—run to the very top of Burma's military junta. Wei has been
spotted a number of times at military sites and political meetings.
Always escorted by several of his well-armed troops—the United Wa
State Army has between 15,000 and 35,000 troops under arms—Wei
seems to have little fear of being captured. But in the event of a strike
against him, he's never in company with his brothers, ensuring that
their operations will never be without a Wei at the helm.

Observers believe that the days of the UWSA and the Wei brothers
are numbered. The American indictments and the damage done
to Thailand are expected to lead to some resolution of the warlord
situation. Border clashes, in effect mini wars, between Wa troops and

the Thai military have continued. U.S. special forces teams have gone into the northwest territory to train the Thais, and the U.S. government has sold Black Hawk helicopters to the Thai government.

Despite the Burmese government's promise that drugs in the country would be eradicated by 2005, Wei's organization blithely continues to farm opium. His factories are turning out ever more shipments of methamphetamine and synthetic designer drugs. Confirmed links have been found between the UWSA and Chinese Triads, particularly the 14K based in Hong Kong and operating in Rangoon and Bangkok.

Endnotes

1. The homicide of Wong Zong Xiao may not after all be tied to the Ecstasy case. A long-time heroin trafficker involved in some of the world's most notorious cases, Wong had plenty of enemies on both sides of the law. He was a central figure in the 1988 Goldfish case, a joint U.S.–Chinese–Canadian global drug investigation that probed the smuggling of heroin hidden in the bellies of dead *koi*, an exotic ornamental goldfish. The case netted several senior members tied to the Triads in eastern China, including Wong Zong Xiao, who was arrested in Shanghai. After being severely beaten by Chinese authorities, Wong was turned over to the Americans to be a star witness in their prosecution. He testified that he was brutalized during interrogations in China and told that he was "like a piece of meat on our chopping board; we can chop you any way we want..." if he didn't testify falsely in the American trial. The case sparked an international incident, since it was revealed in court that the U.S. authorities may have covered up evidence that supported his story. During several investigations by Chinese authorities, it was found, he was dragged through the streets, blindfolded, shocked with an electric cattle prod, and refused food or drink. When he fell asleep he was awakened with the cattle prod.

Wong was freed from custody; an American appeals court refused to send him back to China because it was feared he'd be executed. For several years after the Wong debacle, the Chinese government refused to cooperate in major cases with the Americans.

And although there were other criminal ties that might have contributed to Wong's murder, it might have been as simple as "saving face": detectives at the murder scene were told that Wong had been involved in a fight just moments before the murder inside the Subway Café nightclub.

Wong Zong Xiao's activities in the heroin trade are the subject of the "125" case that follows.

2. *Trail of Misery* by Lee Lamothe and Richard Dickins (HarperCollins Canada), to be released in 2006.

3. The owner of the home was Upen Biswas, a former senior director of the CBI, India's criminal investigation bureau, who was famous as a fighter against corruption in India. Biswas denied any knowledge of the narcotics operation at his house and the Indian parliament absolved him of any wrongdoing. The motion sparked a walkout of Parliament by members of the Opposition.

4. Tom Schieffer in a speech to the National Press Club in Canberra in 2003, as quoted by Jonathan Fenby in *Sunday Business*, London Knight Ridder/Tribune Business News.

5. Both quotes are from *U.S. News & World Report*, February 15, 1999, in an article by Steven Butler. A third quote, from Phil Williams, a professor at the University of Pittsburgh, was even more pointed: "We've rarely seen a state use organized crime in this way. ... This is a criminal state not because it's been captured by criminals, but because the state has taken over crime."

6. Kil Jae-Gyong's defection, like everything to do with North Korea, was wrapped in mystery, charges, and countercharges. The former North Korean ambassador to Sweden was expelled for drug trafficking; he was also booted from Russia for counterfeiting. A defector of Kil's quality—he was said to be very close to the center of the North Korean government—would provide almost conclusive proof of the DPRK's criminal activities. Doubts about the facts of the "defection" were quick to arise, however. North Korea put out a press release stating that Kil had actually died of an "illness" in June 2000 and that his remains were buried in the Patriotic Martyrs Cemetery in Sinmiri, Pyongyang. Of the reports of the defection, the DPRK said: "These are whopping lies and sheer fabrications made by those engrossed in the anti-DPRK smear campaign. ... They will blush themselves with shame over telling the most sheer lies for a smear campaign." Media that reported the initial story of the defection apologized; however, it was noted that the death of a senior government official of Kil's status would have been reported in the DPRK press. No such story was published.

7. Wei Hsueh-kang is known by a variety of names, among them Wei Sia-kang, Wei Xuekang, Chiwinnitipanya Prasit, Cheewinnittipanya Charnchai, and Kadumporn Somboon. Some are Thai versions of his name and others are different spellings of the same name. U.S. indictments and international Wanted bulletins use Wei Hsueh-kang.

8. Wei has two Thai passports issued in his name. One gives his date of birth as June 29, 1952; the other as May 29, 1952. His Thai citizenship card gives his birth date as 1945.

9. Details of the Khun Sa deal remain shrouded in secrecy, but it leaked out that the government offered him an opportunity to live in safety from the U.S. government, who had indictments against him and a $2-million reward for his capture. After turning control of his army over to the Burmese government, Khun Sa was installed in a comfortable house in a government compound in a quiet Rangoon neighborhood. He was given a loan so that he could set up a bus and trucking company; he was awarded concessions to operate in the jade and gem business; he was offered the contract to build a road from Rangoon to Mandalay. As well as giving up his "war" against the government, intelligence sources say that he allowed himself to be thoroughly debriefed about the drug trade. He is said to be terrified that the United States will somehow get hold of him and take him to New York City to stand trial.

PART
THREE
Russian Organized Crime

Crime and Emigration

The modern version of Russian organized crime—the *mafiya*, a bastardization of *mafia*—grew in strength with the tearing down of walls in the early 1990s.

For decades Russian- and Eastern European-born criminals of Jewish background had been operating throughout much of the world, forming their own their own small, informal cartels, primarily in the U.S. where they battled or joined with Italian crime gangs in major cities. With the arrival of Prohibition in the U.S., they, along with the Italian crime gangs, became wealthy; when Prohibition ended, these organized crime groups were flush with money and moved out into the wider society.

Included in successive waves of immigrants from Eastern Europe to North America were many different kinds of criminals. When the Soviet Union eased up on the migration of Russian Jews, many departed to the U.S. Among them were criminals who claimed they were Jewish but weren't; they had simply used the opportunity to escape from the Soviet Union. Intelligence reports state that the Soviet government allowed thousands of gulag prisoners—hardcore career criminals—to emigrate.

In 1983 the U.S. Senate Committee on the Judiciary was told by a New York City police officer that an organized band of Soviet immigrants was loose in his city. The group, mostly made up of immigrants from Odessa, had emigrated to the U.S. and settled in Brighton Beach. Their specialties were the relatively non-violent fraud, pickpocketing, and some extortion. Another group of former Soviets, the Potato Bag Gang, ran a switch con in which a seaman who said he was from a ship docked nearby offered to sell gold Russian coins. When the credulous victim let his guard down momentarily, the bag was switched and instead of receiving gold, the victim received potatoes.

The Committee was also informed about a group of émigrés who had left the Soviet Union posing as Jews. As many as a thousand were engaged in criminal operations ranging from international heroin trafficking and wide-scale frauds to arranged bankruptcies and alien smuggling. Among them, police believed, were several people who had been convicted of murder in the U.S.S.R. Some groups had all the trappings of a "mafia" structure, except for the members' ceremonial initiation. They were spread across the U.S. and Canada and operated in Mexico, Western Europe, Israel, and South America. That they were interconnected when it suited them, and independent when they needed to be, made investigation and enforcement difficult.

✷ ✷ ✷

Vory V Zakone

There are many variations on of Eastern European organized crime—"Russian Mafiya" is the catchall name for various gangs from several countries other than Russia; their only common denominator is that they all speak Russian.

Most secretive—and long hidden behind the Iron Curtain—was the traditional criminal group in which leaders are called *vory v zakone*, or "Thieves Within the Code." Organized Thieves who followed a set of rules of behavior have been traced back for centuries. There were early bands of Thieves—pickpockets, shoplifters, even beggars—who lived outside the margins of society. They, like the more modern Thieves, spoke their own argot, had specific ways of dressing, and helped each other in bad times. There was no Great Criminal Syndicate, but merely small groups of clannish outsiders who lived from day to day and had rejected, or been rejected by, society and all the trappings that went with it. In the 1800s, when poverty was rampant, many were attracted to the freedom and companionship of criminal and anti-social guilds. When miscreants were imprisoned, their outsider status became even more pronounced and, as with the Italian *Camorra*, they took on an enhanced criminal aspect. *Vory* come from all the countries of the former U.S.S.R.; the clannish Georgian version of the *vory v zakone* allows for blood and extended family relationships.

Their criminal underworld is called the *vorovskoi mir*. Heavily tattooed, the *vory* almost without exception spent time in the brutal Soviet gulag system. They have their own slang and silent ways of communicating using hand signals. There are tales of *vory v zakone* who entered prison at a young age and throughout their lives spent only a handful of days in freedom. Many members were initiated inside Soviet prisons.

In the initiation ceremony the applicant is "crowned" at a meeting called a *skhodka*. Accounts of the ceremony range from kissing a knife to swearing an allegiance of fealty before senior criminals. To be accepted into the *vorovskoi mir*, at least two *vory* have to propose the new member and several conditions have to be met. The applicant must never have worked at a legitimate job; he must never have been a policeman or a soldier or tax collector; he must renounce his ties to his blood family; he must never speak to authorities or cooperate with them. The rules of the *vory v zakone* include the following:

- A *vor* must support another *vor* in any and all circumstances.
- A *vor* can only live on what he has stolen or conned from a "citizen" or has won while gambling.
- A *vor* lives above and beyond the rules of State law.
- A *vor* must never serve in the armed forces.
- A *vor* must never defend himself in court, if charged with a crime of which he is innocent.
- A *vor* must take from other prisoners while in custody.
- A *vor* must agitate against the State while in custody; whenever he can he should exploit the weaknesses of his captors.
- A *vor* must find and train new young criminals and, if they're suitable, arrange for their acceptance into the underworld.
- A *vor* must never marry before the State; semi-permanent relationships are permitted; and a marriage involving a *vor* is akin to a master-slave relationship.
- A *vor* must donate money from his activities to an *obshchak*, a fund for the assistance of other Thieves.
- A *vor* mustn't gamble more than he has; all gambling debts must be settled.

Punishments for violating the Code varied from a face slap to death. In a prison with particularly strong adherence to the Code, a *vor* could be expelled for accepting a light for his cigarette from a guard. Because the history of the Thieves is an oral one, a punishment might be as simple as being forbidden to boast about one's activities or adventures.

The Thieves' credo can be summed up as "All for me and none for you" or "Give me everything, and then I want more."

Because of the often-lengthy prison terms the *vory* endured, vices were permitted, such as drinking contraband alcohol or taking drugs, but their use could never be an excuse for violating the Code. Homosexuality, too, was allowed, but the *vor* could never be the passive participant but only the aggressive "taking" one.

For all the violence generated by the *vory v zakone*, contract murder is seen as a negative. While violators of the Code could be put to death—often in gruesome ways, particularly in prison where creativity was needed—those known as having killed for gain were rejected, and could be expelled if they killed for reasons not related to personal honor or in defense of the Code.

Despite the often-told "Thief" tales in books and cinema, a Thief is permitted to remove himself from the underworld and to "walk alone." There are several reports of Thieves who, after the breakup of the Soviet Union, found the widespread criminal anarchy, much of it involving corrupt businessmen, spies, and politicians—the Thieves' traditional enemies—to be a violation of their concept of the pure Code.

All Thieves have nicknames. Those who are brought into the formal underworld may have had nicknames in their former lives; however, when initiated they're given new names or allowed to choose one. Some names describe a physical characteristic—Vyacheslav Ivankov, for example, was called Yaponchik because of the Asiatic cast to his eyes. Others might be for a Thief's attitude: Tank, or Dashing. A home invader might be called Madhouse because of his single-minded wrecking of a victim's home.

Thieves are also famous for their tattoos, even more so than the Yakuza. Thieves' tattoos are often their histories: church spires, for example, denote the number of prison sentences the wearer has undergone. Religious messages are often printed on chests and arms: "O Lord, Save Thy Slave" or "With God I'll Be." Tattoos are found on all parts of the body, including eyelids, faces, necks, and even penises. A tombstone with wings might indicate that someone has died, that "a life has flown away." A black and white diamond, for some reason, means the wearer has pleaded not guilty but was convicted anyway; the diamond means he's a dangerous and angry man. A domino with six spots on it indicates the wearer has come to grips with being a prisoner and has given up any hope of freedom. A suit of cards indicates a professional expert gambler.

The most prominent of the Thieves' tattoos is the eight-pointed star of the *vory v zakone*. It's often worn on the chest of one who's been initiated in the Thieves' world. The same tattoo on the kneecaps means the wearer takes a position of anarchy against the rest of society: "I won't bow to any other power; I cannot be made to fall to my knees." The unofficial wearing of the star—and of several other Thieves' identifiers—often leads to its removal, often by knife or razor blade. Tattoos are also forcibly put on the faces of non-Thief prisoners. A child molester might have a fly inked onto his face; an informer might have the camp slang word for "informant" placed on his forehead.

Inside the prisons, the tattoos—which were banned throughout the gulag system but the rule was unenforceable—were applied in several unhygienic ways. Instruments ranged from needles to broken lightbulbs. One device was made by fitting a knitting needle to an electric razor. Dyes were often made by scorching rubber from a boot or shoe and mixing it with urine. A prisoner might suck on a piece of cloth, mixing the dye with his saliva.

There were always more Thieves, it is believed, inside the gulag system than outside. That changed when the U.S.S.R. began to collapse in the late 1980s and 1990s and a flood of migration ensued. More than two-and-a-half-million Russians, most of them Jews—or claiming to be Jews—made their way to North America and Europe. Among them were hundreds of lower-level members of the *blatnoi*—the Russian underworld. Mostly, they were petty thugs and criminals who make up the bulk of the underworld.

Suddenly the entire world, it seemed, had new citizens; they were in fact iron-souled criminals who, law enforcement agencies warned, would put the traditional mafia groups to shame. They were former gulag prisoners with nothing to lose; they were former battle-hardened soldiers; they were well-trained former KGB agents or predatory businessmen who'd looted the Soviet Union for decades and were going to force-feed hundreds of millions of dollars in the West's economies, polluting it beyond recognition.

"Yaponchik"

Vyacheslav Kirillovich Ivankov wasn't the only *vory v zakone* to make his way out of the chaos of the crumbling Soviet Union. He wasn't even the first. But he was the one who captured the imagination of the public and the attention of police in several countries. His is the story of a man bridging an old tradition—the *vory*—and the New World, where a former pickpocket could loot millions.

Ivankov was known as Yaponchik, or "Little Japanese."[1] He was born in 1940 in the Soviet Republic of Georgia and raised in Moscow. From the time he was 14 he was a rebellious creature of the streets, stealing and picking pockets and paying homage to the criminals throughout his neighborhood. He was aggressive in everything he did, from wrestling to acrobatics.

By the 1960s he'd developed into a member of the Mongol, a band of gangsters led by Gennadiy "the Mongol" Korkov, a notorious *vor v zakone*. The group specialized in a gamut of criminal activities, from relatively peaceful frauds and pickpocketing to strong-arm extortions and violent home invasion-style robberies in which victims were often tortured. The Mongol spotted Ivankov's talents early and, in the manner of the traditional *vor*, began observing him and grooming him for entry to the formal underworld.

Physically strong and a competent wrestler, Ivankov received his first criminal charge in 1966 after partaking in a brawl in a nightclub. Although his lawyer said he was defending the honor of a female acquaintance, Ivankov was convicted and briefly jailed. While in prison, he was exposed to the in-custody underworld of the *vory v zakone*. When he was freed he concentrated his activities on the widespread black marketeering that was the underpinning of the day-to-day Soviet economy. Russian files sketchily detail an arrest in 1974 for extortion.

In 1980 in Russia, according to the MVD—*Ministerstvo Vnutrennikh del*, or Ministry of Interior—Ivankov became involved with the *Solntsevskaya*,[2] a criminal group based in south Moscow and founded by legendary *vor* Sergei Timofeyev, known as "Silvester."[3] The early criminal activities of the *Solntsevskaya* centered on gambling, frauds, firearms, and forgery. There are also, in Ivankov's MVD files, allegations of drug trafficking. The group became notorious for committing a series of home invasions in which Ivankov and his gang used false militia identification to conduct "searches" in the homes of wealthy Russians. During these searches, valuables and cash were taken.

On May 13, 1980, acting on complaints from several victims of the MVD scam, the Moscow Criminal Investigation Department moved in to arrest Yaponchik for robbery. So many shots were fired at his car as he tried to flee that it was riddled with holes and the tires were blown flat. It took several officers to remove the stubborn Ivankov from his small vehicle. Somehow he escaped from custody and when he later surrendered and went to trial, all charges were dropped, either through corruption or inept prosecution.

After his release he was arrested for a particularly savage home invasion, convicted of robbery, and sentenced to 14 years. He spent hard time in Tulun, a tough Siberian prison in the bleak Urkutsk region, and fell in with the imprisoned *vory v zakone*. He certainly acted the part, racking up more than 60 serious violations for knifing other inmates, beating guards—one fatally—and a litany of riotous behavior.

In 1986 or 1987, he underwent the Thieves' ceremony and had two eight-pointed stars tattooed on his chest. (Some reports indicate Ivankov was initiated as a *vory v zakone* some years earlier, in 1978, while serving a sentence at Moscow's Butyrskaya prison.) In 1991, a coordinated letter-writing campaign was orchestrated by civil rights champions, artists and athletes who called the 14-year sentence too harsh. A judge on the Russian Supreme Court took a hefty bribe from mysterious "major forces" in criminal, judicial, and political circles,[4] and Ivankov's sentence was reduced. In February 1991 he was freed on probation after having served 10 years of his sentence. Legend has it that he was flown from the prison to Moscow aboard a private jet and that a grand party was held at the Metropol Hotel to celebrate his release.

At the time Ivankov was released, not only the Soviet Union was in shambles but also the underworld, where relations between Russian criminals and Chechen gangsters had erupted in widespread violence. At a meeting of the most powerful *vory v zakone*, Yaponchik came out firmly in favor of vanquishing the Chechens, whom he called the "blacks." The Chechens, known as fierce fighters, had killed more than three dozen of the "whites."

His activities in the "First Chechen War" again made Ivankov a target of the government. He was gaining a reputation as a powerful criminal leader and had become a legend, especially among young men who wanted to enter the underworld. Senior militia officials looked for a way to overturn his release, and at the Tulun prison they discovered that the positive reports and letters they'd received about Ivankov had been forged. The entire staff at the prison was replaced, but the forgeries weren't enough to re-incarcerate the famed Yaponchik.

Russian authorities allege that he was involved in a wild shootout in the cloakroom of a Moscow restaurant in 1992 in which two Turkish men were killed and another badly wounded. Even though police didn't suspect Ivankov's involvement at the time, he went into hiding. His other activities and increasing notoriety sparked a plan to catch him violating his probation, but as police activity intensified their plans started to leak out. Ivankov's powerful supporters began planning to get him out of the country, to either the U.S. or Canada.[5]

* * *

In the years following the beginning of the outflow of criminals from the collapsed Soviet Union, police across the world were finding themselves up against a threat they didn't truly understand. Modern police thinking was along La Cosa Nostra or Triad lines, structures that had a hierarchal leadership and a flow of orders down to "workers" and of profits up to "bosses." Few law enforcement agencies had heard much about the massive criminal conspiracies operated by Soviet businessmen, politicians, spies, and the *vory v zakone*. But as Russian émigrés appeared in cities across the world, violence erupted: there were gruesome murders, mysterious kidnappings and disappearances, wild public shootouts, and suspects being picked up who were as unlike traditional organized crime figures as possible.

Within Moscow, at the purely criminal level and not counting massive black-market schemes, corruption, bribery, and financial fraud—in 1993 Russian entrepreneurial criminals had made $12 billion vanish from the banking system—a free-market underworld was going full tilt. The union of Soviet states had been transformed from a communist kleptocracy into a capitalistic free-for-all. Drugs were pouring in from all sides and there was a strong export business for heroin, which was easily available. Foreign businesses, looking to capitalize on a massive emerging market, scouted investment opportunities and found themselves victimized by a seemingly institutional corruption. Illegal weapons brokers worldwide seized upon a vast supermarket of firearms and military equipment—and, some said, nuclear materials—available at bargain prices. Joint ventures with Colombian cartels were formed. The entrepreneurial criminal could now connect with traditional crime groups from anywhere.

So began the criminal migration from the Soviet Union, and the ramifications would be felt around the world.

Brighton Beach

In the 1970s and 1980s, before Vyacheslav Ivankov made his way West, several Russian gangs were in operation in Brighton Beach, a Russian-speaking enclave near Coney Island in Brooklyn. Former Soviet and Israeli gangs, usually mustered under a few leaders, had long wreaked havoc throughout the community. Such legendary leaders included Monya Elson, a prolific killer and extortionist who had emigrated in 1978; Evsei Agron, another extortionist, murderer, and thief who'd arrived in 1975; the Nayfeld brothers, massive thug-like drug traffickers and strong-arm men who'd come from Russia in the early 1970s; and the first "Brainy Don," Marat Balagula, who made a fortune through complex frauds, notably a gas-tax scam.

Brighton Beach was a place where people whispered of tortures, kidnappings, rapes, and murder. There were former Russian hitmen who struck in public before sauntering away under the eyes of witnesses. There were gun battles involving Uzis. Law enforcement, reacting to a flood of media reports, began targeting suspected gangsters—loosely called the *Organizatsiya*, the Organization. Except for under Balagula who had strong leadership skills, the *Organizatsiya* was really just a bunch of diverse groups who often fought each other like pre-Prohibition American street gangs.

Larger crimes, though, were being played out on the national and international stages. Within two years of the Soviet Union's collapse,

U.S. Customs had investigated 82 cases involving Russian–Eurasian organized crime. In one heroin investigation, Russian couriers were body-packing multi-kilo shipments of drugs through JFK Airport in New York City. The shipment originated in Bangkok, and the drugs were sent throughout the American eastern seaboard. Customs also found an international pipeline taking stolen American cars—particularly four-wheel-drive and luxury vehicles—overseas. Several models of high-end cars, notably Jaguars and Mercedes, were seized as far away as Belarus. The need for good vehicles and equipment in the former Soviet Union was sharp: $25 million worth of cars, trucks, and construction equipment was seized by Customs. Seventy-seven suspects were arrested.

In Southern California, two brothers from Lithuania, Michael and David Smushkevich, set up a "rolling medical lab" that brought in huge profits. According to the U.S. Senate's Permanent Subcommittee on Investigations, the scheme was simple:

> *Patients were lured to clinics or sites serviced by mobile vans for comprehensive physical examination with bogus claims of "state of the art" testing offered "free of charge" or at a nominal cost to the patient. Billings for nonexistent services, falsely inflated billings, or billings for unnecessary services, provided the basis of the scheme. ...*

The false billing scam—which quickly spread to St. Louis, Florida, and Chicago, cost private and government health insurers approximately $1 billion. The Senate investigation also found a simple but lucrative scheme involving staged traffic accidents "in which phony medical clinics have been set up in order to submit false claims for unnecessary treatments. In some instances, phony law firms using figurehead attorneys have been set up to further this scheme."

The most famous Russian organized crime initiative was the "red daisy" investigation that looked into a series of companies set up to exploit the weakness of the American motor fuel excise tax law. By creating a complex daisy chain of companies, Russian organized crime figures, some of whom had come to America before the collapse of the Berlin Wall, were able to defraud the U.S. government of hundreds of millions of dollars in fuel taxes. The scheme was so lucrative that La Cosa Nostra went into the business in partnership with Russian crime bosses. In a single 18-month period, law enforcement arrested 136 suspects who had bilked American state and federal governments of an astounding $363 million.

But those were the "thinking man's crimes," and were largely invisible. And while some violence was associated with most of the cases, it was at the ground level that the public and media were introduced to the Wild West of Russian crime.

* * *

U.S. Immigration files show that Vyacheslav Ivankov entered the United States on March 8, 1992, on a suspected forged passport and a business visa that said he was in the film industry. He neglected to divulge his criminal record. He obtained a Colorado's driver's license in his own name and with a Denver address.[6] Ivankov made his way to Brighton Beach, where crime among the estimated 200,000-strong Eastern European community had reached intolerable levels. His arrival sparked hysteria and rumor: that the greatest *vor* in the world had come to conquer the out-of-control elements in New York; that he was met at JFK by a *vor* who bestowed upon him a briefcase containing $1.5 million; that he had recruited two brigades of former Special Forces thugs who'd become battle-hardened in Afghanistan, paying them a retainer of $20,000 a month.

On a more realistic level, he set about making the necessary preparations to begin taking control of diverse criminal elements and to protect himself from possible extradition. He called meetings of the local leaders and extorted them directly: partnerships were offered and, if rejected, violence was used both to gain control and, as was his habit, to build a fearsome reputation. A friend arranged a $15,000 false marriage for him, a move that would allow him to apply for a Green Card and then obtain citizenship. Ivankov swiftly established business interests in Florida, where a powerful *vor v zakone* owned a restaurant and several properties. His money also found its way into a car dealership in Texas and into real estate in the western United States.

In January 1993, the MVD notified American authorities that Ivankov was on their soil and was engaged in organized crime activity in the Russian community; several telephone numbers were also sent to the FBI. The initial notice was met with barely concealed indifference, since the only thing the Russian judiciary had on him was a "violation of the rules of administrative supervision." In short, he was a parole violator.

Ivankov, meanwhile, was busily building both his organization and his legend. As well as the Colorado *vor*, he was in contact with organized crime figures of varying degrees of prominence, including Ludwig "Tarzan" Fainberg, a relatively minor criminal in Florida where he operated a strip club. But Fainberg leveraged his connection with Ivankov, and with others involved in serious Russian organized crime, to inflate himself into an international gangster. He was, an associate said during an interview in Fort Lauderdale, "about as low on the ladder as you could get. But he knew a few people, and when he met Ivankov he manipulated it to his advantage." And the Ivankov name was used by several other formerly minor criminals who came in direct or indirect contact with him. A man who drove him from Brighton Beach into Manhattan, for example, described himself as "Yaponchik's driver and bodyguard." In truth, the man worked for a limousine company and usually drove movie stars around town.

Reports circulated that Ivankov moved freely about the world—one day in Tel Aviv where he and his son met with 50 gangsters to discuss investing in the Israeli economy; the next day in the Middle East. Conflicting reports put him in Brighton Beach at the same time as he was strolling along a Florida beach.

Exaggeration was the norm: a report from Interpol had it that in 1994 he traveled to Bonnat where he "represented Russia" at a meeting of the world's criminal godfathers in which they divided up the entire globe for criminal activities. Also represented at the meeting were Colombia, Italy, China, and Japan; together the underworld titans agreed to cooperate and, to avoid bloodshed, to divide the world into territories. There followed two more similar meetings, Interpol said, at which the division of Europe was discussed. This crime consortium had at its disposal "five-hundred-thousand-million US dollars."[7]

This report was swallowed whole, with little question of its veracity.

* * *

In May 1994 the FBI formed C-24, a Russian organized crime squad in New York City. It got off to a running start, launching more than 35 probes into Russian and Eastern European organized crime, the most coordinated and focused investigation into one crime group at any one time. In addition to Ivankov, who had suddenly loomed on their radar, there were probes into a dozen members of the Moscow-based *Izmailovskaya* criminal group and into small groups involved in continuing criminal enterprises.

Pen registers—devices to record numbers dialed on a specific telephone—were installed on telephones used by Ivankov, including the numbers supplied by the Russian authorities. Reports revealed that Ivankov was in contact with senior Russian criminals around the world. The FBI discovered that he had set up a front company, Slavic Inc., to facilitate money-laundering transactions. Other companies discovered by U.S. authorities included Atkom, in Vienna; Ritual, a funeral service firm in Moscow; and Arbat International, also based in Moscow.

Informant intelligence detailed several of the operations in which Ivankov and his associates were involved, ranging from bribery to the arms trading of military equipment that included machine guns and anti-aircraft defense systems worth $20 million. "He has also engaged in several acts of extortion and, from his base in Brighton Beach, Brooklyn, has overseen his organization's criminal activities in Russia and Western and Eastern Europe," FBI reports noted.

Informants were inserted into the Russian criminal underground. One, dubbed CS-1, said that Ivankov's organization operated in cities in Canada, and the U.S., as well as in the U.K., Vienna, Budapest, and Moscow. The FBI found that he "has two principal groups of enforcers, sometimes called 'combat brigades,' which are headed by Aleksei Petrov and Alexander Inshakov." Inshakov's "chief assistant" was Viktor Sergeyev, a former KGB officer; Sergeyev, the FBI said, "aided" Inshakov in murders, including the deaths of five or six top Russian crime figures who got in Ivankov's way. The "combat brigade" run by Inshakov received a "special allotment of $100,000 per month."

Within four months the FBI was on to an extortion scheme being operated by Ivankov. The victims were Alexander Volkov, a former KGB agent, and Vladimir Voloshin, an associate of a Moscow crime family. The two Russian émigrés ran a shady investment/advisory firm, Summit International, which appears to have been an elaborate fraud that saw investors losing their shirts. Volkov and Voloshin had taken in $3.5 million to invest for a man in Moscow. When the man tried to recover his investment, Volkov and Voloshin refused and the investor turned to Ivankov for help.

Ivankov agreed to recover the funds. A campaign of terror was unleashed on the Summit fraud artists, and after a terrifying visit by Ivankov and two of his thugs to their offices, the men fled to Florida. When they returned to New York they were kidnapped and forced to sign a note promising to pay $3.5 million to an Ivankov associate. But then Volkov and Voloshin went to the FBI to expose Ivankov. The FBI kept him under surveillance and gathered what evidence they could. Unable to turn up enough evidence to get a wiretap on Ivankov's phones, they were at a standstill—until help came from an unlikely source.

Project Osada

As Ivankov was to the U.S., Vyacheslav Marakulovich Sliva was to Canada. Sliva, who is related to Ivankov through marriage, was a notorious criminal in Russia. That he wanted to come to Canada was no surprise; generations of Russian and Russian–Jewish criminals have operated in Toronto and Vancouver for decades. Some were linked through their gambling operations to the Canadian branches of the American Cosa Nostra. For foreign Russian Jews, Canada was a prime gateway to the U.S.—Canada's willingness to accept "refugees" from Israel has long been recognized by criminal elements. Low-level gangster Ludwig "Tarzan" Fainberg, for example, first came to Toronto, where he worked in the furniture delivery business, before embarking to Florida. And Canadian immigration department investigators have long filed their concerns about the country's weak security system that acts as a virtual magnet for major organized crime figures from the former Soviet Union, China, and the Indian subcontinent.

Criminals particularly like Canada—even the prison system. A Russian émigré criminal, a member of a violent robbery gang, summed up how the Russian and Canadian systems compare: "This is better than most of the hotels in Moscow," he said on a tapped telephone line from prison. "I am learning English, they feed me three times a day. I get exercise. They even pay for my lawyer. You should come here, only if it is to come to this prison."

Vyacheslav Sliva lied to immigration officials about his criminal record—in 1964 he'd been jailed for refusing to serve in the army; in 1961 he was sentenced to three months over a stolen watch; and he'd also spent nine years with Ivankov in a Soviet prison—and produced a forged government document to prove he'd never been convicted. He also claimed, falsely, that he was married.

Before Sliva's arrival in September 1994, the underworld in Toronto and several other Canadian cities resembled that of Brighton Beach, although not on the same scale. There'd been murders, public shootings, fire bombings, kidnappings, thefts of high-end cars, and extortions. Several major frauds had been uncovered, including some involving the evasion of fuel oil taxes.

Sliva was granted a visa to Canada by the Canadian Embassy in Moscow. Shortly after he arrived in Toronto, RCMP officers with the Eastern European Organized Crime Task force were well armed with intelligence on him and other suspected organized crime players. The EEOCTF, part of the Combined Forces Special Enforcement Unit made up of several regional police forces as well as the RCMP, Toronto Police, and Ontario Provincial Police, knew exactly what Sliva was up to.

Project Osada[8]—named after the Russian word for "under siege"— was set up and a team of investigators conducted hundreds of hours of surveillance on Sliva and everyone with whom he came into contact. Having obtained wiretap authorizations within days of his arrival, they closely monitored hundreds of his conversations and soon determined that he had brought together elements of the existing Russian underworld in Canada as well as American and Soviet criminals. And he was in constant touch with Ivankov in New York City. Links were also uncovered between Russian mobsters and members of Asian and Italian crime groups.

While in Toronto, Sliva married a Canadian woman in a bid to gain status and protection under Canada's rights and freedoms, just as Ivankov had done in the U.S.

The Osada wiretaps revealed the international scope of the Ivankov organization's activities. There was a discussion about assassinating a Russian newspaper editor who'd written about Ivankov's activities, and there were links to Vatchagan Petrossov,[9] a businessman who headed a Russian crime group in Colorado. There was talk about how Ivankov distributed his illegal profits from arms trafficking among various "shell" corporations and about the disposal of profits from the extortion of a major Russian car and truck manufacturer. There were calls to Sliva from "Alik," believed to be Alimjan Tochtachunov,[10] a powerful *vor v zakone* known as "Taiwanese"; Tochtachunov gloated about the arrest of a Brighton Beach boss—"that faggot Monya Elson"—who'd been arrested in Italy. A man believed to be Ivankov's nephew called him from a wired phone in Toronto to discuss setting up a meeting. And Russian–Canadian mobster Joseph Sigalov was discussed in relation to two powerful Russian organized crime figures in Moscow.

Being so far from his boss, Ivankov, took its toll on Sliva, who increasingly felt isolated in Toronto. "Sliva is absolutely helpless here," his girlfriend, Natalia, told Ivankov's girlfriend. "There's no one here he can trust."

Pressure from law enforcement—and the media, which had recently focused several stories on Russian organized crime and particularly on Ivankov—was also much on the minds of Ivankov and Sliva: "I don't call because I hear lots of news and I don't want to disturb you," Sliva told Ivankov. "The stinking bastards [police] have been bugging me since my childhood."

Ivankov: "That's because you were against the Soviets."

Sliva: "We didn't serve in the army when we were supposed to."

For the FBI, who were stalled in their hunt for Ivankov, the Osada wiretaps were pure gold; they used them as part of a successful effort to get their own wiretap authorizations in the U.S. Transcripts of the FBI's operation provide a rare look into the struggles in the Russian underworld. A man identified only as Sergei, for example, called from Russia and talked to Ivankov about the shooting of one of "our guys":

They went outside; three people came to them and started shooting. One guy that was with him got killed right away, the second one is critical, and our guy is critical too. ... The people who were shooting at him were close to him. And supposedly they raised the question about the Thief code—I know that from A to Z.

Sergei also tells Ivankov that he warned a mutual friend about treachery from a rival group:

We told him: "Be very careful. Don't go nowhere. If they'll kill you then nothing will be changed and nothing will be left, only these motherfuckers. Those animals we have been fighting for will die. Those animals will take over." And then these people called him out and started shooting at him. ... Poor guy, they shoot him in the legs and went down to the ground, that's it. ... The second guy just stood up ... and then started shooting. Head, heart, liver. He died right on the spot.

Other discussions were about *vory* who ran different criminal organizations and how they divided up regions, with one getting "nine locations." There were also several references to a criminal who appeared to be Ivankov's superior in the Moscow-based organization.

But for the FBI, the wiretaps were key in investigating the extortion that would eventually bring down Ivankov and several of his associates.

Throughout May 1995, the wiretaps allowed the FBI to home in on Ivankov and his group. There were threats against the victims' families, gunpoint threats, and meetings at a Russian restaurant where the victims were made to sign a bogus contract to pay up the $3.5 million.

By June 8, the C-24 had gathered enough evidence—through the wiretaps, surveillance, and victims' complaints—to bring up Ivankov and five members of his crew on charges of extortion. Some conspirators however had fled to Russia.

Ivankov was arrested just after 7 a.m. An FBI team, heavily armed and wearing bulletproof vests, quietly made their way to his 21st-floor apartment on Surf Avenue in Brighton Beach. When they began banging on the door they heard a woman screaming in Russian. At first she refused to let them in; then, when a Russian-speaking FBI agent threatened to take down the door, she opened it.

Ivankov and a second man were inside. Ivankov, wearing a black T-shirt and underpants, swore repeatedly at the agents. He was handcuffed, allowed to dress, and then hustled out to a waiting car. Searchers found a pistol and bullets wrapped in plastic in the shrubbery below the apartment window. Inside they found a three-quarter-inch stack of $100 bills, a key to a safety deposit box, address books, and cellular phones and beepers.

After his arrest Ivankov refused to be interviewed by Pre-trial Services, and a permanent order of detention was entered by a magistrate.

* * *

In the weeks and months following the Summit arrests, a propaganda campaign in both U.S. and Russia broke out, claiming that Ivankov wasn't a master criminal at all but had been set up by the FBI so they could show that a major Russian *vor* had been taken down. There were claims that Ivankov was framed by an FBI and MVD combined conspiracy. Prominent community leaders in the U.S. and Russia, and even some journalists and law enforcement personnel, gave interviews supporting the argument that Ivankov was being railroaded; that he had been inflated into a criminal titan.

In Moscow, a group of businessmen asked the mayor, Yuri Luzhkov, to petition for the return of Ivankov, arguing that he was the only figure who could bring some semblance of civilization to a city still under siege from bloody underworld assassinations and massacres. The mayor's office had even gone so far as to urge lawmakers to create special legislation that would allow law enforcement and organized crime figures to negotiate a remedy for the violence.

And in the U.S., several people came forward offering to provide bail. Ivankov's lawyer, Barry Slotnick, told the court that his client had $4 million—tied up in real estate—available as collateral for his bail. One man pledged his restaurant, land, and home in Colorado; a residence in Manhattan Beach, Brooklyn, was put up; a prominent surgeon in

Manhattan came forward and offered his assets. Slotnick said that the U.S. government had seized Ivankov's travel documents and, alluding to Ivankov's legal problems in Russia, said he was *persona non grata* there and had nowhere to flee if he was granted bail. Ivankov's son, his wife, and his granddaughter were all residing in the United States. Letters praising Ivankov were presented, including two from members of Parliament in Moscow.

Ivankov's role as a freedom fighter for Russia was mentioned. His lawyer noted, "We've also had letters from associations, signed by various individuals ... the Boxing Association of Russia, in which they say that Mr. Ivankov was one of the fairest people who stepped forward against the Chechen mafia in 1991 and was later forced to leave the country by these people."

Slotnick said that Ivankov had become "a pawn" in political intrigue between Chechens and the Russian MVD:

> In this case the Chechen criminal structures are trying to lead you away from the real heads of mafia who reside in the United States. ... [The MVD] is trying to prove its own irreplaceability, since they actually can do nothing with this country and they are trying to revenge Mr. Ivankov for leaving his country and never agreeing to collaborate with the communists.
>
> He is someone who fought against the communists. ... He is known as someone who helped build the church and fights for the rights of free religion in Moscow.

Slotnick went on to describe Ivankov as "a revolutionary" who wanted "at great risk to himself to bring democracy to the Soviet Union." He said Ivankov hadn't left the U.S. in the past three years; that he was involved in litigation with the immigration authorities about his status; that he had a consulting company which assisted people who were interested in doing business in the Soviet Union; and that he had a book contract to write about his life. He had filed income-tax returns and paid his proper taxes.

In rebuttal, the U.S. government lawyer pointed to the numerous documents seized during the raid at 501 Surf Avenue, including passports from Russia, the U.K., and Poland under false and fictitious names with Ivankov's photograph attached, and to the $80,000 in cash that was found. The lawyer also pointed to Ivankov's extensive criminal record in the former Soviet Union, including a sentence for gunpoint robberies during which Ivankov and his crew wore militia uniforms. He also read from an FBI report indicating that Russian authorities had discovered a contract had been taken out on agents involved in the Ivankov investigation. Ivankov was ordered to be held for trial without bail.

On July 8, 1996, Ivankov and several of his henchmen were convicted of extortion and conspiracy. He was also convicted of arranging a fictitious marriage to enable him to stay in the U.S. In prison, Ivankov presented two faces: the gulag-hardened *vor v zakone* who kept to his Code and was caught with heroin, and the cerebral individual who read Greek philosophy and studied a wide variety of interests.

In a handwritten note to the late journalist Robert Friedman—who had written extensively about Russian crime—Ivankov wrote: "Friedman! You are a dirty fucking American prostitution liar! I will fuck you! And make you suck my Russian dick!" The note was signed "Ivankov" and dated April 29, 1998. Ivankov, who was then being held at a medium-security federal prison near Lake Placid, was moved to maximum-security quarters at Lewisburg, Pennsylvania. And although Ivankov's release date was initially going to be moved up, after he was involved in a fight at the facility, he was ordered to serve his entire sentence.

In 2000, prosecutors in Moscow received information that Ivankov had been involved in the 1992 shooting of the three Turks in a Moscow restaurant. Their case was sketchy, one witness having since died and another having returned to Turkey, but in July 2004 the Moscow Office of the Public Prosecutor announced that an agreement had been reached with U.S. federal officials whereby Ivankov would be handed over to Russian authorities for the 1992 Turkish shootings the moment his American sentence was completed.

And so, when he was released in July of that year, Ivankov was taken directly from maximum security in the U.S. Penitentiary at Allenwood, Pennsylvania, and put aboard a special flight to Moscow.

But nor did his anger at the media coverage prevent him from giving interviews to journalists. In the summer of 2004 Ivankov told a reporter for the *Gazeta* daily that he'd sue the Russian media, claiming they'd inflicted "moral damages" on him: "In the nearest future I intend to invite my representatives who will file dozens and hundreds of court suits demanding public apologies in writing," he said. He added that when he was in prison in the U.S. "I was deprived of the possibility to resist your mad attacks. ... Now I am bored to the limit. You have soiled me so much I will never wash myself clean again."

In July 2005 Ivankov's trial on the double homicide charges began in Moscow. Almost immediately things began to go badly for the prosecutors when their key eyewitness—a police officer doing security work at the murder scene—testified he'd been mistaken when he identified Ivankov's photograph in 2000. Other witnesses said they couldn't identify Ivankov. He was acquited.

Vyacheslav Sliva, "the Canadian Yaponchik," was arrested by Project Osada officers and held on immigration charges: he'd failed to disclose his criminal record and criminal activities. A deportation hearing was ordered. At first Sliva fought the government, claiming he'd been framed by Moscow police after he'd refused to become an informant. He admitted he'd spent more than a dozen years in prison in Russia but said he'd been pardoned—but he had no documentation to back up his claim. He also admitted he'd lied about his marital status by listing his brother's wife and children as his own. As far as the notorious Ivankov was concerned, Sliva said they were both from the same neighborhood and that Ivankov had married Sliva's cousin. The barrage of media coverage of the hearing took its toll on Sliva: disheveled and frustrated he agreed to accept his deportation and went voluntarily back to Russia. His final words were: "I am not a monster."

Semion Mogilevich and the YBM Scandal

While debate continues to swirl around Vyacheslav Ivankov and his role in the international Eastern European underworld, there is little doubt of the power of his vast criminal organization. But his reach and power pale compared with the operations of Semion Mogilevich.

The FBI "Wanted" poster shows a gray-haired, heavy-set, jowly man with thuggish features further marred by pockmarks. His aliases are many: Seva Moguilevich, Semion Yudkovich Palagnyuk, Semen Yukovich Telesh, Semjon Mogilevcs, Shimon Madelwitsh, and Shimon Makhelwitsch. He is a heavy smoker. His primary residence is Moscow, but he has ties to the U.S., the U.K., and Canada. He is, the FBI notice emphasizes, "to be considered armed and dangerous and an escape risk."

Mogilevich, like Ivankov, came to power in the post-Soviet world. And even discounting the bogeyman legends—hit squads traveling the world to do his bidding, robotic bodyguard brigades trained to kill at his command, the torture chambers and hideous butchery of enemies, cornering this criminal market, controlling that one—Mogilevich has emerged over the past 25 years as a truly global criminal.

The son of a middle-class family in Kiev, Ukraine, Semion Mogilevich was born on June 30, 1946. Considered by some to be brilliant—at 22 he earned an advanced degree in economics from the University of Lvov—he chose to live by his wits outside the edges of the Soviet Union's strict and pervasive laws, linking up with the *Lybretskaya*, a Moscow gang, in the early 1970s. He engaged in various black-market currency schemes and served two prison terms, one for three years and the other for four. An early con Mogilevich successfully worked was to convince Jewish refugees leaving Russia in the mid-1980s to leave their assets with him; he promised to sell them at fair market value and then send them the profits in hard currency. The victims, of course, were left high and dry in Israel. His profits were substantial and were reinvested in criminal ventures.

A natural networker, he connected with both professional criminals and criminal politicians. In the vein of Meyer Lansky, the financial brains of the American Cosa Nostra, when Mogilevich made money, everyone around him made money.

In 1990 he left the chaos of Moscow—much as Ivankov had fled the wars wracking the city—and headed to Israel with several of his associates. He prospered there, gathering together diverse criminal elements and providing financial services. He reportedly owned an Israeli bank and used it to launder proceeds of crime.

In 1991 Mogilevich married a Hungarian national, a move that allowed him to legally live in Budapest. This made him a legitimate citizen of Russia, Ukraine, Israel, and Hungary. Again he surveyed the local underworld and began forging alliances. He rapidly bought or gained control of several nightclubs—venues, police believe, for prostitution. Working with organized crime groups in Italy, he went into the weapons and drug trafficking trade, using banks in the U.K. to launder the profits. He arranged to buy stolen art; he created bogus Fabergé eggs. He was a master at bribery and corruption and was able to exploit most Customs officials' weaknesses.

And, like many Eastern European criminals with international connections, Mogilevich was able to insulate himself from arrest by cooperating with intelligence and police agencies across the world. Unlike traditional *vory v zakone*, it's common for businessmen-entrepreneurs from the former Soviet Union to trade intelligence on the business activities of Russia's new multimillionaires, particularly with U.S. agencies and the Canadian Security Intelligence Service. Mogilevich is also heavily rumored to have worked for the Mossad, Israel's spy service; he was in a good position to assist them because he'd been dealing arms and military matériel into the Middle East for years.

Mogilevich's reach into the upper chambers of finance and the judiciary became apparent in 1990 when he successfully bribed a judge to free Vyacheslav Ivankov long before his sentence in the gulag was up. He maintained his connection to the *Solntsevo* criminal organization, and it became clear that although he was immensely wealthy, he was far from a powerful leader of the umbrella organization. In 1994, for example, the boss of one of the major crews hounded him for not making a payment into the *obschak*, the Thieves' fund. Mogilevich apparently owed $US5 million.

His talents as a major financial wizard were to come to light in the 1999 Bank of New York money-laundering scandal in which as much as $10 billion was illegally transmitted through the prominent financial institution. An indictment filed in the case said that several suspects—at least one with ties to Mogilevich, who figured in the background of the case—brought in as much as $250 million a month, much of it moved through accounts on a daily basis. The money was moved out just as quickly, ending up in as many as 50 countries. There were more than 85,000 separate transactions.

According to filings in New York federal court, security officers at the bank raised red flags and told executives about ties between Mogilevich and the husband of a bank's senior vice president in the Eastern European division. Further, it was learned, two Hungarian banks that had been under investigation by the FBI for their connections with Mogilevich were linked to the money moving through the Bank of New York. Transactions out of Latin America were also being probed after it was alleged that a bank executive had received wire-transfer instructions from the Cali cocaine cartel to move profits through Brazilian banks to offshore firms. Paper trails led directly into the Kremlin as well as several Russian banks and prominent financiers in Eastern Europe.

Throughout the Bank of New York investigation Mogilevich's name came up repeatedly, an investigative auditor said. "There was such an outflow of money from Russia it only stood to reason there were mafia types behind it," she said. "Mogilevich was only one of many. But he was the toad that ran the pond."

In the wake of the scandal, the Bank of New York agreed to improve security and oversight and to toughen its customer screening process. It also agreed to report suspicious activity and practice enhanced due diligence.

The Bank of New York operation provided a peek at the breadth and power of Mogilevich's financial acumen and methods. Complex paper trails ran through several companies, individuals, and countries. Those who followed the story learned for the first time of the existence of the "Brainy Don" who would become the public face of the Red Mafiya. But in the U.K., investigators who'd been following his activities for several years weren't surprised. It was their information that had uncovered the money trail into the Bank of New York.

Semion Mogilevich routinely created companies that could be used to facilitate the movement of criminal profits—not only his own but those of other major criminals and entrepreneurs—around the globe. Scarcely a country in the world was without some weakness he could exploit. His elaborate holdings, either in his own name or those of colleagues, created a massive "spaghetti jungle" of financial transactions that stopped investigators in their tracks, particularly when enforcement jurisdictions conflicted. Following a money trail through 20 firms in nine countries, involving a dozen banks and perhaps hundreds of bank accounts, was an almost impossible task.

But British authorities were on to Mogilevich's money-laundering activities in the early 1990s. In 1995 Operation Sword, conducted by Britain's National Crime Squad, found that Mogilevich was moving funds from the U.K. to Hungary then on to the U.S. and into Canada. According to the report, "Canada has been used purely to legitimise the criminal organization by floating on the stock exchange a corporation which consists of UK and USA companies whose existing assets and stock have been artificially inflated by the introduction of proceeds of crime."

One company used by Mogilevich was YBM, a firm ostensibly manufacturing magnets and bicycles. With a seemingly endless flow of cash and a record of ever-increasing sales, YBM, based in Pennsylvania, went public and began trading on the Toronto Stock Exchange. Despite information that the company was a front for organized crime activities, in just four years YBM went from being a penny stock to a firm worth almost $1 billion. And with a board of directors that included prominent Canadian business and political figures, YBM's shares went through the roof. But there were no bicycles and no magnets: the books were cooked and YBM's "profits" were actually the proceeds of crime. And so on May 13, 1998, federal search warrants were executed at YBM's headquarters in Newtown, Pennsylvania. Trading in YBM was then suspended by the Ontario Securities Commission.

Five years later, on April 24, 2003, prosecutors at the Eastern District of Pennsylvania unsealed an indictment charging Mogilevich and three of his cohorts, Igor L'Vovich Fisherman, Jacob Bogatin, and Anatoli Tsoura, with 45 counts of racketeering, securities fraud, wire fraud, mail fraud, and money laundering in connection with the YBM fiasco. Rather than referring to the Red Mafiya, the indictment more accurately summed up the organization as "the Mogilevich Enterprise." Profits to each of the participants were significant: Mogilevich made $18.4 million, Fisherman made $3.3 million, Bogatin made $10.3 million, and Tsoura made $1.3 million.

And the money trail uncovered by American investigators was global. It led through the Republic of Nauru in the South Pacific, the Cayman Islands and Nevis in the Caribbean, and through Canada, England, Hungary, Israel, Lithuania, Ukraine, and Russia. In all, the investigators hunted evidence in 25 countries. FBI, IRS, and Customs agents arrested Bogatin at his home in Richboro, near Philadelphia. Mogilevich, Fisherman, and Tsoura had left the U.S. and were believed hiding in Russia. International arrest warrants are out for each of them.

Mogilevich is believed to be dividing his time between Russia and Israel, often traveling on a private jet. Cannily, he made a point of not operating against Israeli interests, almost certainly guaranteeing him a safe haven. British investigators say that his name still comes up in financial and Russian organized crime cases but that he uses a series of front men to act on his behalf. "We know there was an attempt on his life not too long ago," said a U.K. investigator when interviewed at a money-laundering conference. "He's made a lot of money, he's made a lot of people rich. But I think that now if I were him I'd be concerned that I'd outlived my usefulness." He went on to say that, for criminals like Mogilevich, "the world is his neighborhood. ... No place is new to them, there are friends and associates everywhere."

In Toronto, the Ontario Securities Commission, which regulates the markets, sanctioned and fined two brokerages and several individuals involved in YBM's activities. But curiously—and this is likely why criminal organizations enjoy looting Canada's stock markets—the OSC panel determined that the YBM debacle wasn't a matter of criminal activity: "This case is not about organized crime [or] money laundering. ... It is about disclosure of risk."

Endnotes

1. Ivankov is also known as "Yaponets" and "The Assyrian Son-in-Law" because he had reportedly married an Assyrian woman. He's also been called The Red Godfather and the "Father of Extortion." In the Russian underworld nicknames are important; they tell a lot about a person. Ivankov likely chose "Yaponchik" because that was the name of a legendary Russian–Jewish criminal from Odessa. Some believe, though, that the nickname was because of his distinctly asiatic eyes.

2. Solntsevskaya Brigade—or Solntsevo—takes its name from a Moscow suburb. It is the largest and most powerful of the criminal brigades of Russia. There are an estimated 9,000 members of the group and, although they're spread around the world, they maintain strict territorial control both in their neighborhood. The leading figures in Solntsevo were/are Sergei Mikhailov—"Mikhas," Viktor Averin— "Avera," the late Sergei Timofeyev—"Silvester," Yura Samosval—"Yurii Esin," and Vyacheslav Ivankov, who was the group's representative in the U.S. Vyacheslav Sliva was the group's representative, under Ivankov, based in Toronto.

Semion Mogilevich, one of the FBI's most wanted Russian criminals, is considered the Solntsevo representative for operations in several countries of the world. Solntsevo maintains many of the rules of the Code of the *vory v zakone*—notably a community fund to assist members who require money—but has modernized itself on several fronts. In Italy, for example, there are female operatives who carry out many of the traditional roles of Solntsevo members.

Even within Moscow—the group's home base—"crews" are allowed to operate under the Solntsevo umbrella with a great degree of independence. Of the crews—police have identified a dozen—each crew leader belongs to a council that orchestrates operations and ensures that no one is jeopardizing others' activities. While Ivankov was in the U.S., several of the Solntsevo council members attended a meeting in Miami. Most entered the U.S. undetected.

3. Silvester was one of the most charismatic and notorious of the murder *vory v zakone*. He had interests in the oil business, sports, and several of Moscow's financial sectors. A colleague of Ivanokov's, Silvester died in an explosion in September 1994 when a bomb planted in a Mercedes went off. The blast was so powerful that authorities could identify him only through dental records.

4. Among those involved in the campaign to free Ivankov were Josef Kobzon and Otari Kvantrishvili; Semion Mogilevich was in charge of bribing the judge. Josef Kobzon is known as the "Russian Frank Sinatra." He's been banned from entering the United States and, according to a classified FBI report, is considered the "spiritual leader of the Russian mob." Kobzon has repeatedly denied the allegations.

Otari Kvantrishvili, who'd known Ivankov since they were youths, concentrated his criminal activities not just on run-of-the-mill extortions and violence but on penetrating the world of sports teams and charities. He was murdered by a sniper in early 1994; his funeral, which was broadcast on television, was attended by MVD generals. The musical theme was from the film *The Godfather.*

The other man involved in the campaign to free Ivankov was the legendary Semion Mogilevich, known as "the Brainy Don." Mogilevich has an advanced degree in economics and is one of the most wanted men in the world. He first came to light in the West in connection with the Bank of New York–Russian money-laundering scandal in the 1990s. He is most well-known for his involvement in the YBM scandal that left victims holding the bag for millions of dollars.

5. The reasons for Ivankov going to the West vary, ranging from the logical to the ridiculous. That he was fleeing the closing circle of investigators trying to overturn his early release is likely; that he was fleeing the murder of the Turks is plausible; that he feared he would become the latest in a series of *vory v zakone* to be assassinated by the Chechens is also reasonable. That the leaders of the underworld—the famed Circle of Brothers—"gave" him the U.S. as a "prize" for leading a ferocious battle against the Chechens is ridiculous; another report that he was told by the Circle to "Go to New Land and invade America!" is ludicrous.

6. That Ivankov has connections to Denver, Colorado, and several other locations in that vicinity is no surprise, according to several police reports. A powerful *vor v zakone* lives there and has amassed millions of dollars in real estate and businesses. From Colorado he runs criminal operations on the U.S. West Coast, and he's also well known to Canadian law enforcement agencies. Ivankov has been a visitor to the area: monitored use of his cellular telephone showed that in March 1995 he made calls from the Denver vicinity.

7. The global criminal consortium report is common in law enforcement circles. But the "Board of Directors of Crime" stories are generally either untrue or grossly inflated. An example—detailed in the authors' book *Bloodlines: The Rise and Fall of the Mafia's Royal Family* (HarperCollins Canada, 2001)—proved that a long-believed story about the Sicilian Mafia, the Colombia cartels, and the Calabrian *'ndrangheta* meeting near Venezuela to organize the entire global cocaine trade had a kernel of truth but was overstated. The meeting wasn't in fact a secret high-level summit, but rather four traffickers meeting over lunch to discuss a drug shipment to Europe.

8. Project Osada became known as Osada… I when a subsequent project—Osada II—ended with the largest roundups of Eastern European criminals in North America. On December 9, 1999, CFSEU teams raided homes and businesses in Toronto, Windsor, and Montreal, arresting 38 suspects and naming 17 others in arrest warrants. Among them was a man believed to be a powerful *vor v zakone*. The accused were charged with Ecstasy smuggling from the Netherlands; immigration fraud from Eastern Europe; smuggling fake diamonds from the U.S.; casino frauds in the U.S., the Bahamas, Aruba, and the Dominican Republic; and the widespread manufacture of counterfeit credit cards that were distributed in North and South America and in Europe. Intelligence gathered during the Sliva investigation sparked the crackdown.

9. Vatchagan Petrossov was twice banned from getting a U.S. visa at the American Embassy in Moscow. U.S. officials were told that Petrossov was a dangerous criminal in the Russian underworld—he'd served 15 years in a Soviet prison for rape and rioting. However, Petrossov went to Latvia and presented a clean passport and received a visa. He didn't reveal his criminal record. In June 1997, however, he applied for a visitor's visa to Canada and was refused. And Petrossov wasn't the only Russian crime figure wanting to get to Canada: between 1994 and 1998, Canadian immigration officers refused entry to 807 known or suspected Russian crime figures out of 44,665 visas issued.

10. Alimjan Tochtachunov—also spelled "Tokhtakhunov"—who is known in the Russian underworld as "Taivanchik" or "Little Taiwanese," came to prominence during the Winter Olympics in 2002 in Salt Lake City. He was accused of bribing judges. Tochtachunov, a colleague of Ivankov, is carried in North American and European intelligence files as a *vor v zakone* and part of the *Solntsevskaya* crime group, the same organization to which Ivankov is attached. His name came up several times on the Ivankov wiretaps. Tochtachunov was later detained by police in Italy but was released without charges.

PART
FOUR
Israeli Organized Crime

The Ecstasy Connection

Israeli organized crime groups are unlike traditional ones in that they're not cemented by an honor code or blood ties; their activities are motivated purely by profit. Although some groups have political agendas or have formed along family, religious, or political lines, the profit-making *raison d'être* makes most Israeli organized crime groups unique. It also renders them vulnerable to members who become informants purely to save their own skin.

Israeli organized crime groups operate both locally and internationally. Home-based activities focus on illegal gambling, extortion, and the sex trade. Internationally, the Ecstasy trade is a major money-maker, followed by traditional crimes of jewel theft and money laundering. Believing themselves to be safe from extradition—or at least serious police attention—by staying in Israel, members of Israeli organized crime groups have built organizations that encircle the globe. Their Ecstasy networks reach across Europe and into North America; massive shipments of pills spill into the two largest drug markets in the world.

Six main crime groups operate in and/or from Israel. The most powerful is the Yitzhak Aberjil organization, followed by the Ze'ev Rosenstein organization. In order of power, the remaining are the Yehiyeh Hariri, the Jarush, and the Bar-Moha groups, and a mixture of Bedouin tribes who operate in the south of Israel.[1]

Until recently, the activities of these organizations—or gangs, in some cases—haven't been a high priority for the Israel police. Individual crimes such as murder or robbery or extortion were vigorously investigated, but the actual structures of organized crime were seldom scrutinized and attacked. Some observers attribute this to the strong ties between the powerful Israeli bosses and religious groups and political organizations; others to the counterproductive structure and mindset of Israeli policing. Whereas Israeli crime groups operated throughout the country, police were confined by narrow jurisdictions. And while crime organizations collaborated in their efforts, operational restrictions tended to smother a police investigation.

Internationally, law enforcement agencies are increasingly aware of the activities of Israeli organized crime groups. Police in Germany, the U.K., Eastern Europe, the Baltics, the U.S., Canada, South Africa, and Australia have disclosed that Israeli organized crime groups are operating on their turf. In every country one constant was the drug Ecstasy; and in most cases the manufacture and export trail led to Israel. The criminal organizations responsible were loosely dubbed "The Jerusalem Connection" although the back ends of the networks were based in several Israeli cities.

One of the earliest and most prolific Israeli Ecstasy dealers was Oded Tuito, who was the first Israeli to be put on the White House list of foreign drug traffickers under the Narcotics Kingpin Designation Act. The Kingpin category dilineates traffickers whose activities make them a threat to American national security.

Like most Israeli criminals who operate outside the Middle East, Tuito maintained dual citizenship, in his case Israeli and French. He was born either as Oded Tuito on July 25, 1961, or on July 27, 1959, as Eliyahu Mamo. He kept documents in both names. Beginning in the mid-1990s, he organized massive Ecstasy operations that exported millions of pills into the U.S. from France, Belgium, and Germany. Tuito made huge profits by buying the entire output of laboratories in the Netherlands; by buying in such large quantities, he was able to turn an investment of as low as 50 cents per tablet into a retail price of $28. His product was sold along the American eastern seaboard as far south as Miami and as far west as California. He moved his profits back to Israel and parts of Europe. Tuito himself moved easily throughout the world, at times living in New York City, California, and France.

Tuito moved his product in innovative ways. He recruited dozens of couriers at a time, often using women from strip clubs to charm Customs officers. Each courier carried between 30,000 and 60,000 pills at a time; they were also used to body-carry hundreds of thousands of dollars out of the U.S. for laundering. He used conservatively dressed Hasidic teens in yarmulkes to bring pills back from Europe; he also used elderly men and women.[2]

In 1999, in response to a request from the U.S. government, German authorities set up wiretaps on the telephones of members of Tuito's organization and gathered a detailed dossier of intelligence. The data was sent to the U.S., and in November 1999 a grand jury in Brooklyn brought down an indictment charging Tuito with conspiracy and related Ecstasy offenses. Four months later, a superseding indictment added charges of operating a continuing criminal enterprise as well as conspiracy to commit money laundering.

In January 2000, Tuito was arrested by French authorities in Fresnes, near Nice, and held on a U.S. provisional arrest warrant. His lawyer filed a certificate that showed he had French citizenship, his father having had Algerian citizenship dating back to pre-Algerian independence from France. Given that as a French citizen Tuito couldn't be extradited to the U.S., he was released from custody. But the DEA, through Interpol, kept track of his movements, and on May 28, 2001, he was captured in Barcelona and held pending extradition. Tuito began a lengthy battle to avoid being sent to America.

While he was in Spanish custody, police in Los Angeles arrested eight of his subordinates; two weeks later a federal indictment named him and 11 associates with running a major Ecstasy network that pumped a blizzard of 100,000 tablets a month into the city.

After almost two years, in March 2003, the Spanish Council of Ministers granted the U.S. extradition request. On April 15, in the custody of U.S. marshals, Tuito was flown to JFK International Airport and taken to jail. But before he could be brought to trial, he died of a heart attack in his cell at the Metropolitan Detention Center in Brooklyn. He was also awaiting trial in Pittsburgh and Los Angeles.

* * *

The Oded Tuito Organization wasn't the only Israeli group under investigation by U.S. federal officials. With primarily young people in the States consuming Ecstasy in alarming amounts, the drug has showed all the signs of running rampant. In 1998, for example, police in Florida broke up an Ecstasy ring and seized 40,000 pills that had landed at Miami International Airport carried by two Israeli men connected to an Israeli-based organized crime ring. Suspects from the same organization were later charged after police seized 30,000 pills from another courier heading into Miami and Fort Lauderdale airports. And in 1999 a cell of traffickers linked to Tuito were arrested in Holland during a Europe-wide investigation. Most of those suspects—including an Israeli–Canadian and an Italian trafficker—were tied to Israeli mafia. Police in California broke up an Israeli–American Ecstasy ring that pumped more than nine million tablets and pills into the U.S. market between 1997 and 1999. In 2001, in one of the largest Ecstasy busts ever, police in New York arrested two men who had in their possession a million Ecstasy tablets; a follow-up investigation led to the seizure of a FedEx package containing 200 kilograms of the drug and Israel police consequently extradited three Tel Aviv residents to the U.S. Arrests were also made in several American jurisdictions, including Los Angeles, the Midwest, and on the eastern seaboard. More arrests followed in Canada, Germany, Holland, Australia, and South Africa. Each investigation had an "Israeli component."

Another factor in the Israeli underworld has been the influx of Russian organized crime figures, particularly those who used real or bogus "Jewish roots" to gain entrance to Israel. From Israel it's easy for citizens to apply for visas to go to credulous countries—most notably and almost without exception Canada—on the grounds they were persecuted in Israel because of their Russian roots. Every major Russian organized crime group has members on the ground in Israel, and most of them are involved in money laundering or in brokering young Eastern European women to work in Israeli-run brothels. For the Russian criminals, getting their illegal profits into the Israeli financial sector was relatively easy; the money is then sent to other jurisdictions without the taint of Russia's notorious reputation as a source of criminal profits.

The Israeli government has had to focus its resources on fighting terrorists, so despite the many criminal organizations settled in or using Israel as a base, until relatively recently organized crime wasn't a priority for law enforcement. News reports would periodically point to money-laundering schemes or to links between criminals and politicians, but for Israeli police—and for the public—mafia-like activities weren't of great concern.

All that changed in December 2003.

The Rosenstein–Aberjil War

Ze'ev Rosenstein's nickname is "The Cat." It's not a particularly appropriate handle, since he looks anything but feline and sleek. In his early 50s, he wears his hair in a now-famous crewcut; his face is fleshy and his body bulky. And although he's Israel's most well-known crime figure, he has only a single criminal conviction on his record—an armed robbery committed 20-odd years ago when he was barely out of his teens. He served five years in jail. Since then he's been arrested several times but never convicted; witnesses would turn out to be unreliable or evidence was found wanting.

Friends say Rosenstein is a likable fellow. He enjoys attending sporting events, and he's always willing to discuss a business venture or buy a round of drinks. On the streets of Tel Aviv he's moved around in an armored car flanked by a convoy of bodyguards. He's instantly recognized and is willing to sign autographs when asked. His daughter's wedding was shown on television.

Ze'ev Rosenstein is called The Cat because a cat has nine lives. And on a Thursday afternoon in December 2003 he used up his seventh.

In the 1990s a simmering gang war was taking its toll on the Israeli underworld; victims were killed, beaten, and kidnapped. On one side were Ze'ev Rosenstein and his supporters and on the other was the Aberjil organization, the largest and most powerful criminal group in Israel. The Rosenstein organization was less powerful than the Aberjil and held onto their number-two status solely because of Rosenstein's charisma, ruthlessness, and savvy.

The Aberjil group, based in Lod, is a family affair. Yitzhak, or Itzik, Aberjil and his brothers, Meir and Abe, run the organization. Their father, a major Israeli criminal, was the victim of a gangland murder. The Aberjil brothers run dozens of gambling sites in Israel and abroad and reportedly have a stockpile of weapons at their disposal. Among their allies are some of the more powerful of Israeli's smaller crime gangs.

No one's quite sure what started the Rosenstein–Aberjil war, but it's clear that a lot of money was at stake. Control of local gambling outlets, junkets out of the country, and prostitution—much of it in conjunction with imported Russian sex-trade workers—were multimillion-dollar businesses. Murders, shootings, bombings and beatings were committed as the two sides struggled for control of local gambling and prostitution operations. The Israeli underworld was split along Rosenstein and Aberjil lines. Smaller gangs were quick to align themselves with whomever they thought would survive.

One of the leaders of a small gang who chose sides was gang boss Yehezkel Aslan; he joined the Aberjil team. That cost him his life: in

1993 he was murdered outside a Tel Aviv restaurant. Rosenstein was picked up by police in connection with the shooting, but after 30 days in custody he was released for lack of evidence. And although three other men were charged with the slaying, police believed Rosenstein was behind it.

The Aberjil brothers agreed. On an early morning in June 1996, Rosenstein was driving down Tel Aviv's Rehov Ibn Gvirol when gunmen in a passing car opened fire on him. Struck twice by bullets, Rosenstein managed to drive to Ichilov Hospital where he was treated and put in the trauma unit. Among those arrested for the attempted murder were Ilan Aslan, the brother of Yehezkel Aslan, and gangster Ya'acov Kahalon. Both were charged but later released from custody. Aslan disappeared; Kahalon was later found executed, killed by a gunshot to the back of the neck.

The Rosenstein–Aberjil wars continued. Different gangs and organizations swore their allegiance to one side or the other, a move that usually sparked some retaliation. A bounty of $1.5 million was reportedly put on Rosenstein's life.

Despite the tit-for-tat murders and attempted murders, both organizations still needed to do business, if only to make money to continue their warfare. And the Ecstasy trade, with its low investment for high returns, was a perfect money-maker. Both the Rosenstein and Aberjil organizations had people situated throughout Europe and in North America.

In June 2001 police in Tel Aviv began a probe into the Ecstasy trade. They discovered that criminal organizations in Israel—notably the Rosenstein group—were shipping several million pills into Europe and the U.S. The organization was directed from Israel and had been operational for several years. International investigations turned up increasingly large quantities of Ecstasy and—no coincidence here—Israeli gangsters. In November 2001, 1.6 million Ecstasy pills were seized in Germany and 29 suspects, including the Dadush brothers, were arrested. Baruch Dadush—who'd been Rosenstein's right-hand man—and Alan Dadush refused to cooperate with authorities; they were charged with financing the purchase of the drugs and arranging the deals. Police found evidence at an Ecstasy lab in Europe that suggested

Ze'ev Rosenstein was involved in the operation, but they didn't have any cooperative witnesses or substantive evidence to act upon.

Ze'ev Rosenstein did emerge in connection with a sting operation run out of Florida in which the U.S. Drug Enforcement Administration used an informant to arrange the purchase of 65,000 Ecstasy pills. The price was $393,000 and, because the pills were at a stash house in New York City, the transaction would have to be made there. First, a sample of the drug—13 pills—was handed over by a courier to the DEA's agents; police teams followed the courier to an apartment in downtown Manhattan. Armed with a search warrant, police raided the apartment and arrested David Roash and Israel Ashkenazi on conspiracy and possession charges. More than 700,000 pills and $187,000 in cash were seized. Both men quickly cooperated and told investigators that they'd been sent to New York to distribute the Ecstasy for Israeli organized crime figures. In the days after the arrests, police learned that Rosenstein had called Mordechai Cohen, an Israeli Ecstasy trafficker living in Spain, to discuss the New York arrests. Cohen was subsequently arrested and began cooperating. Using the information from the three informants, the DEA had Rosenstein in their sights.

International investigations into Rosenstein's trafficking activities weren't his only problem. He'd been shot at, bombed, and even, it was said, fired at with a shoulder-launched missile. In one case nine citizens were injured when a bomb was activated. In each attempt Rosenstein escaped unscathed or with minor injuries. Police warned him of a credible plot to use an Arab suicide bomber to assassinate him. For his part, Rosenstein, working through one of his partners, Shem-Tov Mahtabi, hired two Colombian mercenaries to assassinate Nissim Alperon, one of his archrivals; however, police were tipped off and they followed the would-be killers until they left Tel Aviv without completing their mission. Police believe there may have been other attempts on Rosenstein that went unreported.

Rosenstein was making other moves of his own. In June 2003, a professional assassin from Georgia was arrested and charged with conspiracy to murder Yitzhak and Meir Aberjil. Police were also told of several schemes to pick away at the crime groups who had allied themselves with the Aberjils.

On December 11, 2003, Israelis woke up to the turmoil tearing the underworld apart. Rosenstein was having lunch in a restaurant when a bomb exploded in a currency exchange shop next door. Three citizens died in the blast and two dozen were injured. Rosenstein and his bodyguards ran from the restaurant, jumped into his Mercedes, and drove to a nearby hospital to be treated for minor injuries. Rosenstein, who'd taken on folk hero status as "the man they can't kill," had just used up another life.

Four men were arrested after the bombing. All were tied to the Aberjil Organization, and all were later released for lack of evidence.

Police response to the fatal bombing was swift but ineffectual. Poorly funded and understaffed, they'd long had an unofficial agreement with organized crime figures that as long as their activities didn't directly affect the public, they'd be left in relative peace.[3] But in the wake of the bombing, they were forced into action. They investigated and arrested several members of Israel's criminal organizations. Seventeen hundred gambling clubs and 1,400 brothels were shut down. Almost a thousand foreign prostitutes were picked up in the six months following the bombing, most of whom were deported to countries of the former Soviet Union. Several major criminals left the country and lay low in Western and Central Europe. Some went to Canada and the U.S. Rosenstein, meanwhile, didn't do much except express wonder that anyone would want to kill him.

The "crackdown" by Israeli authorities had little effect. Within days of the currency shop bombing an underworld figure tied to the Aberjils was shot dead; a man suspected in an underworld-related double homicide was himself killed; and a bomb was found in a Tel Aviv parking lot adjacent to a house where a man linked to organized crime lived.

By November 2004 Rosenstein's international Ecstasy network was falling apart. Police in several jurisdictions had ongoing investigations and some had successfully closed. Gang members were in custody in the U.S., Spain, Bulgaria, and Western Europe. Many of them had given police information about Rosenstein in return for lighter sentencing, and some had already been extradited to the U.S., where Rosenstein had been declared a Top Tier drug trafficker by the DEA.

The Dadush brothers, Baruch and Alan, were convicted in Tel Aviv District Court and sentenced to 18 years in prison. Although both had declined to cooperate against Rosenstein after their arrest, local police visited them in custody and told them that the U.S. Drug Enforcement Administration was aware of their roles in the July 2001 New York City drug transaction and that the DEA was going file for their extradition. Their lawyers conducted several months of negotiations and, in an agreement with the DEA and the Israeli police, the two agreed to go to America to testify against Ze'ev Rosenstein. Their sentences were drastically reduced, and the men and their families went into the Witness Protection Program.

At 2 a.m. on November 8, 2004, Tel Aviv police arrested Rosenstein outside a Tel Aviv bar on an American extradition warrant for drug charges. U.S. authorities called him "the worst of the worst" of the international traffickers. He appeared in court wearing sunglasses, handcuffs, and leg shackles and surrounded by dozens of heavily armed police. His daughter, Sarit, an actress who'd coincidentally been chosen to play a gang boss's daughter in a television program, was in the courtroom to give her father moral support.

While Israeli laws of extradition had initially forbade sending accused or convicted citizens to other jurisdictions, in 1999 the government added a rider to the law saying that Israeli citizens who lived in Israel would be extradited only if the country seeking extradition allowed the suspect to serve his or her sentence in Israel. The U.S. agreed to this stipulation.

Rosenstein was ordered held in custody. His notoriety caused him problems in jail; other prisoners refused to be his cellmate, fearing both retribution from the Aberjils and being forced to testify in court about anything Rosenstein said. Rosenstein, for his part, complained he was lonely and was losing his mind. He remains in custody, vowing to vigorously fight the U.S. government.

Meanwhile, the Aberjil family suffered problems of their own. Yitzhak, who exiled himself to live overseas after reaching an agreement with the courts, was arrested in September 2004 with seven other Israelis in Amsterdam on suspicion of several drug offenses. Meir is being held in Germany on drug charges, and Abe is serving a four-year prison sentence, also for drug offenses. But prison walls haven't slowed down their war against Rosenstein; in March 2005, a grenade was thrown at a building where he kept an office. One man was killed.

Nor has the crackdown by Israeli officials slowed down the gangs' criminal operations. The brothels and gambling clubs are up and running, and laboratories in Europe are turning out Ecstasy in ever-increasing amounts. Competition from Asian groups is chipping into the market, however, particularly from Big Circle Boy labs in Canada.

One result of the enhanced interest in homegrown Israeli gangsters is a noticeable surge in activities of Russian organized crime members who continue to enter Israel as returning Jews. Police sources in Israel note that the smuggling of sex-trade workers from Eastern Europe is increasing, and they anticipate a muscling-in on brothel operators for extortion payments.

Internationally, law enforcement agencies are finding that Israeli criminals are becoming ever more sophisticated; they've reportedly created a barter trade with Colombian cartels whereby cocaine, which is plentiful in Colombia, is exchanged for synthetic drugs, which the Colombians expect to profit from within North America.

There are few if any probes into Israeli organized crime anywhere in the world that don't involve organized crime groups from at least two other countries. International cooperation will be required to conduct local investigations and then to follow them back through multiple jurisdictions to catch the main players and seize their assets.

Endnotes

1. The Yehiyeh Hariri group is an offshoot of Taibeth, a nationwide criminal organization, according to an Israeli police intelligence report. The report also says Hariri members control a vast gambling market in northern Israel and are prime suspects in several murders. The Jarush family—run by brothers Zayad and Khatam—are powerbrokers in the drug trade in the Lod region; they also engaged in widespread extortion. Yitzhak and Moshe Bar-Moha's organization is considered violent and often at odds with other groups; their main income is from illegal gambling. And in the south, the intelligence report says, the Bedouin families are involved in extortion protection and the trafficking of women for the sex trade.

2. The use of young Hasidic Jews as mules very quickly became notorious and caused a scandal in New York's Jewish community. When a Hasidic teen—one of several arrested in courier operations with a Tuito colleague—appeared in Brooklyn federal court, dozens of Hasidic men and women attended the hearings to testify on his behalf. This prompted Judge I. Leo Glasser to comment angrily from the bench, "I don't know where this community was while all of this was going on."

3. This courtesy didn't extend to all criminal organizations. Russian émigré mafia suspects are quickly rounded up and held for expulsion. In 1996, for example, 33 Russians were awaiting expulsion. Several were suspected of money laundering through the Israeli financial system, but the main fear, some observers believe, is that with their huge wealth they'd corrupt the political system. "We expect corruption," an Israeli financial crime investigator said, "but we don't want Russians coming in to do it with their black money. We're quite capable of bribing our own officials, thank you."

PART
FIVE
Albanian Organized Crime

The Balkan Connection

Law enforcement authorities in several countries—most noticeably in the U.S.—have set their sights on Albanian-based criminals as the newest potent organized crime threat. They're listed, along with Serbians, Montenegrins, Croatians, Bosnians, and Macedonians, under "Balkan Organized Crime."

As did, for instance, the Vietnamese gangs of the 1980s, the Chinese Fuk Ching of the early 1990s, and the Eastern Europeans throughout the 1990s, Albanian organized crime has become the newest magnet for police attention. "Bloodthirsty," "ruthless," and "the newest mafia" are phrases used in recent press clippings to describe this group. And while the phrases might be hyperbolic, the emerging groups all share common traits: they've come from countries suffering from serious social and political disrepair; they operate in a culture of violence resulting from sharp change; and many of their members have military training under harsh conditions. Those who were criminals and incarcerated before arriving in North America or Western Europe had been imprisoned in the cruelest of circumstances. And those who bent or even broke the law on a daily basis just to survive were thrilled at the opportunities created by democratic freedoms in the West.

Law enforcement faces the same problems dealing with Albanian crime groups as they did with the waves of other ethnic gangs that arrived earlier: the language and slang are new and few translators are available; the ties that bind the gangs together are familial as well as social and difficult to penetrate; the countries they've fled are corrupt and finding prior intelligence on their operations is nearly impossible; and they've survived such harsh military and police punishment that any sentence that a civilized judicial system metes out is considered laughable.

But the most difficult problem to overcome is an ancient code that rivals the loyalty oaths of the Italian Mafias and the Russian *vory v zakone*: the *besa*.[1] *Besa* is at the heart of Albanian culture, rooted mostly in the rugged north; to give your *besa* is to swear on your blood that you'll keep your word. It's a concept that encompasses a range of human behavior: loyalty, fidelity, honoring one's word, the face of dignity. *Besa* is a part of day-to-day transactions—for example, if one man promises another that he'll pay tomorrow for food today, he has given his *besa*. On a higher level, cooperation with authorities is a violation of *besa* and can lead to *gjakmarria*, the taking of blood in a vendetta. These blood feuds can go on for generations. If a man who gives his *besa* dies before he can carry out his obligation of honor, his family is honor-bound to carry it out for him—the promise is "in the blood."

Because many Albanian criminal gangs are based on *fis*—the family or clan—the same social and cultural ties that bind non-criminal groups are naturally covered by the laws of *besa*.

"The Corporation"

In the U.S., a series of stories began appearing in 2004 detailing how a group of Albanians—dubbed "The Corporation" and directed by their alleged ringleader, Alex "Alley Boy" Rudaj—orchestrated an attack on the American Cosa Nostra. According to American indictments filed in New York City, in 2001 the 37-year-old Rudaj led a crew of six of his henchmen on a raid on a social club where a powerful New York City LCN family operated a gambling racket using Greek front men. Armed with guns, Rudaj's crew swarmed into the mob-controlled club and violently attacked the workers. Afterwards The Corporation began muscling at least six Astoria-area gambling clubs; these were added to several other clubs Rudaj's crew operated, bringing the total number of clubs to 50 and yielding $5.75 million in profits. They also attacked several associates of both the Lucchese and Colombo crime families.

The opportunity for the Rudaj group to make aggressive moves on the American mob was the success by the FBI in a series of coordinated attacks on La Cosa Nostra's five families in New York. The constant police pressure allowed groups like the Albanians to push the envelope and take several bold steps against LCN. And so, capitalizing on the disarray and the sheer number of LCN members in prison, the Corporation conducted a four-year reign of terror against established mob families and independent criminal networks. They seized former mob turf in Queens, the Bronx, and Westchester County from three of the city's five Families: the Gambinos, the Luccheses, and the Colombos.

Even the social life of LCN members has been under assault. At Rao's, a famous Italian restaurant where many powerful LCN mobsters eat, 20 Albanian gangsters, unable to get seats, demanded to be seated at the table of the late John Gotti. "They were aggressive, they were ready for anything," a witness said. "They got the table."

Subsequently, Arnold Squitieri, acting boss of the Gambino Family, demanded a sitdown with Rudaj and his associates at a New Jersey gas station. When Squitieri pulled a gun during the meeting, one of the Albanians pulled his own weapon, aimed it at the gas pump, and said that if the Italians didn't back off they'd all go up in flames. The Gambinos, it was reported, gave in. The Albanians had become a power to be reckoned with.

"We've seen over the years groups such as this, be it Russian or Albanian, step into the turf of organized crime," U.S. Attorney David Kelley said. "This happens to be the most extensive we've seen." Organized-crime watchers observed the rise of the Rudaj organization with some interest and a lot of skepticism, particularly when authorities went so far as to call The Corporation "the sixth family." "They're a hardened group, operating with reckless abandon," said an FBI official, echoing comments made for the previous 30 years as criminals from Vietnam, China, and the U.S.S.R. made their way to North America among law-abiding immigrants.

Albanian criminals have been part of the American underworld, particularly in New York City and the eastern seaboard, since the 1970s. Mostly they were recruited as low-level couriers, enforcers and, in some cases, hired hit men for LCN families. In the 1980s, however, law enforcement uncovered a "Balkan Connection" involved in shipping more than $100 million worth of heroin from Afghanistan and Turkey through to Kosovo and then into the U.S. The emergence of the Balkan Connection was the downside of the success the FBI had had in their persistent attack in the mid-1980s during the Sicilian Mafia Pizza Case: Albanian criminals, until then in the lower echelon of American organized crime, had recognized and exploited a gap that suddenly appeared in the heroin-smuggling business.

More recently, some cases have emerged involving more sophisticated Albanian crime figures. One Albanian criminal, for example, organized a

$19 million Internet theft for the Gambino family. Typical growth pains and hubris are suspected as being behind the sudden aggressiveness in the local Albanian–American underworld; the weakening of the traditional LCN Five Families under the U.S. government's seemingly relentless assault is likely another factor.

As the prosecution against the Rudaj organization unfolded, Rudaj's lawyer described his client as a hardworking family man and philanthropist. Rudaj, who's an ethnic Albanian from Yugoslavia, and his followers remain before the courts. And while the investigation into the activities of Albanian criminals in New York City may be somewhat overstated—it is, after all, their turn for police and media scrutiny—Albanian organized crime on the global stage is an emerging threat to be taken seriously.

On an international level it's very difficult to overestimate the activities of Albanian organized crime. An FBI report has listed the group as in the top tier of global underworld threats, a list that includes Triads and Chinese syndicates, the Yakuza, and Eastern European organized crime.

Since the early 1990s, when Albania was freed from 40 years of communist rule and quickly fell into chaos and anarchy, Albanians have fled the country and settled throughout the world, primarily in Western Europe. Among them were criminal gangs that had, since 1945, operated under the thumb of despot leaders. Suddenly they were liberated, and the entire world was rife with possibilities. Albanian communities sprang up across Europe along with a sharp increase in petty crime, from pickpocketing to burglaries, extortion, fraud, and migrant smuggling. By 2000, when an estimated 500,000 ethnic Albanians were living in North America, 400,000 in Germany, and 30,000 in the U.K., the state of Albanian organized crime in Europe led Italian prosecutor Cataldo Motta to declare the Albanians as a major threat to Western society.

As in Russia after the collapse of the Soviet Union, a mix of warlords from Albania's rugged mountainous region, along with corrupt police, military, and government officials; and out-and-out gangsters, drug traffickers, and black marketeers were able to run loose. And with unrest and upheaval in nearby countries—notably Croatia and Serbia—disrupting heroin-trafficking routes from Central Asia and Turkey, Albania was perfectly geographically situated to become an essential part of the pipeline. It also had the matériel to support the new heroin-trafficking gangs; the complete breakdown of civil authority in Albania in 1997 led to widespread anarchy in which military arsenals were raided and thousands of automatic weapons were liberated. Anyone who wanted to arm themselves suddenly had the benefit of a full marketplace with competitive prices. Having accumulated firepower, some criminal organizations set themselves up as paramilitary units. Then, in 1998 and 1999, the war in Kosovo broke out, and again the traffickers were able to capitalize on chaos by organizing smuggling operations to support the cause.

During the communist years the Fifteen Families—"fifteen *fis*"—had controlled organized criminal activity in Albania, primarily through smuggling and corruption. But with the collapse of the communist government and the military, the Fifteen Families were in essence the only groups that didn't descend into anarchy and chaos. This paradox echoes that of Sicily after World War II; when the Americans looked for leaders of strength who could govern there, they had only the Mafiosi to choose from.

One of the most prominent criminals among the fifteen *fis* was Daut Kadriovski. Kadriovski was originally from Macedonia, but his activities spread quickly throughout the Baltics and into Western Europe and the United States. His specialty was moving heroin and he used an almost impenetrable family cloak to conduct his business. With Turkey as a base, he put together an international network that employed some unique methods of transit. In one instance he stuffed a hollowed-out accordion to move his product. A member of an Albanian folk troupe carried the accordion into the United States.

Kadriovski quickly became notorious as an associate of the Magliana criminal organization based in Rome. He created a partnership with the *Sacra Corona Unita*—the SCU—which received his shipments of heroin once they reached Italy. Then, in 1984, police in Germany cracked down on the increasingly public Albanian criminal activities and arrested several of his traffickers. A year later authorities arrested

Kadriovski himself on heroin possession charges. Several villas, boats, and cars were seized during the investigation.

In 1993 Kadriovski escaped, using the tried and true method of bribing a prison guard. He turned up in the U.S. with an Australian passport and blended into the growing Albanian communities, particularly in New York, New Jersey, and Philadelphia. Intelligence files show that he worked with several La Cosa Nostra families along the northeastern seaboard on heroin operations. He set up a system of repatriating drug profits to criminal and political groups to Albania and Kosovo. Two years later, he was again operating from Albania—by which time 13 countries wanted him for drug trafficking and numerous Interpol warrants were out for his arrest. He was finally re-arrested in September 2001 in Tirana—Italy, it turned out, had an extradition warrant on him; he'd been found guilty and sentenced *in absentia*. He is now serving a 12-year sentence for heroin offenses.

The story of Daut Kadriovski is, in essence, the story of the rise of Albanian criminal groups who see a world of victims without limit. His involvement in the heroin trade coincided with the American dismantling of the Pizza connection. He had a strong familial network that followed the concept of *besa*. He moved with ease throughout the world, easily shrugging off one identity and assuming another. Wherever he went he was able to connect and coexist with whatever powerful organization he came into contact with.

That Kadriovski and other Balkan, particularly Albanian, criminals were able to insinuate themselves into Italy, for example, can be attributed to the similarity of both groups' mindsets. *Besa* is not far from *omertà*, the Sicilian concept of behavior and manliness.

A Terrorist Connection?

The successes of the Albanian "mafia"—particularly on the global stage—can also be attributed to the command structure of the groups that make up the wide federation. A Leadership Council oversees, but doesn't necessarily dictate, both local and international operations. The council is made up of elders who are the leaders of the *fis*, the family networks that govern individual groups. Some *fis* operations are controlled according to territory, particularly in the Baltic region, while others are built around *fis* members and their opportunities and specialties, such as a source and route for the transit of firearms, or alternatively, all activities in a specific region of influence. Many Albanian politicians and former military and espionage agents are believed to be members of individual groups, but *gjak*, or blood relatives, form the hard kernel of each cell. Family attachments, such as through marriage, make up a close but less trusted outer circle.

Overseas, the Council's power is somewhat diluted, particularly in areas where members from several *fis* operate in a small geographic area and where opportunities to earn large profits might be limited. In New York City, for example, or Toronto, joint operations are either allowed or not, apparently at the sole discretion of the *bajrak*, or committee, that directs each "family." The *bajrak* is made up of the heads—the *krye*—and inner circle of the *fis* operating in that area. Under the *krye*—the equivalent of the Sicilian *capo*—are the *kryetar*—the equivalent of the "underboss" in traditional Mafia groups. A liaison officer, or a *miq*, is charged with monitoring all operations of his family and determining if the activities encroach on the operations of other *fis*.

There are reports that a financial officer is appointed whose job it is to invest and launder the group's profits as well as to identify and exploit methods of repatriating funds overseas, particularly in groups with strong ties to their Albanian mother-*fis*. This may or may not be the same person who's called a "coordinator." The coordinator is a trusted blood relative who travels the world carrying messages, passing information, and assisting Albanians who want to emigrate to either America or Canada. Often the coordinator has a public role, usually as a member of a cultural or social-awareness group. When a member of the group gets into legal difficulty with the law, it's the coordinator who navigates the judicial system, finding lawyers, arranging payment of fees and, when possible, corrupting or bribing police or judges.

The bulk of the Albanian crime family is similar to the LCN "crew." Directed by the *kryetar*, or underboss, each crew has a leader and may comprise as few as four or five members; some crews identified in Europe have more than a dozen members. Crews, unlike modern LCN cells, directly involve themselves in traditional criminal activities at the street level, ranging from organized robbery and ATM machine rip-offs to lightning-fast gang burglaries and small-quantity drug trafficking.

The decentralized makeup of the vast number of crews makes it almost impossible for law enforcement to climb the ladder to the next level. And the blood loyalty of the Albanian criminal groups makes them virtually impenetrable. "This is the key," a Canadian law-enforcement officer said.

> *If a guy rats here, his entire family back in Albania is blamed. When we get a traditional organized crime informant in Vancouver, we can generally take him and his wife and kids into protective custody, into the [witness protection] program. With Baltics, there's no way we can even begin to identify relatives, never mind get a corrupt foreign government to protect mothers and fathers and children. Right away the entire clan goes "in the blood" and there are bodies falling for generations to come, long after anyone even remembers why it all started.*

He added that the current law enforcement offensives against traditional "headline groups"—including the Mafia, bikers, and Triads—means that resources will continue to be focused in that direction. "Some of these Baltic names, you can't even say them. The Albanians don't have the media drawing power of a mafia hit or a Triad heroin-smuggling ring. People don't know about the Albanians. And the Albanians like it that way." He went on to say that getting a "wire" on Albanian hangouts or suspects' telephones is difficult because few translators are available to work their way through the tapes, let alone understand the slang.

Although no hard evidence has emerged, American authorities have raised concerns that a nexus might exist between the Albanian *fis*, who are primarily Muslim, and al-Qaeda. Terrorist financing trails from several parts of Europe and the Middle East are being examined for linkages to the financial channels used by Albanian criminal organizations. Also under investigation are Albanian criminal "safe houses" used to smuggle illegal migrants into the U.S. They might also be used by terrorists sent West to form sleeper cells. Within Albania dozens of Wahabi mosques have been built since 1999 as well as a hundred primary and secondary

Wahabi-funded schools. Wahabism forms the Salafi strand of Islam, which, according to Dr. Rohan Gunaratna, "strives to revive Islamic thought within the boundaries of Islamic principles (meaning the presentation of realistic Islamic solutions to contemporary problems) and to establish a true Islamic society governed by Allah's laws. It is pure and free from any additions, deletions or alterations."[2] Additionally, at least one al-Qaeda member was caught entering Dubai with a false passport manufactured by an Albanian crime group.

Endnotes

1. *Besa* is part of a primitive set of tribal laws known as the *Canon* (or *Canun*, or *Kanun*) *of Leke Dukagjini*. During the communist years in Albania, the Canun, formulated 500 years ago, was rarely followed except in some remote areas. But with the fall of the communist regime, Albanian watchers have noted a sharp return of the laws. The *Canon*, which is patriarchal, emphasizes that family blood is above all other ties, whether political, social, or cultural. Fathers have the right to beat or even kill their children; a man can abduct a woman he wants to marry. A husband may cut his bride's hair and return her to her family if he discovers she isn't a virgin on her wedding night. Under the *Canon*, a woman with her hair cut in this manner can be killed. And although rape, for example, is an act that can be punished, it was seen as an act against the woman's husband or family rather than a violation of herself. Similarly, and more sensible and less sensational, a person who's a guest of a family is protected not for his own sake but because an insult or injury against a guest is an act against the host. Believers around the world subscribe to the *Canon*.

2. Rohan Gunaratna, *Inside Al Qaeda: Global Network of Terror* (New York: Berkley Books, 2003), p. 36.

PART
SIX
Colombian and Mexican Cartels

The Border Economy

Cocaine shipped by Colombian cartels to Mexican organized crime groups, then trans-shipped by the Mexicans, along with pharmaceuticals, anabolic steroids, and precursor chemicals (used in the production of "date rape" drugs and other synthetics), is increasingly flooding across the Mexico–U.S. border. Organized crime groups also smuggle Mexicans who want to work in the United States; South and Central Americans hoping for a better life; and even Chinese migrants whose journey has taken them halfway around the world to the southerly doorstep of America.

The southern border itself—as does the northern border along Canada—creates the opportunities for organized criminal activities. As in other jurisdictions in the world, wherever a border causes an imbalance in availability or cost of an item, organized crime exploits the differences. When increased taxes on cigarettes in California resulted in hefty price hikes, for example, Mexican crime groups stepped in and began producing counterfeit cigarettes that were sold throughout central and southern California. For Americans who had difficulty accessing steroids, an open market was created in towns like Tijuana where the product is available only a few hundred feet from the border. And the lack of jobs in Mexico sparked a cottage industry in smuggling workers that has since grown into complex organized networks. These networks in turn expanded into drug smuggling as the human traffickers—called "coyotes"—realized that their routes could be used as a pipeline for any number of products.

In addition to prohibited, restricted, and over-taxed or over-legislated goods, the underground economy also led to an export in corruption and violence. Some places along the southern U.S. border resemble war zones.

And of all the illegal industries, narcotics is the most active and violent. While the southern border is heavily guarded (certainly compared with the Canadian border), it too is porous, and having the world's largest illegal drug market only a few miles away is naturally tempting to criminal organizations. And because organized crime prefers to position itself between the source and the market, control of both sides of the border is necessary.

Money laundering, long a by-product of successful organized criminal activities, is also carried out on both sides of the border. Real estate investment and the purchase of luxury items have in some cases actually been beneficial to local economies. For example, on the northern U.S.–Canada border along Ontario and Quebec, and on Native reserves, the influx of sudden ready cash has changed entire communities, bringing in auto dealerships and hotels and restaurants and creating a leisure economy fed by criminal profits. The failure of governments to adequately provide protection, investment, and stability has long been recognized as a primary factor in the growth of organized crime in border communities.

For Mexican cocaine traffickers, the major factors in the growth of their trade were the Colombians' retreat after the successful extradition of Colombian traffickers to the U.S.; the death of Pablo Escobar and the destruction of the core of his cartel; and the increased control of Mexico itself by crime groups that already had ways and means of penetrating the U.S. border. Success against the Colombian cartels—long expected to reduce the movement of cocaine into America—merely created a corrupt and criminal culture right on America's southern edge.

Colombian Cartels

Like the recent emergence of Mexican crime syndicates, Colombian cocaine cartels didn't start out as drug-trafficking powerhouses. The country had never been much of a source country for cocaine; its production nets only 10 percent of market demands. In contrast, Bolivia and Peru had vast cocoa fields and laboratories that turned out an adequate supply. But Colombia does have a long history as a base for smuggling. From refrigerators to quinine, from coffee to tobacco, and from fashion goods to perfumes and watches, organized smuggling groups in Colombia operated illegal import/export rackets for more than a century before the demand for cocaine hit the radar.

In 1974 the U.S. National Household Survey found that more than five million people in America had tried cocaine, even if only on an experimental basis. Colombian criminals found themselves in a prime location to exploit the transportation of cocaine out of South America: their country not only had easy access to prime cocoa-growing regions, but also good weather, busy seaports, endemic corruption, and an underworld well experienced in smuggling all manner of goods. At first the trade in cocaine was chaotic and wracked with murders and massacres, hijacked shipments, and kidnappings, all carried out with a ruthlessness that shocked even the usually violent Peruvian and Bolivian criminal organizations.

Then, throughout the 1970s, several small independent smuggling gangs formed themselves into cartels. The most powerful, initially, were the Medellin and the Cali. The Medellin quickly established itself as a criminal organization as famous for its violence as for its product. The Cali cartel kept to more businesslike methods. Whereas many of the Medellin cartel leaders were purely criminals, many of the Cali were both legitimate businessmen and criminal entrepreneurs. Between them they would control or influence as much as 70 percent of the cocaine shipped into North America.

Using a variety of methods, the cartels were able to simultaneously work backward to the cocaine producers and forward into the American distribution markets. Alliances were formed and broken. Throughout the 1970s and 1980s parts of America were exposed to a series of cocaine wars over control of territory, and the ruthlessness of the Medellin and Cali cartels became legendary. Victims of the "Colombian Necktie" became much talked about; the victim's throat was cut and his tongue pulled out through the hole. South Florida—the prime trans-shipment route to the rest of the U.S.—was particularly hard hit by violence as Colombian distributors fought over turf and supply lines. There were daylight shootouts and bodies dumped in public, messages of terror and power. Police seized "war wagons" containing automatic weapons, grenades, bulletproof vests, and masks. California underwent a similar but more subdued campaign of violence as the cartels used ships and boats to carry their product up the Pacific Ocean to be off-loaded either with legitimate goods at ports or from mother ships anchored offshore and unloaded by smugglers in small, fast craft. There was cocaine-related violence as far north as New York City and Canada. And as the demand for cocaine grew, so did the wealth and power of the cartels.

Organization of the cocaine networks wasn't a matter of hit and miss. The Colombians brought to the drug underworld a business plan and a system. Shipments were organized so that if one load was confiscated by authorities, several others were almost guaranteed to make it through. If one trafficking unit was taken down by police, the members could give only limited information because the units were isolated, both from each other and from the primary command structure. Any seizure or arrest of members was "investigated" by cartel people to determine whether mistakes were made, how to prevent them in the future, or if someone was greedy or sloppy. And since the Colombians used a cell system, often based on families, many of the traffickers who were assigned to consumer countries were in effect hostages; this guaranteed that they wouldn't talk to police if caught because they all had families back in Colombia who were vulnerable.

A former cartel-related cocaine dealer interviewed at a Toronto leather goods shop he operates said that every arrest or loss had to be justified. "I was all the time sweating," he said. "If a package didn't arrive, you had to prove it didn't arrive. If the one before you [in the network] became greedy, he would just say it was delivered. If he had more friends than you, you would be in trouble." He said that losses due to investigations by police were acceptable, "but if you were the one who allowed a policeman to make a purchase, you were responsible."

Loss of money was always treated more seriously than loss of product. "At first I had a thrill, here," the shopkeeper said, touching his chest. "So much money, it was beautiful. But after a time it was just paper and was always a problem to get rid of it." And he was never comfortable dealing with his customers, he went on, because they were from other groups, usually Italians or bikers. "I know, I know. The movie image is that Colombians are fearless, Colombians are vicious killers. But it isn't true most of the time. You come here to do a job for a specific length of time. Canada isn't the best of places. The weather, and not too many Spanish people here. The police, too, were very hard to give money to."

Distributors in foreign countries were carefully trained in setting up their operations. They were instructed to live quiet lives with their families, showing no sign of wealth or power. They were to blend into their neighborhoods, operate small businesses, drive modest cars, and keep their homes in good repair. Houses with specific features were sought out for lease—electricity meters should be on the outside of the house to prevent meter-readers from having to gain entrance; garages should have direct access to the main body of the house. Never was any business conducted with children around; they might talk at school or to friends.

Local "bosses" were in every major city to maintain security and support, often scouting out the city in which their group would be set up. They would determine from local underworld players which lawyers were loyal, and which accountants and banks were amenable to taking cash in large quantities. They also looked for opportunities for corruption among police and the judiciary.

The path the cocaine took from its inception as cocoa plants in Peru, Bolivia, and to an increasing extent Colombia required management, maintenance, and enforcement of security. Transit teams retrieved the cocoa paste from the grow fields and took it to remote laboratories, often housed in rundown shacks, where it was processed into cocaine hydrochloride, the famous white powder. Then it was taken to the stockpiles, where it was held until shipment out of the country was arranged. Often shipments from several fields were warehoused until a secure system was devised to get the product to market, whether North America or Europe. Airplanes, ships, trucks, and commercial buses were all used to move it across borders.

When the cocaine arrived at either the market country or a transit country—Bahamas, Mexico, Venezuela—it was kept secure by heavily armed cartel "security forces" until it was sold off in smaller loads to brokers, who acted as middlemen, and the stash was depleted. These smaller loads—in the hundreds of kilograms—were bought up by middlemen who often arranged sale of their own cocaine as well as that supplied by the cartel. The prices rose at each point of distribution as each point required profit. Credit was often granted, and this allowed each wholesaler to negotiate for the next shipment as he amassed profits from a current deal. Funds were then repatriated back to the cartels in Colombia either by cartel members in the chain of supply or by the customers themselves.

The size of shipments increased throughout the late 1980s; in one instance, considered a record at the time, law enforcement seized 47,554 pounds of cocaine in Sylmar, California, in 1989. Once the cycle of inflated payment and repeated dilution of the product was completed, the shipment would have generated more than $3 billion.

While the Colombian cartels could maintain a high profit margin by shipping their drugs themselves, using their own supply chain—ships, body bulkers, swallowers, and even convoys on the long trail to North America—they farmed out some of the routes, hiring non-Colombian criminal organizations to do the actual transit and security until the drugs were across the U.S. border. The Mexican gangs brought into the cocaine trade weren't usually paid in cash; instead, they were given a portion of the load. This was good business sense on the part of the cartels; if the load was lost then their transit people, the Mexicans, lost their own product and profit as well. It also allowed the Mexicans to create their own powerful criminal organizations.

The Rise and Fall of Cartels

The 1980s and early 1990s were days of profit and power for the Colombian cartels. But their activities generated attention from law enforcement, notably the Americans who were waging a war on drugs. Cartel leaders became notorious. Pablo Escobar, who ran the Medellin cartel, was a lifelong criminal who worked as a kidnapper, thief, and con man before going into the cocaine trade. In 1976 he was arrested for smuggling, but within a few years the police officers involved in arresting him, their boss, and the judge who signed the arrest warrant were all assassinated. As the Sicilian Mafia did in the early 1990s, Escobar had declared war on the state; in the ensuing years more than a thousand members of the judiciary and police were killed.

Escobar had been named in drug-trafficking warrants in the U.S. and so, aware that extradition meant death in an American prison, he negotiated his surrender to Colombian authorities on outstanding local drug charges. Convicted, he was put into a low-security facility. This was a win-win for Escobar and the Colombian government, which by then had all the trappings of narco-state; Escobar was now immune from the American warrant and could easily run his growing empire, and the Colombian government could point to his incarceration and say they'd locked up a major drug trafficker. But the government's move fooled no one, and especially not the U.S Drug Enforcement Administration. After a public outcry, Escobar escaped from his jail when he learned he was to be transferred to a military prison. He lived on the run for 18 months before he was tracked down and killed by heavily armed Colombian drug agents.

The death of Escobar took some of the gilt off the lily for the cartels. As much a legend as a man, his death at the hands of the government demonstrated that he didn't have a monopoly on power. And ever-increasing numbers of investigative teams, usually at the urging of the U.S. DEA, were taking down cartel operatives and making massive seizures.

The Cali cartel, founded in the 1970s by Gilberto Rodriguez Orejuela and Jose Santacruz Londono, also found itself in difficulty. Initially powerful and wealthy—as early as 1980 the Cali was raking in tens of millions of dollars every year—it used a business model that concentrated on small, independent cells to traffic the cocaine and another, separate group of cells to launder the profits to either Colombia or offshore banks. Like any successful business venture, the Cali had spin-off franchises that bought their product from the cartel in Colombia but were allowed to handle their own outbound smuggling routes as well as distribution down to the retail level.

Law enforcement pressure from the U.S. made life difficult for the Cali and Medellin cartels. Some cartel leaders relocated to Spain and Panama and continued directing their operations at arm's length. American authorities went after them with a vengeance. General Manuel Noriega, who had accepted millions of dollars to let narco-traffickers into Panama, was snatched up and taken to the U.S. where he was tried and convicted. Traffickers were lured from their new locations by sting operations and arrested.

When a short-lived extradition treaty with the U.S.—signed in 1979 but lasting only until 1987—was reinstated in 1997, many cartel leaders were arrested and jailed in Colombia and others were finally sent to America for trial. The Rodriguez–Orejuela brothers and Londono were arrested; Londono later escaped and was killed in a shootout with authorities.

These successful initiatives against the Colombian cartels led them to retract some of their operations. The absence of many leaders of the cartels, whether by death, extradition, or imprisonment, weakened the organizations; every success of the Colombian or American government diminished their mythic power. They reduced some of their operations and formed smaller, more low-profile cells.

According to a U.S. government report, the transit flow of cocaine has changed. "A smaller but growing cocaine smuggling method is to use small civilian aircraft from clandestine airstrips in southeastern Colombia to fly cocaine to Brazil, Suriname or Guyana," the 2005 report says. "From these countries the cocaine is either consumed locally, as in Brazil, or transferred to maritime vessels for shipment to the United States or Europe." The use of "go-fast" boats is also increasing, with small speedboats being used to carry loads from mother ships offshore; the go-fast boats employ refueling ships at sea to extend their range and allow them to reach Central American countries.

Current intelligence reports show that Colombia remains the source of 90 percent of the cocaine and half of the heroin entering the U.S. Of all the countries in the world that import precursor chemicals—used in the production of many illegal drugs—Colombia tops the list. Corruption is so endemic in the country that schoolchildren in the ninth grade are taught a course in The Culture of Lawfulness—a civics class to steer youth away from crime. American-sponsored crop planes regularly fly over illegal crops to spray chemicals that eradicate the cocoa plants; many fields are so well hidden, however, that even satellite surveillance fails to locate them.

New cartels have rushed to fill the gap created by the retreat of the two traditional prime cartels. The Norte del Valle Cartel (NVC),[1] operating near the Pacific coast, has become a major target for law enforcement. The NVC uses both marine and air transit methods to move product out of the country, either up to the American west coast or into Mexico or Central American countries for reshipment. As well there are hundreds of smaller cartels who operate quietly to prevent attracting too much attention.

The trafficker-terrorist nexus has become the latest focus of U.S. and Colombian security and police agencies. Rebel and anti-government groups are funded by the cocaine trade, and the U.S. sees them as a threat to the stability of the region. On December 31, 2004, Juvenal

Ovidio Ricardo Palmera Pineda, a leader of the Revolutionary Armed Forces of Colombia (FARC), was extradited to the U.S. on both drug trafficking and terrorism charges. Today other narco-terrorists dubbed "high-value targets" by American authorities are either close to being caught or, like Omaira Rojas Cabrera, the chief of finance for FARC, in custody awaiting decisions by the Colombian Supreme Court on American extradition requests. There are also joint U.S.–Colombian intelligence operations under way to locate and capture some 300 cocaine-terrorist kingpins called *Cabecillas*. Since the *Cabecillas* task force was set up in August 2004, nine targets have been arrested in four separate operations.

From Colombia the cartels continue to control the production and sale of huge loads of cocaine, sending shipments not only to the U.S. and Canada, but also to Western and Eastern Europe. While some money flows back to pay for past purchases and to make down payments on future ones, the bulk of the profits make by traffickers of Colombian cocaine are laundered throughout the world's financial systems.

One of the beneficiaries of the shift in Colombia to narco-terrorism are the Mexican cartels. For years, working as transit groups for the Colombians and carrying their product over the last leg of the route to the U.S., Mexicans organized crime groups that have grown wealthier—and have become dangerous and significant.

Mexico

While Colombia is by far the most prolific producer and shipper of cocaine out of South America, 90 percent of the cocaine that enters the U.S. is moved through Mexico. Mexico is also a major producer of heroin, methamphetamine, and marijuana. And as a gateway for illegal migrants, it rivals Canada for being the primary human smuggling entry point, once day workers and labor migrants are eliminated from the equation.

The power of Mexican organized crime, particularly narco-traffickers, has been deemed a threat to both national security and public health by the Mexican government. But despite massive and continual seizures of product—in the first 10 months of 2004, 25 metric tons of cocaine, 300 kilograms of heroin, and over 2,000 metric tons of marijuana were interdicted—the drug trade, and the gangs that run it, have continued to grow and thrive. Criminal organizations trafficking in precursor and synthetic drugs have concentrated their activities along the borders with California, Arizona, and Texas. Huge methamphetamine laboratories in northwestern Mexico have been set up to feed the American market. And an ongoing series of gang wars for control of sectors of the market has led to gangland slayings targeting law enforcement officers, journalists, lawyers, and politicians. Several border towns have been terrorized after gangs conducted running gun battles, often in broad daylight. Bodies are found dumped along roads or in isolated desert areas; many have been horribly tortured, burned, or dismembered and left stacked in piles.

Even though during the current Vicente Fox administration Mexican officials have arrested more than 36,000 suspects on drug charges, there's no shortage of players in the Mexican underworld. And despite the U.S. government's lauding of Mexican authorities' successes in the fight against drugs, the country is for the most part a narco-state, with corruption rampant in both law enforcement and the judiciary. Investigations have found that the police, particularly anti-drug officers, are heavily involved in the drug trade. They either form criminal groups among themselves and take bribes from cartels, or hire themselves out as security guards for shipments or as hit men. And several high-profile cartel members, when they're arrested, seem to be able to escape custody with ease.

In short, Mexico—despite hundreds of millions of dollars in American drug-control funding—is a country out of control.

The Arellano–Felix Organization (AFO) has historically been one of the most powerful of the Mexican drug cartels. Operating from strongholds in Tijuana and Mexicali—where they're firmly entrenched and protected locally by systemic corruption—the AFO oversees the import and distribution of multi-ton shipments of cocaine and marijuana as well as the movement of large quantities of heroin and methamphetamine into the United States.

Unsatisfied with merely moving its own product, the AFO in the mid-1990s instituted a taxation system that allowed other criminal organizations to move their product along its routes on the Baja

California border. They apparently charged 60 percent of the value of large shipments to allow their turf to be used as a gateway into the United States. The AFO has traditionally positioned itself to reach into Colombia and Peru to make large purchases and has extended its distribution and sales areas deep into the U.S., reaching as far as Michigan and into Canada.

When the Mexican police and the U.S. DEA focused their attention—successfully—on arresting members of the top AFO leadership in 2002, rival gangs who felt they'd been the victims of predatory taxation by the organization years earlier began to encroach on their turf. This has sparked battles for control that continue into 2005.

The Carrillo Fuentes Organization, also known as the Juarez Cartel, has emerged as the most powerful of the Mexican groups. The CFO, like the Arellano–Felix Organization, has a long reach back to South American cocaine sources and ahead into the distribution markets of the United States. And as the main beneficiary of the crackdown and the warfare disrupting the Arellano–Felix group, the CFO is constantly making changes to their structure as well as solidifying their direct connections to the most powerful Peruvian and Colombian cartels. To protect themselves, the primary cartel managers almost never leave Mexico, relying instead on lower-level traffickers to risk arrest in the U.S.

Another top cartel in Mexico is the Cardenas Guillen Organization (CGO), based in the northern states of Tamaulipas and Nuevo Leon and with operations in several other Mexican states. Its activities are vast. The CGO, like the Arellano–Felix and Carillo Fuentes cartels, has members throughout the U.S., including in New York City. And in the cities of Matamoros, Reynosa, and Ciudad Miguel Aleman, it's locked in a savage fight with another breakaway faction originally of the same group.

It's that ongoing bloodshed that has given Mexico a new face before the world.

✳ ✳ ✳

The rapidly deteriorating law enforcement situation along the U.S.–Mexican border in Texas goes back to the story of a former policeman who became the leader of the powerful Gulf Cartel.

Osiel Cardenas Guillen was born in Matamoros, Mexico, on May 18, 1967. He's remembered by friends as an aggressive and violent young man who later became a police officer. He resigned or was fired under undetermined circumstances and ended up working for Juan Garcia Abrego, who ran the Gulf Cartel from a base in Matamoros. Abrego built the modern Gulf Cartel, extending his contacts and influence into South America and the Caribbean and, through Brownsville, Texas, into the U.S. A notorious corrupter, Abrego operated with impunity, often drawing Mexican police and Customs officers into his network. He was considered the Mexican equivalent of Pablo Escobar.

Abrego was suspected in dozens of homicides—on the 17th of each month he ordered a murder to commemorate his brother's death. Through his pipelines in the Matamoros area, he was believed to be responsible for as much as 70 percent of cocaine entering the U.S. He was arrested in 1996 and sentenced to 11 life terms the following year.

Following Abrego's extradition, Osiel Cardenas Guillen took control of the cartel. He ruled the Gulf Cartel in much the same way as Abrego had. Through murder, kidnappings, torture, and bribery he expanded the scope and wealth of the cartel. Encased in a pod of heavily armed bodyguards, Cardenas moved through Matamoros like royalty. Working with Mexican immigrants who had made their way throughout America, he created pipelines that saw his product delivered as far as the Atlantic northeast.

On November 9, 1999, Cardenas and about a dozen of his crew came across a car in downtown Matamoros. Inside were two U.S. federal agents and an informant. The heavily armed cartel members surrounded the car, brandishing automatic weapons. An attempt was made to kidnap the trio, but the agents managed to talk their way free. When U.S. officials were told of the incident, they immediately turned their attention to Cardenas and his cartel, putting a $2 million reward on his head. Cardenas moved to the top of the American most wanted lists.

A former federal agent interviewed in Laredo remembered the tense anger along the border at the time. "Ozzie [Osiel Cardenas] was just one of a bunch of them we were looking for. If he'd kept his head down, we would have got to him sooner or later, probably later, maybe never. But when he went off on the agents over the border, well that was it. For him to confront us head on, that wasn't part of the game." Pressure was put on informants, he said, to find Cardenas and his inner circle. "Money was paid, charges were dropped, heads were banged. We weren't accepting excuses from the Mex [Mexican government]; getting Cardenas had become personal. If the government protected him or interfered with his arrest, things were going to get ugly. It was time for a show of force."

The crackdown worked. Members of the Gulf Cartel were tracked down and rounded up. One, Gilberto Garcia Mena, listed as Cardenas's number two man, was found in a hidden compartment behind a cupboard in his bedroom. When he was taken to Mexico City he was accompanied by a contingent of heavily armed soldiers for security. Overall, 21 members of his group were arrested. An army general, a captain, and a lieutenant who had been corrupted by the cartels were taken into military custody and a shipment of 17 tons of marijuana and 183 kilograms of cocaine was seized.

On March 14, 2000, a federal grand jury in Brownsville, Texas, returned a sealed indictment charging Cardenas and several of his cartel members with drug-related offenses.

In 2003, working from intelligence provided by arrested Gulf Cartel members, Cardenas was confirmed to be in a house in Matamoros. More than a hundred troops—to prevent leaks to Cardenas, none knew where they were going that day—raided the home, expecting little resistance. But at 9 a.m., when the military strike force attacked the home, cartel members—including Cardenas's personal security team of elite ex-army officers and former federal police officers—began fleeing the house in several vehicles with the soldiers in pursuit. A barrage of car-to-car gunfire ensued as the traffickers and soldiers sped through the streets. Houses and businesses, including a daycare center, were riddled with bullets. Miraculously, no one was killed. Cardenas was taken into custody under heavy security.

After the arrest, Mexican federal officials said it might be a long time before Cardenas makes it to an American courthouse to face 17 counts of drug trafficking and money laundering. He's also charged with a host of crimes ranging from extortion to attempted kidnapping to murder.

Cardenas continues to run his cartel from inside prison walls, arranging purchases and deliveries as well as directing a bloody war of attrition against the Juarez cartel members who've tried to take advantage of his incarceration by moving onto his turf. He's teamed up with Benjamin Arellano Felix, who once headed a Tijuana-based cartel, to conduct joint operations both inside and outside La Palma prison. Their power inside the prison was so solid that a team of Mexican federal agents with 30 tanks raided it to wrest control out of the trafficker's hands.

Cardenas's hatred of the U.S. government is unabated. At the end of January 2005 an internal FBI memo warned that he was plotting the kidnap and murder of American law enforcement agents. Part of the Gulf Cartel, police warned, were the Zetas,[2] former members of the Mexican armed forces and fanatically loyal to Cardenas. They're suspected in three drug-related murders in Dallas and of carrying out the murders of six workers at Matamoros maximum-security prison who were found shot to death, their bodies stuffed into a van outside the prison's walls. In Nuevo Laredo, the Zetas are also suspected in at least dozens of murders and disappearances that are terrorizing the town. In March 2005, in response to the cartels' infighting, the government sent 600 federal agents and troops to patrol the streets of Nuevo Laredo.

Throughout Cardenas's turf his enemies and perceived enemies have been attacked, including a mayor and his two sons who were murdered and dumped on a highway; the kidnapping of 20 fishermen who were beaten by traffickers who suspected they'd stolen drugs; a police officer and his uncle found dead beside a highway with a warning note from the Zetas pinned to their clothing; the hostage-taking of 40 guests at a hotel reception by narco-traffickers looking for a rival; the disappearance of a former mayor; and the murder of a civic advisor found on the Monterey highway.

And those incidents cover only a two-week period.

Violence, murder, and kidnapping along the border have not abated, and the U.S. State Department has issued a travel alert about the deteriorating situation. Putting a positive spin on the bloodbaths, U.S. ambassador Tony Garza said it merely highlighted that the violence was a result of the Mexican government's success against the cartels.

Despite widely trumpeted successes by U.S. and Mexican authorities, the power and violence of the Mexican cartels shows no sign of letting up. In early January of 2005 media outlets reported on the body count of the cartels and said that by the end of the second week of the year the death toll was already at 33, primarily along the U.S. border. There were reports that the cartels were amalgamating their power and resources and were expected to become an even greater threat than in the past.

In March, 19 suspects, including federal, state, and local police officers, were ordered to stand trial after five people were executed the previous November outside Cancun. All the victims had been shot in the head; two were members of the Federal Agency of Investigation, Mexico's FBI. And just hours after the five were found, four more bodies were found in the trunk of a burned-out car near Cancun airport.

On April 5, Dolores Guadalupe Garcia Escamilla, a radio reporter, was shot nine times after she aired a live report about a cartel-related murder. She survived—barely—and became the latest victim in a war of terror that was increasingly targeting journalists. According to the Center for Journalism and Public Ethics, four journalists were killed in Mexico as a result of their coverage of the drug trade. One journalist disappeared; others were picked up by traffickers and warned to cease reporting on the cartels. Mexico, media watchdogs reported, was behind only Iran, Bangladesh, and the Philippines for the number of reporters killed.

The cartels' activities are expected to continue unchecked, with a populace paralyzed by narco-terror and a government unable—some say unwilling—to root out the corruption that facilitates the cartels. To some observers it's become clear that the cartels are waging a war against the state, much as the Colombian cartels did, killing and attacking everyone from policemen to lawyers to journalists.

"It's not a case of mere corruption, of evil judges and evil policemen," an investigator said in an interview in early 2002. "It's *plata o plomo.*" *Plata o plomo*: silver or lead. The bribe or the bullet. "Which would you choose, eh?"

International Criminal Networks

Drug cartels aren't the only groups operating in Mexico; international organized crime families and syndicates also use the country as a base of operation.

Several Russian organized crime groups, including the Solntsevskaya, Tambovskaya, and Izmailovskaya, have been at work in the country and are involved in trafficking in drugs, weapons, and women from Central Asia. All the Russian groups have been documented as being in contact with the top six or seven Mexican cartels. And on the American side of the border, particularly in southern California, federal investigators have found cooperative distribution arrangements between Eastern European and Mexican crime groups.

Asian crime groups, including offshoots of Triads and syndicates, use Mexico for the final leg of their migrant-smuggling operations. And because Asian countries are exporters of vast quantities of precursor drugs, natural partnerships have formed over the past decade. As well, in the late 1990s Mexican authorities found a Yakuza criminal network enticing gullible and desperate young local women into traveling to Japan to work as hostesses, singers, and actresses. Upon arrival, the women—an estimated 1,200 in one instance—were forced into prostitution. Korean organized crime too has been detected at work in Mexico, particularly in the field of counterfeit goods. In one case, involving the Kookh Kim Sung Hol/Hyo Sun Park group, police seized 180 tons of phony merchandise that had been manufactured in Asia.

MS-13

When a smuggler and the three aliens he was transporting through Matamoros, Mexico, was caught on February 10, 2005, the specter of America's newest and likely most powerful gang emerged.

The smuggler was a leader of MS-13—Mara Salvatrucha—and his arrest led to worries that the El Salvadorian gang might be in league with al-Qaeda. "There has been some intelligence that al-Qaeda has talked with Maras to help smuggle someone into the U.S.," said John Naland, chief officer at the American Consulate in Matamoros. "The

Maras are certainly a threat to the United States . . . it's kind of the logical open door that could be used and the Maras are just ruthless enough to do it."

Until recently, few in the U.S. had ever heard of the Mara Salvatrucha.

For generations the Crips and the Bloods have been the most notorious of America's street gangs. Their activities and their absolute control over turf in many American and some Canadian cities have led to bloody street battles, organized cocaine trafficking, and associated criminal activities. The two gangs are so entrenched, particularly in their California base, that several younger members are actually the grandchildren of original members.

The newest "most dangerous gang in America," to quote a *Newsweek* article published in 2005, is MS-13. Mara Salvatrucha is named for a notorious organization that began in the 1980s as a relatively small outfit on the streets of Los Angeles. Its original members were Salvadorans who had fled civil strife; among them were members of the El Salvadorian street gang La Mara and paramilitary groups. In America they—and their children—found themselves taunted by and preyed upon by local gangs in the L.A. ghetto. To protect themselves they banded together in a *mara*, or crew, and as the initial cell grew it attracted many Salvadorians as well as youths from other Central American countries. And like a lot of gangs that form themselves for self-defense, MS-13 soon recognized their own power and evolved into a local criminal organization that practiced extortion, drug trafficking, and violent robberies.

A crackdown by U.S. authorities led to the deportation of several members; the deportees banded together, however, and outposts of the gang popped up throughout Central America. This effectively gave what was a local street gang reach across international borders. Investigators have uncovered a direct U.S.–El Salvador route for the shipment of stolen high-end cars. And it was MS-13—known for the beheadings of their victims—that was behind a bus bombing in Honduras that killed 28 people. In Texas and in several U.S. cities, police did a sweep and picked up more than a hundred members. In northern Virginia, police investigating 11 murders since 2000 found they were connected to MS-13.

Tens of thousands of MS-13 members are estimated as operating in the U.S. and Central America. They range from young teenagers to adults. Between 8,000 and 10,000 gang members have been identified in 33 U.S. states, and tens of thousands more have been identified in Central America and Mexico. U.S. federal reports say that MS-13 members have also been tracked into Canada.

The growth of MS-13 was the result of several factors. Initially the group wasn't taken as seriously as the Crips or the Bloods, and while it was essentially ignored it was able to form a hard nucleus of leaders. After 9/11 resources were cut back, and in the FBI's Washington field office, gang investigators were reduced by 50 percent as agents were reassigned to terrorist-related activities. Now, however, MS-13 has become active in a range of activities, including murders, kidnappings, extortion, gang rapes, and drug and migrant smuggling.

Endnotes

1. The Norte del Valle cartel is notorious because of its connection to law enforcement in Colombia and the U.S. leaders of the group—Danilo Gonzalez, Wilber Varela, Luis Ocampo, and Orlando Henao are all former policemen, according to DEA documents. Gonzalez, a former colonel, has ties to the DEA as well as to a wide range of Colombian law enforcement officials. A master of corruption, he bought off hundreds of officials; those who couldn't be bought were assassinated or forced into retirement by senior officers under his control. Informants within his organization are quickly identified—some say police intelligence is leaked to Gonzalez—and eliminated. Most members have U.S. indictments against them. The extraditions have sparked fierce internal fighting in the cartel, with several members meeting with U.S. officials outside Colombia to arrange surrender; this in turn has led to fears that those who are giving themselves up will cooperate in the arrests of other members. A number of homicides have been carried out, and attrition through an ongoing fight with the Cali cartel has also depleted ground-level "troops" in both organizations, with 1,000 combatants killed. By 2004 police had cracked down on the NVC—and in one investigation seized $100 million in property from Hernando Gomez Bustamante, then leader of the organization. The NVC is reported to be the last of the civilian—non-paramilitary or non-rebel—cartels, according to DEA analysts.

2. The Zetas—*Los Zeta*—are former members of a commando unit formed in the late 1980s under the organized crime unit of the Mexican attorney general's

office. They received advanced training from the American military in the U.S. with a mandate to track down drug traffickers. The original 31 Zetas were trained paratroopers; they were considered the Mexican equivalent of the U.S. Special Forces. Several members deserted the unit and went to work for Osiel Cardenas Guillen. The "Z" comes from their serial numbers—each began with the letter Z.

PART
SEVEN
Outlaw Motorcycle Gangs

Businessmen in Biker Attire

Outlaw motorcycle gangs (OMGs) have been established in North America for more than half a century. At first they were small, relatively benign, almost countercultural groups of disillusioned men, many of whom had served in America's armed forces and returned to a country that was suffering from post-war ennui. To say that OMGs were made up of "disaffected" people seems almost ridiculous by the standard of violence OMGs are known for today, but in the late 1940s and early 1950s they stood out from the non-violent counter-cultural groups.

It was their predisposition to party—invasions of small American towns during motorcycle conventions, beerfests and fights, even rapes and (later) murders—that brought motorcycle gangs to public attention. The ensuing media frenzy sparked the popular imagination and law-enforcement curiosity—old FBI files suggest there might be a "homosexual" aspect to the groups; other dusty old teletypes urge the investigation of the "Hell's Angels" (the apostrophe has long since been removed) for links to Communist activity. Hollywood moved things along by popularizing the rebellious nature of bike gangs with the movie *The Wild One* starring Marlon Brando, and Hunter S. Thompson wrote a book about his time spent with members of the Angels.

Law enforcement saw parallels between the concept of biker gangs and the early war on marijuana. Beerfests and rapes were considered akin to marijuana "head" parties and sex and loose morality. In a society where only police officers got to wear uniforms and practice violence when necessary in the course of enforcing the law when the biker gangs took on that role as well they felt the sting of ridicule.

How bike gangs went from fist-swinging party outsiders to what police today consider a major criminal organization coincides with the rise of illegal drug use throughout North America and Europe. In the 1960s, when marijuana was feeding the American counterculture, biker gang members were drawn to the hippie movement. With the instinct of anyone in a position of power in an underworld, it was only natural that the gangs would insert themselves into the supply/demand chain. For several years the Hells Angels, for example, were seen as benevolent suppliers of a product. As other drugs—speed, particularly—came onstream, the more criminally minded members of OMGs found more markets where increasing profits could be made. Those in the gangs who didn't engage in trafficking nonetheless supported those who did, bound by loyalty to their "brothers."[1]

When OMG members end up in jail or prison, the crossover of contacts in the underworld leads to expansion of business. And despite the common perception that OMG members are brain-dead Neanderthals, there are some highly intelligent gang members who recognize joint ventures and profits to be made with an instinct that would make a venture capitalist blush. So in an underworld where physical force and organizational self-protection are the keys to maintaining power, no one should have been surprised when OMG members entered into liaisons with mafia groups, especially those involved in the international drug trade.

Broadly speaking, the OMGs' structural underpinning is the "chapter." A chapter controls the defined geographic area in which it conducts its activity. Each chapter is headed by a president and has varying degrees of independence from other chapters. Members are almost always Caucasian males—there has long been a racist and misogynist element to OMGs—and new members undergo an initiation. Prospective members are subjected to a security review to weed out those who are police officers or informants. Some reports suggest that in order to identify police and police agents, the prospective member must commit a murder or be involved in carrying one out. (There's no basis to this belief, and it's likely rooted in rites of initiation used by other traditional organized crime groups such as the Mafia.) Loyalty to the club is demanded; most gangs have bylaws or a constitution that governs behavior both inside and outside the group. Mutual support among all members in all circumstances is paramount. This extends not only to backing each other up in a bar fight, but to facilitating the criminal activities of members when required.

It's in the criminal activity jurisdiction that OMGs get the most attention. While spokesmen for clubs and those who reluctantly give interviews to the press deny the hierarchical criminal structure of their gangs, even the most skeptical reading of crime reports and police dossiers shows that to varying degrees almost all OMGs have an organized, top-down structure in place. Not every member necessarily belongs to the criminally active group or is directly involved, but the existence of patch-wearing members who publicly display their membership supports the idea of a criminal structure. And while on the one hand the OMG spokesmen deny it, on the other police inflate it to gargantuan proportions.

The OMGs' criminal activities range from supplying stripper/ prostitutes to night- and dance clubs, to weapons trafficking, drug trafficking, extortion, organized theft, fraud, money laundering, and contract murder.

Hells Angels

The oldest, largest, and most well-known—even notorious—OMG is the Hells Angels, which operates more than 150 chapters worldwide. The Angels are voracious, either battling and domineering smaller gangs to take over their territory or absorbing them in patch-overs. Somewhere between the perception of police and media that they're the modern equivalent of the Mafia, and the Angels' own PR campaign that media and police smear them, lies the truth. In several countries the Angels qualify as full-blown criminal organizations, specifically in drug trafficking.[2]

While police, media, and gang experts disagree on whether the Hells Angels are a criminal organization or a motorcycle club with some— perhaps many—criminals in it, the frequency with which club members and/or close associates turn up in drug cases is almost endless. Most states where there are Angel chapters have seen members rounded up in several investigations, usually involving huge quantities of drugs or the laundering of drug profits. Undercover operations have found linkages between chapters: in December 2003, for example, a probe into drug and firearms trafficking resulted in raids from California to Alaska.

In Canada, as this book was going to press, the Hells Angels suffered a major legal setback when a Supreme Court judge ruled the club was "an identifiable criminal group." It was the first time a national precedent was set regarding the status of the Hells Angels.

The Canadian case involved an extortion attempt by two full-patch Hells Angels who, the judge found, were both wearing the Hells Angels death-head insignia when they arrived at the home of an extortion victim. The Angels, the judge said, "presented themselves not as individuals," but as members of a crime group, specifically the Hells Angels.

The proliferation of Hells Angels clubs around the world has created a built-in network for drug trafficking; ties have also emerged between Angels and organized crime, including the Colombian cartels, the Italian mafias, and even Asian-based trafficking organizations. Reviews of confidential U.S. immigration files show periodic surges in the movement of Hells Angels members from the United States to Europe, Thailand, South America, and Australia and New Zealand. "There are meetings held in all these places," a U.S. Senate investigator said.

> *We look at them and we go: ah, another drug network. I admit, this is a guess. There are trips we thought were related to narcotics trafficking that turned out to be anniversaries of chapters, that were related to funerals. That were to show support for OMG members on trial in various jurisdictions. Do we believe the OMG travelers are also planning criminal activities? Yes. Can we prove a global criminal organization with money flowing from all these places back to the mother chapter? No.*

He went on to say that reports—"hard surveillance, hard wiretaps"— indicate that several meetings were held, particularly on the U.S. eastern seaboard, between La Cosa Nostra members and known Hells Angels drug traffickers. "Almost without exception they've made contact with each other through either neighborhood affiliations or through being in prison together." Referring to a Canadian audio surveillance of a cocaine trafficking associate of the Montreal Sicilian Mafia meeting with a Toronto Hells Angels leader, he said: "There's absolutely no reason why the mafias in Canada and the OMGs in Canada wouldn't work together. The audio showed a strong friendship U.S. DEA files show the movement of Québec Hells Angels in Colombia and the U.K., it showed international links as far away as Thailand."

Despite several high-profile drug investigations, mostly involving cocaine and synthetic drugs, events do occur periodically that manifest the real roots and foundation of the club. The infamous Laughlin Run 2002, for example, revealed a face of the Angels reminiscent of the riotous Angels of old. When the dust finally settled at Harrah's Laughlin Casino three bikers were dead and several Angels and members of the Mongols bike gang were charged with murder.

The feud had begun more than 25 years ago, when the Angels and the Mongols, a primarily Hispanic club rooted in East Los Angeles, fought over the use of "State of California" on their jackets. The Angels had the phrase on their jackets and the Mongols wanted to have it too; the Angels resisted. The "phrase war" escalated quickly and saw murders and beatings. Two Angels were killed, shot off their bikes, and there were tit-for-tat retaliations. Occasionally there were minor turf battles and, with members of both clubs involved in the methamphetamine trade, some fighting over market share.

The feud underwent periodic flare-ups, but had generally settled down by 2002, and the Laughlin River Run motorcycle rally was an event usually immune to violence by a mutually agreed upon truce. River Run had been going on for more than 20 years and was an economic boom for the businesses in Laughlin, a town 80 miles south of Las Vegas. Tens of thousands of bikers, ranging from old-time graying Hells Angels to modern-day RUBBIES—Rich Urban Bikers—flooded into the area, blazing their way across the Mojave Desert.

No one's certain about what went wrong at the April 2002 Run. It might have been connected to the death of a Hells Angel that same day, apparently shot off his bike on the highway from Southern California to Laughlin. Or it might have been the escalation of a minor disagreement that got out of hand. But whatever it was, it ended with a wild melee of gunfire, stabbings, beatings, and two Angels and one Mongol dead. Most of the violence was captured on surveillance cameras in Harrah's Laughlin Casino. Bodies were seen falling onto blackjack tables; bikers were seen pulling guns and firing almost indiscriminately. There were knifings and attacks with hammers and wrenches.

After the battle police recovered 13 guns, 107 knives, 2 hammers, 2 wrenches, and 9 flashlights that had been used as weapons. "Throughout the casino there were weapons being found pretty much everywhere, in stairwells, on top of stairwell landings, in casino machines" an investigator said. "We were receiving information on a regular basis for about two days, another weapon being found, another weapon being found." Witnesses were uncooperative, and it took two years to bring indictments in the case. Seventy-three counts were laid, charging seven Hells Angels and two Mongols with murder and multiple other charges. As this book goes to press, trials are pending.

The Laughlin Run killings show that while some members of the Angels—and other biker clubs—may indeed be involved in large-scale drug trafficking. But they also show that the outlaw origins of the clubs are never far below the surface.

✳ ✳ ✳

Hells Angels have operated in Canada for decades, particularly in British Columbia, where they've been involved in the usual gamut of criminal activity—extortion, prostitution, drug trafficking—but also in ventures into the stock market, real estate, and control of the west coast docks. So financially savvy were the bikers, the Royal Canadian Mounted Police (RCMP) said in a report on the club, that other chapters were told not to continue borrowing money from them.

Vancouver is one of the few places where police warnings that bikers have donned suits and ties and infiltrated wider sections of society have proven true. That isn't to say they've turned their backs on the traditional use of violence; when a group of Eastern European traffickers decided to take over the cocaine trade in Vancouver in the 1980s, a brief gang war left the encroaching leaders dead. On the West Coast of Canada, however, some Hells Angels chapters are exactly what the police say they are: a fully operational criminal syndicate with influence or control in every segment of society.

But while these chapters were the Canadian public's first introduction to financial activities of the Hells Angels, it was a lengthy battle for control of Quebec's lucrative drug market that brought the club to notoriety. Hells Angels in Quebec—whose motto seemed to be Gun-and-Run—displayed little subtlety. In fact, in interviews with club members and associates in Toronto and Vancouver, the Quebec Angels were described as a different breed of biker altogether. "The Crazies," a B.C. biker called them. "*Les Hells ... les nuts,*" said another. "They party like Angels but they wear the colors for dealing (drugs). ... But they wear the colors and we support them." And both men believe that the Quebec underworld's instability was a result of the well-organized flow of cocaine into eastern Canada courtesy of the Caruana–Cuntrera–Rizzuto trafficking axis. The seemingly endless supply made fortunes for the participants, and when fortunes are to be had, wars ensue.

For the citizens of Montreal, the bloody war in the late 1980s between the Angels and the Rock Machine, a drug-trafficking gang, was greeted at first with disinterest. But for how long? The lucrative drug markets of Montreal demanded a large flow of drugs that yielded tens of millions of dollars a year in profits. Both gangs wanted to position themselves between the Mafia groups who smuggled the drugs into Canada and the retailers. But while the gangs had a fierce reputation as high-flying international drug barons, the reality was that they only sought a place in the chain of distribution, as close as possible to the international importers where the prices were the most reasonable. Of course, along with controlling the drug turf were other rackets ranging from prostitution to extortion. And, in the underworld's "you're the dog or the dog food" mindset, not controlling the turf made them mere guests in the Montreal underworld. Power was everything, even when it came to wearing club colors in public. And by the mid-1990s the war had escalated into a cycle of violence that rivaled Chicago in the Roaring Twenties, with bombings, beatings, gruesome murders, and disappearances on both sides.

The leader of the Angels in the province was a media-savvy former street thug who had the charisma of Al Capone during Prohibition. Maurice "Mom" Boucher joined the Hells Angels in 1987 and quickly rose to lead the club. Often photographed—and even sometimes inviting press to events he was attending—Boucher appeared to be a congenial front man for the Angels. Behind the scenes, though, he was close to the Rizzuto Mafia family. Positioned at the receiving end of the Caruana–Cuntrera cocaine pipeline, they were operating out of Venezuela where they brokered massive shipments of cocaine into Canada and the U.S. (Hells Angels had been active in the drug trade with the Caruana–Cuntreras dating back to 1980, notably involving the importation of hashish and heroin from the U.K.)

Sophisticated and even protective when it comes to organized crime, Montrealers viewed the battles with interest and even bemusement. As long as the bikers were only killing each other there was no great public outcry, even as the murder tally passed a hundred. The police seemed unable to quell the battles or control the gangs. Mom Boucher took on folk-hero status in the province and planned a media campaign that blamed everyone from the police to the media for the Angels' misunderstood image. He endured minor arrests and shrugged off attempts on his life.

The benevolent image of Mom Boucher and the Angels changed in the summer of 1995 when a bomb planted in a vehicle owned by a Rock Machine member exploded, killing a young boy nearby. The public mood swiftly turned to outrage and, within weeks, a special anti-biker squad, the Wolverines, was formed to go after bikers on both sides of the war. But bodies continued to drop: bikers kept killing each other, but then they also shot prison guards in a violent public display of power. The Hells Angels had, in essence, declared war on the state. Even the intercession of Mafia boss Vito Rizzuto, who urged the gangs to settle their differences and go about making money, fell on deaf ears.[3]

An informant, himself charged in the prison guard murders, identified Mom Boucher as the man who'd ordered the killings. At his first trial, in November 1998, Boucher was acquitted. The violence continued: in September 2000, veteran Montreal crime reporter Michel Auger was ambushed and shot several times as he arrived at work at *Le Journal de Montréal*. Auger, who had written about organized crime and the underworld for decades, was one of Canada' best-known crime reporters. His shooting renewed public outrage; demonstrations were held not only against the bikers but the government's failure in dealing with them.

In October 2000 Boucher was re-arrested for the prison guard murders. Five months later police launched Operation Springtime and arrested more than a hundred bikers, seizing a host of firearms, including an Uzi machine gun and a rocket launcher. Then, in March 2002, Boucher went on trial again for the prison guard murders and was convicted and sentenced to life in prison. Mega-trials for Hells

Angels members were held in a specially built courthouse. Groups of Angels were convicted of drug-trafficking offenses, murder conspiracies, and gangsterism.

Canadian police carried out other successful initiatives against bike gangs, using intelligence from Operation Springtime and from a number of informants. Profits flowing to the Québec Angels kept currency counting machines going around the clock. Puppet gangs—smaller groups of bikers used by the larger organizations—were targeted, and police were able to unravel several conspiracies. Operation Shadow, aimed at the Alberta Hells Angels, yielded impressive results: 51 people were arrested in the Calgary area, among them six members of the Hells Angels and 39 associates. Two hundred and seventy-five charges were laid, the bulk of them for drug offenses.

But while the successes effectively stopped the raging war in Quebec, they did little to quell the Hells Angels' ambitions to expand their empire. For years law enforcement agencies warned the public of the incursion of the Hells Angels into Ontario, particularly Toronto. Statements reminiscent of the early FBI investigative documents that called the Angels "huns" and "hordes" and "tartars" raised the specter of Canada's most lucrative drug market overrun by the same bloody violence that had wracked Quebec.

Ontario, and particularly Toronto, has long been home to a quiltwork of motorcycle gangs, Mafia families, and drug organizations. Most of the OMGs had ties to cells of the Calabrian and La Costra Nosa–related organized crime groups. Police investigations determined that bikers were used as enforcers by Mafia families and that bikers had long been involved in the production and distribution of methamphetamine. Biker associates were found investing in the stock market through straw men. Stripper bars were either owned or controlled by OMG members; women were rotated through the bars as part of a circuit that included parts of the U.S.

Battles of varying degrees of violence raged over the years in Ontario, but nothing came close to the meltdown of bikerdom in Quebec. And although journalists and police gave dire warnings of a bloodbath, when the Angels came to Toronto the takeover, with little violence and a lot of negotiation, was almost seamless. Four bike gangs were absorbed into the Angels, and suddenly the presence of the Angels was felt throughout the province.

Coincident with the Angels' arrival was the incursion of Montreal's Sicilian crime families. Relations between the Angels and the Caruana—Rizzuto—Cuntrera group were deep and strong, and intelligence reports noted negotiations between the Sicilians from Montreal and several Mafia leaders in Ontario in preparation for the Angels' Ontario move. Key to the expansion scheme was to first attempt to co-opt OMGs in Ontario, particularly in Toronto. Meetings were held to negotiate patch-overs between some Toronto biker gangs. According to a confidential police report in 2002,

> *Vito Rizzuto has long planned a move of his Family's influence into Ontario, particularly in the Toronto area, and Niagara Peninsula areas. Younger members of the Rizzuto Organization in Montreal have strong ties to several OMGs, particularly the Hells Angels. With a move into the Toronto/Ontario markets, confidential sources say Rizzuto will want to make certain the Angels' activities don't cause publicity. ... Relations between 'ndrangheta families and non-Angels groups will be examined and negotiated.*

The report goes on to note several meetings in the Toronto area between 'ndrangheta bosses, several Sicilian drug traffickers, and local OMG leaders. "It looked easy," an intelligence officer said of the bloodless takeover.

> *But like anything that looks easy, it was a tough road with a lot of issues to be resolved, old scores to be worked out. No matter how powerful some OMGs are, the Italians are still the dog wagging the tail; it'll always be that way. The Angels are superb middlemen. But there's no powerful component of any OMG anywhere in the world that can set up the deals the Italians can with the Colombians. The Italians in Ontario or Quebec could put their thumb on the spigot and the flow of relatively cheap cocaine would be shut off. They*

could decide, "No, we'll give a better price to someone else," and the Angels would be out in the cold. With peace everybody makes money; with war, everybody loses.

The Intelligence Officer went on to say that without the negotiations of the Sicilian Mafia, the Hells Angels could never have taken over in Ontario.

This excerpt from the 2004 report of the Criminal Intelligence Service of Canada gives an overview of biker crime in Canada:

- *There were five hundred members across 34 Hells Angels chapters, of which two in Quebec were listed as "inactive";*
- *In British Columbia, Quebec and Ontario the Angels "remain sophisticated and well-established," but in other Canadian regions they are being challenged by law-enforcement attention, internal conflict and competition from other organized crime groups;*
- *Outlaws and Bandidos have kept a low profile since crackdowns in 2002; the Outlaws had seven chapters in Ontario but only three of them had any degree of stability; the Bandidos had one full chapter in Ontario, and a recently-established probationary chapter in Alberta—sparking fears the move indicates a potential move against the Hells Angels;*
- *While the Angels' influence is growing in British Columbia—their most stable location—and in Ontario—through ties to Italian organized crime groups—it appears to be waning in Alberta, Manitoba, Quebec and Atlantic Canada.*

In the spring of 2005 the stability of the OMG scene on Canada's West Coast was shaken by the murder of William John Moore, who was the president of the Renegades, a Hells Angels puppet club that operated in Prince George, British Columbia. In January 2005 four Angels and six Renegades had been arrested after police had placed an agent/informant into the group. Moore may have been killed because his co-conspirators believed he'd cooperate with police.

Moore's murder was typically gruesome. He was put behind the wheel of his pickup truck outside his newly built home. His hands were reportedly tied to the steering wheel and the vehicle was parked facing the house. Before his eyes the house was burned to the ground. Then he was shot dead.

∗ ∗ ∗

While the OMG situation in Canada has settled down, at least temporarily, a 10-year battle between the Hells Angels and the Bandidos motorcycle gangs has raged in northern Europe. Rather than a turf war about drug trafficking, the ongoing battles are about ego and power: the toughest of the two controls the turf.

Violence between the two OMGs began in a minor way in 1994. The Angels, who'd established themselves in late 1980 in Copenhagen, became angered when the Morticians motorcycle club began meeting with the Bandidos motorcycle club. In 1993, when the Morticians became Bandidos MC/Denmark, clubhouses were quickly strafed by gunfire. Then there were biker murders, and in retaliation an anti-tank rocket was fired into the Hells Angels clubhouse in Helsingborg, Sweden. More shootouts broke out, resulting in more killings. In Finland the president of the Klan Motorcycle Club was shot and killed by a Hells Angels associate; in Sweden, the president of the Bandidos was shot and killed. More anti-tank rockets were fired at the clubhouse of Hells Angels–associated gangs. Between January 26, 1994, and mid-June 1997 more than 75 incidents of OMG-related violence occurred in northern Europe, including 11 murders and 75 attempted murders.

A tenuous peace was brokered, and to a degree the war has been put behind the two main combatants. Both have expanded throughout Europe and are heavily involved in a range of activities, from drug trafficking to migrant smuggling and extortion. OMGs in northern Europe are receivers and distributors of cocaine shipped either directly from South America or rerouted through Canada. Several European Union justice officials point to the OMGs as producers and out-shippers of methamphetamine and Ecstasy, products that aren't at the mercy of overseas shippers or rivalries between competing crime groups.

Greed, however, has surpassed loyalty and brotherhood in some parts of the OMG underworld. In March 2005, 12 Hells Angels in Amsterdam were convicted and each sentenced to six years in prison for killing three members of their club. Among the victims was the club president, Paul de Vries; two other victims were believed to have stolen a 300-kilogram cocaine shipment sent from South America by a Colombian cartel.

Recent reports warn that the Denmark Bandidos have set up an official chapter in Thailand—where Hells Angels already have a chapter—and that other Scandinavian groups will likely follow suit. International drug officers believe that the moves are the beginning of a pipeline from Asia to northern Europe that will give OMGs a direct conduit for heroin trafficking.

* * *

While OMGs do battle in parts of the world, in Australia a cooperative spirit seems to prevail—all in the name of making profit. Despite their racist views, OMGs have formed partnerships with several Australian and New Zealand organized crime groups, including Asians.

But becoming mature money-makers in the underworld wasn't achieved without some strife. In 1984 a western suburb of Sydney, experienced a wake-up moment when the Bandidos and Comanchero motorcycle gangs had a showdown in which seven people were killed and dozens injured. For the next 15 years similar incidents occurred involving several gangs.

In August 1999 police in Adelaide responded to a surge of inter-gang violence by calling a special meeting of federal police officers. Similar to events in other parts of the OMG world, Australia had undergone a wave of arsons, bombings, shooting, torture, and homicides. One of the roots of the warfare was reportedly an attempt to reduce the disparate gangs—there were more than 50 at one time in the mid-1990s—to just a half-dozen, thus creating a more controlled and stable underworld. Police intelligence officers were told of one meeting held in Sydney in 1994 among leaders of the most prominent gangs in which they established a policy of negotiation to absorb some smaller groups. Over the next six or seven years the number of "outlaw" outlaw gangs was radically reduced.

The primary revenue stream for OMGs in both Australia and New Zealand is the methamphetamine trade. Throughout the states of Queensland, New South Wales, and South Australia the OMGs have set up factories—similar to the bikers' speed labs in the western and southwestern U.S.—to produce tens of millions of dollars in synthetic drugs. The OMGs also use the facilities to make Ecstasy, using quick but dangerous methods that requires extreme caution in preparation of materials. Obtaining the precursor chemicals involves cooperatng with Asian crime syndicates whose members operate from both Southeast Asia and Australia.

The inflow of profits to the motorcycle gangs has sparked a need for money-laundering services that has led to the OMGs' co-opting of accountants and financial advisors. Money invested in legitimate businesses gives the gang members a veneer of respectability. Corruption too has emerged, with a confidential report stating that some members of the armed forces have been caught selling their weapons to the gangs and that some active police officers have even become members of one OMG.

In 2004 heavily armed police raided locations in rural NSW, Queensland, and south Australia. The targets were members of several OMGs—including the Hells Angels, the Outlaws, and associates—who were operating a massive methamphetamine laboratory. Almost $25 million worth of speed was seized and more than $1 million worth of marijuana. Twenty people were arrested.

Government reports released the same year showed that police had uncovered 314 Ecstasy and meth labs in 2002 to 2003 and seized $334 million's worth of product. Imports of chemical precursors rose sharply. Data was obtained that indicated ties not only to Asia but to the U.S., Canada, and Europe, where most of the OMGs have chapters or connections.

Chapters of the Hells Angels, the Bandidos, the Gypsy Jokers, Rebels, Nomads, and Outlaws are present in Australia; the FBI has told Australian authorities that the main gangs have ties to the U.S. Three dozen other gangs of varying strengths, and with an estimated 4,000 members, also operate across Australia. Federal police are currently unraveling ownership and investment in such businesses as bars and restaurants, security firms, auto dealerships, and financial companies.

* * *

In New Zealand, ties are strong between OMGs and the 14K Triad, the Wo Group of Hong Kong, and the Big Circle Gang syndicates—the primary criminal organizations in the region. The most powerful OMG is the Hells Angels, which is well established compared with the smaller and newer gangs. Angels are cautious, even fastidious about allowing new members into their chapters. And the Angels of New Zealand are world travelers, visiting brother chapters around the globe, including California, Canada, and South Africa. Within New Zealand the Angels have become wealthy, primarily from their activities in the early 1980s in the methamphetamine trade.

There may be a challenge in the wings, however, and it comes from a familiar foe. The Bandidos have long been in the process of identifying a local gang with an aim to patching over with them to gain a foothold in New Zealand. The most likely gang is Highway 61, an active OMG. The meetings are said to be ongoing and the Hells Angels are preparing, if necessary, to do battle to keep the Bandidos out.

Meanwhile, meetings between high-ranking Asian kingpins and members of several gangs, including the Head Hunters, have been monitored. Batches of speed and Ecstasy are cooked by the gangs' chemists and packaged for either local consumption of overseas shipment. Because New Zealand isn't a high-priority source country, packages originating there don't undergo much scrutiny.

The OMGs operate, much as they do in Canada, as a distribution arm for the Chinese-supplied product. With a strong economy, New Zealanders work hard and play hard and the drugs are in great demand—in fact, New Zealand ranks third, behind only Thailand and Australia, as a market for amphetamine users. The New Zealand marketplace is so notorious that police believe the influx of Israeli and Eastern European criminal groups is a direct result.

Globally, law enforcement expects that outlaw motorcycle gangs will firm up their operations both independently and in conjunction with local criminal organizations. Quick to exploit an opening, new-style drug-trafficking organizations will form and then fall away, regrouping when another initiative arises. There'll never be harmony in the OMG underworld: the profits to be made are too huge and the loyalty to the colors worn by members too egocentric.

Endnotes

1. Two interviews by the authors illustrate this point. In Toronto, a current Hells Angel—known by one author since the early 1970s—who joined the club through a patch-over in which his previous club was absorbed, was asked about drug-trafficking activities. "It's nothing to do with me. I'm a grandfather for Christ's sakes. I smoked in the sixties and seventies, who didn't? I've been pinched once for [stolen motorcycle] parts, that's it. I make a decent living. I don't do drugs, my kids don't do drugs, and I'll fucking kill my grandkids if they start." He was candid about trafficking in the club: "Nothing to do with me, what other people do. Go ask them. But if a brother needs help, I'm gonna help him, that's it. That's how it started and that's how it is."

A second interview just outside San Francisco with a paroled member of a local bike chapter yielded much the same: "I know guys who do things; that's their business. I don't and never did. I'm in it for the parties, even at my age, and the broads and my friends and my bike. I just got out [of prison for assault with a weapon] and when I got home there was a bunch of money with my wife. I'm opening a business, detailing bikes, chroming. Was some of that drug money? Sure. Maybe. I guess. Will the fucking cops call my store a front for bike gang drug trafficking? Sure they will. Big laundering scheme—I'm going to use my 6,000 wrinkly bills to fire up a lease."

2. Having powerful Mafiosi—who want only a stable distribution system and little police attention—intercede in strife between local drug organizations involved in a turf war is common. In the late 1990s, when the Pagan motorcycle club and a local drug organization, the Tenth-and-O gang, were at loggerheads in South Philadelphia, Ralph Natale and Joey Merlino, two powerful La Cosa Nostra figures, brokered a peace accord between the groups. Fearing a Quebec-style all-out gang war, Natale and Merlino convinced the Pagans to back off; in return, he guaranteed that the Hells Angels, who the Pagans feared would move into the area, would be kept out. The result was a settling down of violence; that the Pagans were now indebted to them was an added benefit for the LCN.

3. In his 2004 book *Crime School: Money Laundering*, RCMP officer former Chris Mathers offers a reasonable and realistic perspective on outlaw motorcycle clubs and criminality: "Bike gangs don't deal drugs. Bikers deal drugs. Certain members of the club simply use the club structure and some of its members to carry out their task. ... The reality is that very few other members of the club will know anything about the activities of the ... bikers who are selling drugs, other than that they are doing it. ..."

PART
EIGHT
African Organized Crime

The Black Hole

Non-traditional organized crime groups are emerging throughout the world. Africa, because of its tribal unrest and institutionalized government corruption, is now a major conduit for drug- and human-smuggling organizations.

The most notorious of the African organized crime groups are the Nigerians, who are particularly adept at heroin trafficking and international fraud. The ease of getting drugs in and out of Nigeria—through porous borders and co-opted customs officials—has turned the country into an international hub for heroin trafficking. With the exception of marijuana and related products, Nigeria isn't a source country for narcotics, but criminal groups—including Asian syndicates, Italian organized crime, and Colombian cartels—operate throughout the country. Known as a drug-transit hub, the Murtala Mohamed International Airport (MMIA) in Lagos is under the control of crime figures and corrupted officials. And when the Nigerian government implemented passenger and luggage searches at MMIA in response to demands from the U.S. to stop the drug shipments, the drug traffickers merely shifted their efforts to Port Harcourt Airport, which happily for them is used by British Airways and other international carriers. Air travel is a popular conduit for moving heroin into the U.K.

The use of Nigerians as couriers for drug shipments is well known. International routes—avoiding specific highly monitored airports—have been followed with some variation for more than a decade. Corruption of airport workers and customs officials is a technique the smugglers have perfected. Disabled travelers, mothers with children, diplomats, and student groups have all been used to carry heroin throughout Europe and North America. In one case, couriers were given visas to travel with a sports group to the Special Olympic Games in the U.S.; they passed on the heroin and returned to Nigeria with the same group.

In the mid-1990s, the Operation Global Sea takedown demonstrated the sheer quantity and breadth of a single Nigerian heroin smuggling operation. Over an 18-month period, the U.S. Drug Enforcement Administration tracked an Asia-to-America Nigerian network that moved drugs from Thailand to Pakistan, Chicago, New

York City, and Detroit. The organization had smuggled $26 million worth of top-grade Southeast Asian heroin, as well as several hundred kilograms previously sent along a route from Thailand, through Europe, Guatemala, and Mexico and into the U.S. Agents uncovered several sophisticated components of the drug ring ranging from acquisition to transit to security/intelligence and distribution. It also emerged through Global Sea that women were used as couriers, and that female Nigerian immigrants were actually in charge of the Chicago end of the operation.

To maintain control of the shipments' flow, each pipeline was broken down into parts: one group was used to carry the drugs to point A where they were received by an in-place conspirator, and they were then carried to point B, where again they were held before being passed on to courier C. This allowed the route to remain relatively secure if a breakdown occurred at any part of the chain.

In one 10-month period in 2004, seizures at Nigerian airports, border points, and seaports were relatively high: more than 90 kilograms of cocaine, 53 kilograms of heroin, and almost 200 kilograms of psychotropic drugs. "Those numbers look pretty good," said a researcher who worked on a study of organized crime in the region for a U.S. government intelligence agency. "But you have to wonder two things: how much did get through, and how many of the seizures were because government officials weren't paid to facilitate the smuggling?"

Several U.S. government reports note that despite the seizures and arrests—and most arrests result in convictions—corruption is entrenched at all levels of Nigerian society, politics, the financial sector, and law enforcement. Money laundering is rampant and Nigerian banks are used by crime groups from throughout Africa.

Nigerian organized crime is most famous for the fabled "Nigerian Letter Scam," or 4-1-9 frauds, which involved the mass mailing of letters to individuals and companies around the world.[1] (These letters were often poorly written. But when the Nigerian fraudsters used word-processing technology and even spell-check programs to improve their quality, the success rate dropped sharply and they went back to badly written, typed pleas for help. Observers believe that victims were initially drawn into the scam because they thought they were dealing with uneducated and naive Nigerians; once it appeared that they might be dealing with something other than dupes in a backward country, they became more cautious.) The letters usually purported to be from businessmen who'd stolen or otherwise appropriated huge amounts of money and had to find a safe haven in a Western bank. A percentage of the money was offered for the use of Westerners' bank accounts, and all that was required of the victims was some banking information to ensure that they themselves weren't crooks. Once this banking information was transmitted to the Nigerian fraud artist, it was used to clean out the victims' accounts by co-conspirators in the victims' countries. Cautious respondents who sent a query letter but no banking information found their letterheads copied and used to get American or European travel visas or to commit frauds against other companies. Victims who seemed exceedingly greedy were invited to meetings in Nigeria, where they were terrorized and held hostage while more financial information was extracted. Once more money had been taken from the victims' personal and country bank accounts, the victims were either released or murdered.

With advent of the Internet a new wave of Nigerian scams is appearing across the world, and despite repeated warnings, victims in Europe, Asia, and North America continue to respond and be victimized.

Most of the Nigerian criminal groups have some degree of organization, with a leader at the top and lieutenants below him, and almost all have connections to government agencies. Rather than being modeled on a mafia per se, the Nigerian groups are cell-like syndicates, often breaking apart and reforming in other criminal initiatives with interchangeable members. A noticeable trait that's fairly constant is formation of small groups along tribal lines or family ties. The diaspora of Nigerian migrants in communities across the world provides an infrastructure for both fraud and drug dealing rings.

In East Africa, Chinese smuggling operations routinely use ports to facilitate the movement of illegal migrants. Criminal organizations, meanwhile, use several cities—primarily Nairobi, Mombasa, and Addis Ababa—as transit points for drug shipments from Asia and South America. A major drug seizure in Kenya in December 2004 proved how attractive Africa is to global traffickers. Eight suspects tied to criminal organizations from Italy, Colombia, Venezuela, Holland, the U.K., and Germany were either arrested or named in warrants after the seizure of 700 kilograms of cocaine worth tens of millions of dollars.

As in Nigeria, rampant corruption makes it almost effortless to ship people or drugs. "It's a black hole," one African researcher observed. "There's absolutely nothing you can't do in East Africa." She said that investigations have found, in addition to Chinese criminal syndicates moving people and drugs, Eastern European, Baltic, Colombian, and Italian criminal organizations using the East African countries for transit routes.

South Africa, too, has become a flashpoint in international organized crime. More than 200 crime groups operate in the country, ranging from prison gangs and tribally based theft and murder groups to traditional organized crime figures from throughout the world, notably affiliated with Chinese, Russian, and Israeli mafia organizations.

Recent events in the region's Asian community point to fully entrenched Triad-like organizations involved in drug smuggling and extortion activities. The Asian groups are mostly part of far-flung international syndicates that assist in the highly lucrative "snakehead" trade—the shipment of illegal aliens out of Asia into the U.S. The most prominent Asian organized crime groups in South Africa are the Sun Yee On, the Wo Shing Wo, the 14K-Ngai, and the 14K-Hau. All are involved in a host of criminal enterprises ranging from extortion and drug trafficking to money laundering and the smuggling of endangered species.

Almost always quiet "mafias," the Asian syndicates' power came to light in late 2004 when Pretoria businessman Jia-Bin Lik and his wife and two children—aged three and 15—were found murdered. While four arrests were made in the case, the slamming of the Chinese community's doors was deafening. Years of being preyed upon had taken their toll on the polite but reticent leaders in the community. Nonetheless, whispered rumors of entrenched extortion, money laundering through Asian firms, and a growing number of migrants held in debt bondage to pay the snakehead gangs suddenly gained substance. Jia-Bin Lik, investigators discovered, had been involved in a financial dispute with a Triad member who had given him investment money that appeared to have been stolen.

According to a study by researcher Peter Gastrow published by the Pretoria-based Institute of Strategic Studies,[2] over the past 15 years Chinese criminal groups have become "well-organized entities, modeled on the Triads societies of Hong Kong and China." Gastrow found that Triads were active in major cities like Johannesburg and Pretoria, and that once they established a base they engaged in fraud, drug trafficking, firearm smuggling, extortion, money laundering, prostitution, illegal gambling, migrant smuggling, and importation of counterfeit goods. Contract killers appear to be active as well: "There have been a number of what appear to be contract killings of Chinese business people in different cities in South Africa," Gastrow told the *Pretoria News*, adding that the assassins appear to be "professionals brought in from China."

Chinese criminal involvement in the local drug trade has emerged over the past three years with huge seizures of Mandrax powder. Mandrax, a sedative-type downer drug, is popular in South Africa, along with "dagga"—cannabis—and "tik"—crack cocaine. In July 2003 the Scorpions, an elite unit of the South African police, seized four tons of Mandrax after a shootout with members of an Asian drug syndicate. Investigators found a network of vacant houses used to store the drug in powder form preparatory to being pressed into pills. A year earlier another network had been taken apart by the Scorpions, and in that case just under three tons of chemicals used to produce Mandrax were seized. International investigations have shown that chemicals used to produce Mandrax and other synthetic pills are often imported from China.

Warfare between Asian and Nigerian traffickers has led to crackdowns on both criminal groups. In May 2005, murders and bombings were sparked, police believe, by Chinese and Nigerian criminal organizations seeking control of distribution channels into several neighborhoods.

The International Organisation for Migration (IOM) also found that Asian criminal elements are involved in the sex trade. Young rural women from China are taken in an established circuit through several countries; when the women reach South African cities they're deprived of their passports and essentially become sex slaves. A circuit of sex rings throughout Africa is structured so that the victims can be moved on a regular basis after being sold and resold to different groups in different countries.

South African-based criminals will likely continue to emerge as both a growing local threat and an international hub for transnational organized crime. With a full complement of organizations—outlaw motorcycle gangs, Triads, Nigerians, and Italian Mafia money launderers and drug traffickers—it's predicted that after a few years of "shaking out" the groups will create joint ventures and even mergers. "South Africa is a Petri dish for global criminal organizations," said an American crime analyst working in the region. "There's no one that's not there. There are, increasingly, Russians, and we're seeing a lot of Israelis. This violence they're undergoing now—once it settles down I think there'll be sharp increase in the use of South Africa as a transit zone for everything from drugs to people to precious stones."[3]

Endnotes

1. "4-1-9" is a designation of the fraud offense in the Nigerian criminal code.

2. *Triad Societies and Chinese Organised Crime in South Africa* by Peter Gastrow, published by the Institute of Strategic Studies, Pretoria.

3. Interview in Thailand with syndicated crime analyst.

PART
NINE
Narco-Terrorism

Brothers in Arms and Drugs

In many parts of the world, drug trafficking— once an industry purely in the criminal domain—has emerged as a key source of funds for terrorists. Long before the September 11, 2001, attacks in New York City and Washington, U.S. authorities found that rebel insurgents, terrorists, and corrupt governments were involved to various degrees in a host of criminal activities, not only in the production, smuggling, and trafficking of drugs, but also in the weapons trade, counterfeit goods manufacturing, and cyber crimes. Since 9/11, state-sponsored and commercially funded terrorism have sharply decreased; many countries that would have once refused to cooperate with American financial and criminal investigators have become more vigilant in tracking the transfer of large amounts of money through their jurisdictions. These countries are now making a point of being seen as anti-terrorist and even sometimes pro-American. Increasingly, terror groups have turned to other avenues to finance their activities.

The U.S. State Department's Bureau for International Narcotics and Law Enforcement Affairs (INL) has already targeted groups in countries that were funding terrorist and anti-government activities in fields formerly controlled by organized crime. "Although the sources of funds may vary between terrorists and other criminals/drug traffickers—for example, terrorists may obtain funding from 'clean' sources such as contributions to charities that are diverted or from front company operations—the methods used by terrorists and drug traffickers to transfer funds are similar," says Deborah McCarthy, deputy assistant secretary for International Narcotics and Law Enforcement Affairs.[1] Terrorists' methods and those of organized crime groups are essentially the same, she said, even though the end goals are different: "[T]errorist and criminal organizations, which have fundamentally dissimilar motives for their crimes, may cooperate by networking or subcontracting on specific tasks when their objectives of interest intersect. For example, certain South American kidnapping gangs frequently sell custody of their victims to larger terrorist groups on what amounts to a 'secondary market.'"[2]

Latin American countries are the most direct examples of the nexus between terrorist groups and organized crime. Operating in key cultivation areas and as chains in the cocaine and heroin supply system, groups in Colombia, Peru, and Paraguay have emerged as key players in the drug trade. With heavy armaments—some are as well equipped as small armies—the terror/drug armies and militias are able to provide growing fields, security on shipping routes, and infrastructure support for traffickers. That most of the rebel groups are anti-American gives impetus and "legitimacy" to their activities, even though drug trafficking isn't strictly a political initiative.

The Revolutionary Armed Forces of Colombia (FARC) collects "taxes" from traffickers to raise funds to finance their lengthy war against the government of Colombia. In some regions, U.S. sources believe, FARC also protects jungle laboratories and maintains airstrips for planes that carry cocaine out of remote areas for several of the cartels. They're paid either in cash or in weapons.

At the end of the 1990s, FARC operated from a "schedule" for their services to the cartels, charging $15.70 per kilo of basic paste produced by cocaine laboratories, $4,210 per hectare of poppy field requiring security and protection, $5,263 for protection of international flights, and $2,631 for each militiaman required to protect landing strips. In a region where literally tons of drugs are produced annually, the inflow of money to FARC is stunning. With the cash they're able to buy increasingly sophisticated resources for their cause; in 2001, Colombian National Police arrested three Irish Republican Army members who were said to be providing demolitions training to FARC cells. The severe decline of the several dozen cocaine cartels in Colombia has given FARC almost total control of cultivation, production, and shipping of cocaine in several areas of the country.

Similarly, along the northeast border of Colombia and Venezuela, the National Liberation Army (ELN) operates with prominent drug-trafficking organizations. ELN soldiers are used to guard marijuana and opium poppy fields; they too are reported to collect a transit tax from cartels. More socially aware, the ELN is less involved in the drug trade than FARC, having declared their disdain for narcotics as a source of income. They do, however, oversee control of the movement of drugs out of their areas.

AUC—the United Self-Defense Groups of Colombia—is an umbrella organization that includes several Colombian paramilitary forces. They've used the cocaine trade to finance counter-insurgency projects. Although a commander of AUC, Carlos Castano, admitted in 2000 that he received 70 percent of his funding from the drug trade—"a necessary evil," he said—he announced plans to shift his financial underpinning away from the industry. One difficulty he faces is the myriad paramilitary groups under the AUC banner; several appear to be criminal organizations that use political aims as justification for their illegitimate activities.

The expansion of cartel–terrorist partnerships into the heroin market over the past several years has provided a much-needed boost to paramilitary operations in South America, especially Colombia. Although farmers, particularly in Peru, are paid more money for their efforts, the profit margin for heroin, as opposed to cocaine, is much higher because of the proximity of the American drug marketplace compared to Asian or Middle Eastern sources. The cocaine infrastructure of internal transit, international transit, corruption and bribery, and crop protection and security remains essentially the same for both products, allowing heroin to be "piggy backed" along existing routes.

In Peru, the Shining Path—Sendero Luminoso (SL)—maintains its operations in remote areas of the country where government authority is almost nil. During the 1980s and 1990s the Shining Path grew into one of the most wealthy, powerful, and violent anti-government groups by providing security and protection to drug traffickers and collecting transit taxes from traffickers; today, however, its influence has been reduced. U.S. intelligence reports say that several middle- to high-level members of the Shining Path are focusing purely on the profits to be made from drug trafficking and are less concerned about their sway over political and social agendas.

In addition to these and several other rebel and paramilitary groups, many smaller armies with varying degrees of power in smaller territories are involved in the drug trade at the "farm gate" level.

In 2002 and 2003, concentrated law-enforcement pressure led to the exposure of several ties between drugs and terror. The 2003 arrest of the cousin of Assad Ahmad Barakat[3]—the head of Hizballah in the Tri-Border area of South America (Argentina, Brazil, and Paraguay) who had in his possession five pounds of cocaine powder—revealed a link between the drug trade and Mideast terrorism. Authorities believe he was part of a scheme to sell the drugs in Syria, with the profits accruing to Hizballah.

In November 2002, eleven members of FARC were indicted for murder, hostage taking, and drug trafficking in a conspiracy that saw huge quantities of cocaine being shipped into the U.S. In the same month a separate probe in Houston, Texas, uncovered four members of AUC trying to exchange cash and cocaine for firearms. The money and drugs were to be used to purchase military-grade weapons, including shoulder-fired anti-aircraft missiles, more than 50 million rounds of ammunition, 9,000 rifles and rocket-propelled grenade launchers, and 300,000 grenades.

South America isn't the only territory with a nexus between terrorism and narcotics. In Afghanistan, which accounts for as much as 70 percent of the world's supply of opium, links between narco-traffickers and terrorists have endured for several decades. With the defeat of the Taliban, many opium kingpins are re-emerging, using their anti-Taliban—and thus pro-American—profile to facilitate their activities. Operating on the "my enemies' enemies are my friends" principle, U.S. policies in Afghanistan may be giving rise to an entirely new political culture based on drug trafficking. Although unsubstantiated, there are reports that al-Qaeda is funding its operations by taxing opium traffickers.

One example of the power of kingpins in the Afghanistan drug trade emerged in 2005 when American authorities arrested Bashir Noorzai in New York City. Noorzai is charged with smuggling more than $50 million worth of heroin into the U.S. over a 14-year period. Noorzai, who was added to the American narcotics kingpin list on June 1, 2004, was reportedly supplying al-Qaeda operatives in Pakistan with 2,000 kilograms of heroin every eight weeks, according to congressional testimony given by Representative Mark Steven Kirk of Illinois. "At the Pakistani price for heroin, this one conduit gives Osama bin Laden an annual income of $28 million," he said. DEA officials dubbed Noorzai the "Pablo Escobar of heroin trafficking in Asia."

According to an indictment filed by the U.S. Attorney for the Southern District of New York, Noorzai, a former close associate and financial supporter of Taliban leader Mullah Mohammad Omar, ran a drug network that ensured the largest profits possible: Noorzai "controlled opium fields in Afghanistan where poppies were grown and harvested to generate opium. After the opium was harvested, Noorzai used laboratories in Afghanistan and Pakistan to process the opium into heroin. Noorzai and his co-conspirators then arranged to transport the heroin from Afghanistan into the United States and other countries." Once, in 1997, when one of Noorzai's shipments of morphine base was seized by Taliban authorities in Afghanistan, it was quickly returned to him, along with personal apologies from Mullah Mohammad Omar, the leader of the Taliban.

The indictment details the relationship between Noorzai's organization and the Taliban: "During the course of the conspiracy, the Noorzai Organization provided demolitions, weaponry, and manpower to the Taliban in Afghanistan. In exchange for its support, the Taliban provided the Noorzai Organization with protection for its opium crops, heroin laboratories, drug-transportation routes. ..."

Arresting Noorzai—and he's only one of dozens of major traffickers operating out of Afghanistan—will do little to slow the narco-terrorism trade. With a per capita income in Afghanistan of only $186, traffickers are welcomed when they deliver seeds to rural citizens and promise more than $225 per kilogram of raw harvested opium. Even a small crop on five acres can yield about $1,000 to the grower.

This involvement of narco-traffickers in the daily lives of average Afghanis mirrors the state of affairs that has plagued several countries over the past century; where the government doesn't provide jobs, the criminal elements will. But that Afghanistan is becoming—or is already—a state driven by narcotics is undeniable. With the economy in tatters, opium production in 2004 increased to 4,000 tons, a fivefold increase from 2003.[4] Despite the U.S. attempt to support—with arms— a pro-American regime in Kabul, a narco-economy has emerged, and with it all the trappings of a criminal state: it is violent, corrupt, and funds terrorists.

Throughout Central Asia, India, and Sri Lanka, authorities have traced profits from drug trafficking to political and terrorist groups. The Liberation Tigers of Tamil Eelam, based in Sri Lanka, has long been a primary player in the heroin trade. Investigators haven't determined specifically whether the upper echelons of the organization are directly involved, but several major arrests have involved the discovery of Tigers' literature and propaganda. As well, financial trails from suspects such as charitable organizations in North America have led to bank accounts and companies known to be fronts for the group.

While initially thought to be jungle-bound traffickers living close to the ground, existing in tents and cut off from the wider world, terror traffickers throughout the world are on the cutting edge of new technology and practices. They have sophisticated systems for creating almost-perfect travel documents and Customs forms and possess state-of-the-art telecommunications systems. There's little hesitancy in bringing in experts from anywhere in the world, from IRA explosives experts to Pakistani agronomists to perfect planting techniques.

Several terror/narcotic groups easily justify their trafficking as an assault on the Great Satan—America. With most of the world's drug addicts in the U.S., the drugs themselves can be seen as a weapon, a force of destabilization.

Coincident to the needs of both traffickers and terrorists is the use of centuries-old ethnic-based underground banking systems that leave no paper trail. Drug profits and terrorist operational funding might enter the money-laundering streams at different points, but these monies do commingle and both are used to further criminal or political conspiracies.

For pragmatic organized crime groups who receive their narcotics from what appear to be the usual sellers—Colombian cartels or Asian syndicates—the politics surrounding the sources are of no consequence. Several reports detailing the connections between the criminal traffickers and the terror traffickers hint at a closed conspiracy; however, most criminal traffickers generally ignore the political or paramilitary goals of their suppliers.

* * *

A Balkan connection for the transit of drugs, weapons, and migrants has evolved over the past decade. The main players are former Albanian guerrilla or terrorist groups, the *'ndrangheta* of southern Italy, and the mafia-like *Sacra Corona Unita* from the Apulia area. Several small splinter groups—well-disciplined and heavily armed—control a vast portion of the heroin routes from Afghanistan through Turkey, Bulgaria, Macedonia, Albania, and on into Italy, where mafia groups distribute the product throughout Western Europe.

Here too are allegations and reports that al-Qaeda is involved in a middleman role between the producers and the destination countries—and most of the reports came out before September 11, giving them some credence. The routes used for smuggling are identical to those used to move Islamic fundamentalists into Europe, and Albania has long been identified by international security services as a key base of operation for extremists from the Middle East.

A terrorist funding network based on drug trafficking has emerged since the settling of conflict in the region. Kosovo Liberation Army members have disappeared from sight—and so have their weapons. An estimated 20,000 former fighters are believed to be active in the underworld, and several of them have moved into Western Europe and into the U.S. With these remote destinations and a strong base in their homeland, the fighters have created international drug networks. American tracking of funds connected to the new networks has revealed that profits were used to arm liberation extremists with strong ties to the Taliban. One purchase of weapons uncovered by police included SA-18 and SA-7 surface-to-air missiles.

Law enforcement agencies throughout the world believe the Albanian and Balkan criminal gangs will continue their joint ventures and partnerships with Eastern European and Italian organized crime groups. Tracking profits through several banks across the world hasn't successfully determined the ultimate destination of the money, but police in Italy believe the terror/drug and criminal/drug groups will eventually merge into one.

Links between Islamic extremists and drug trafficking are being discovered in several countries and regions, particularly in Central Asia, where tons of raw opium are being seized with some increasing regularity. Again, the goal is the lucrative markets of Europe. Several state security apparatuses have joint duties: to keep competitors out of the markets and routes of their own regions and to facilitate the movement of approved shipments. In addition to using their profits to fund the battles against the U.S., many of the groups are involved in regional terrorism, financing Islamic states where none now exist.

In the Philippines, Islamic fundamentalists, wanting to create their own religious state, have strong ties to the 14K Triad Society in Hong Kong. A weapons-for-drugs market between the two groups has found a dizzying flow of precursor chemicals—needed to produce methamphetamine and other synthetics—as well as weapons and finished product. The ties between Islamic leaders in the Philippines and al-Qaeda have emerged over the past several years, particularly in several assassination plots.

The underworld's thirst for profits and the terrorists' need for funding have created a unique economy in which the two sides work as partners but also in a client–patron relationship. Joint ventures between southern Italian Mafias and Balkan terrorists are becoming more common—both sides gain, more or less equally—but the global reach of these entities became apparent in late 2004. During a sting operation, prosecutors in Italy uncovered evidence that the Sicilian Mafia was involved in smuggling weapons-grade uranium after the seizure of an enriched-uranium rod in a Rome suburb. Fourteen suspects, many of whom were thought to be members or associates of the Sicilian Mafia, were taken into custody. The global reach of the organization was exposed during monitored telephone calls between several Catanian Mafia members; police determined that the rod had been imported from the Democratic Republic of Congo by way of the former Soviet Union. Sale price for the rod was negotiated down from $22.5 million to $11.5 million by an undercover agent who penetrated the scheme. And, he discovered, as many as eight other rods had been previously shipped into Italy. The final client for the transaction wasn't determined, but authorities believe the purpose of the rods was terrorist-related.

The terrorists' need for matériel and other equipment has created clients for non-organized crime entrepreneurs. In March 2005, the U.S. Attorney in the Southern District of New York announced indictments charging 18 people with conspiring to import and sell heavy weaponry reportedly destined for terrorists. Among the weapons were rocket-propelled grenade launchers, shoulder-fired surface-to-air missiles, machine guns, and several pieces of Russian military hardware.

The arrests were the result of a two-year sting operation in which a confidential informant (CI) posed as an arms dealer in the business of selling weapons to terrorists. The FBI laid wiretaps on seven telephones and recorded 15,000 conversations.

The indictment charged Artur Solomonyan, Christiaan Dewet Spies, Isoeb Kharabadze, Joseph Colpani, and Michael Guy Demare with several counts of conspiracy to import the weapons from Eastern Europe. "The CI, it is alleged, had multiple conversations with Solomonyan and Spies over the course of the conspiracy," the indictment read, "in which the CI indicated that his clients were terrorists."

The confidential informant also provided specifications and a price list of various weapons that could be delivered within the U.S., "including RPG's Stinger missiles, AK-47s, and claymore mines. ... Solomonyan discussed importing 200 RPGs from Armenia for sale." The CI was given the name of a Russian website, a user name, and a password so that he could access digital photographs of available weapons; included on the site were two SA-7b Strella surface-to-air heat-seeking anti-aircraft missiles, a Russian AT-4 Spigot anti-tank guided missile and launcher, a 120mm mortar launcher, anti-tank guns, and fully automatic assault rifles. During the investigation the CI took delivery of several firearms; three were delivered to New York City, three to Los Angeles, and two to Fort Lauderdale, Florida.

On March 14, as Solomonyan, an Armenian citizen, and Spies, a South African living in New York, were reportedly to leave for Eastern Europe, they were arrested by the FBI. Arrests were made in California and Florida; in Russia and Armenia, law enforcement officials moved to seize the weaponry and arrest suspects overseas. All suspects in the case remain before the courts.

Cyber Crime

The drive for profit combined with modern technology have created new revenue streams and greater opportunity for criminal organizations. And technology, primarily the Internet, has allowed organizations in various parts of the world to communicate and network without having to make actual physical contact with each other. No longer do criminals have to use telephones—which can be tapped relatively easily—or cross international borders to formulate schemes; the use of email and other cyber methods can allow a conspiracy to be formed and activated within seconds. Laptop computers, BlackBerries, the Internet, and other devices give criminal organizations access to instant communications, anonymity and, in the case of telemarketing frauds, a limitless victim pool.

As a tool of extortion, cyber technology knows few boundaries. The Bloomberg extortion-and-hacking case is a perfect example of how geography no longer restricts criminal activities.

Oleg Zezev, also known as Alex, was a Kazakhstan resident and chief officer of information technology for Kazkommerts Securities, a company based in Almaty, Kazakhstan. In the spring of 1999, the Bloomberg company provided database services to Kazkommerts, sending the company the software required to access Bloomberg's business service. A short time later Kazkommerts failed to pay its bill; in March 2000, Zezev used Bloomberg's software to bypass security systems to gain unauthorized access to Bloomberg's computers. In a single month Zezev, posing as a legitimate client of the Bloomberg service, accessed the database and entered various accounts, including owner Michael Bloomberg's personal account. Zezev copied email in-box screens, Michael Bloomberg's credit card numbers, and private information regarding the company's internal functions.

On March 24, Zezev contacted Michael Bloomberg via a Hotmail email account from Kazakhstan; to demonstrate his access, he attached several screens he had copied. Threatening to disclose information to Bloomberg's customers and the media, he wrote: "There's a lot of clever but mean heads in the world who will use their chance to destroy your system to the detriment of your world-wide reputation." He demanded $200,000.

Bloomberg computer specialists, having found where Zezev accessed the system, rewrote the software to prevent further intrusions. The FBI was called in and they traced the Hotmail account back to Kazkommerts Securities, where Zezev was still working.

Because cyber crime has no fixed boundaries and therefore no jurisdictions—and because extradition from Kazakhstan would be difficult, if not impossible—Michael Bloomberg and the FBI set up a sting. They sent a series of emails to Zezev saying that the extortion would be paid but only if Zezev would meet Bloomberg and some of his computer specialists in London to explain how he was able to crack their system. Zezev agreed, and in August he traveled to London and met with Bloomberg, his head of technology, and a British undercover agent acting as a bodyguard. The meeting was taped, and shortly later Zezev was taken into custody and later extradited to the U.S., where he was convicted and sentenced to 51 months in prison.

The global reach of more sophisticated cyber criminals emerged in the spring of 2005 when a five-country cyber pharmacy was taken down by the U.S. Drug Enforcement Administration (DEA). Operating in the U.S., Canada, India, Costa Rica, and Australia, the scheme was run by two Indian nationals who shipped controlled substances, including narcotics, amphetamines, and anabolic steroids, directly to buyers. The "pharmacists" used more than 200 sites on the Internet—what DEA administrator Karen Tandy called "an open medicine cabinet"—to sell millions of dollars of product.

In "Operation Cyber Chase," the DEA in Philadelphia began probing the activities of the Bansal Organization, led by Brij Bhusan Bansal and his son Akhil Bansal. Investigators determined that since July 2003 the Organization had distributed about 2.5 million dosage units of several controlled substances, including steroids and amphetamines, per month. The DEA said that the products were sold "directly to buyers of all ages without the medical examination by a physician required by U.S. law." Investigators feared the drugs may not have been safely sourced, may have been improperly stored, and might not meet safety standards. "Many of the safeguards that exist for brick-and-mortar pharmacies do not exist for Internet pharmacies," John Taylor of the Food and Drug Administration said, "and the potential for harmful drug interactions is magnified."

While tracking the Bansal Organization, investigators from several U.S. agencies found 41 bank accounts in the U.S., Cyprus, India, Singapore, the Channel Islands, the Isle of Man, the West Indies, Antigua, and Ireland used by Bansal.

Not all cyber schemes involving pharmaceuticals are as broad as the Bansals'. In 2004, another DEA project, this one centered in Bangkok, found a similar cyber pharmacy turning out 500,000 dosage units of controlled substances, including Valium, Xanax, Phenobarbital, and codeine. The drugs were sent to customers in 36 U.S. states. Medical "screening" of customers consisted of having them fill out an online questionnaire.

In the U.S., a special task force of federal agencies is currently tracing the paths of illegally supplied drugs back to their sources. One problem is that, given the number of handlers—shipments often pass through 20 or 30 different companies and entities before reaching wholesalers who distribute on the Internet—it's almost impossible to identify the original producers.

Europe too has been hard hit by cyber pharmaceuticals. Several investigations have exposed counterfeit drugs and packaging, making the use of these products a dangerous game of Russian roulette. Graham Satchwell, a former detective in the U.K., said in a written statement to the U.S. Senate Health, Education, Labor and Pensions Committee that the sophistication and care put into the packaging of counterfeit drugs is of an extremely high level: "Counterfeit medicines often appear so like the genuine product that no one, not the best specialist, can tell the genuine packaging from the counterfeit," he wrote. "And no one, not the best specialist, can tell the genuine product from the counterfeit unless the product is subjected to chemical analysis."

Satchwell, who has bought counterfeit medicines from China, Germany, Poland, India, and Pakistan, said it was easy to find foreign sources willing to counterfeit medicines. He was skeptical about Canadian online pharmaceutical businesses' selling over the Internet. "[Drugs] purporting to be from Canada ... frequently came from Malaysia, Vanuatu, or Eastern Europe... [T]he likelihood of drugs being time-expired or incorrectly stored is extremely high."

Endnotes

1. Testimony before the Committee on the Judiciary, United States Senate; Washington, D.C., May 20, 2003.

2. This was chillingly prophetic: kidnappings in Iraq in 2004 and 2005 found a similar pattern, with criminal gangs snatching up foreign workers and selling them to terrorists to either be executed or used for political propaganda.

3. Assad Mohamed Barakat has invested heavily in Hezbolla funding operations from his bases in South America. A rags-to-riches criminal businessman and terrorist, he emigrated from Lebanon when he was 17 years old and went from being one of hundreds if not thousands of street peddlers in Paraguay to a wealthy and powerful businessman. American intelligence files show he is the military chief of Hezbolla. Raids on his stalls in Paraguay turned up training videos and propaganda CD-ROMs. A review of his banking records showed monthly transfers of money to Middle East averaging $250,000 a month, as well as transfers to identified terrorist-linked bank accounts in Canada ($505,200), Chile, and the U.S.

4. United Nations International Narcotics Control Board.

PART TEN

Canada: The Triple-Threat Country

Haven, Transit and Source

It's often said that if organized crime were to create a country, it would look a lot like Canada.

We began this book with a reference to a project we co-authored that was published in 1995: *Global Mafia: The New World Order of Organized Crime*. We noted that little has changed for the better over the past decade. In *Global Mafia*, we had intended to write an international book; however, wherever we looked, our research took us to Canadian criminal organizations and Canadian criminal initiatives in every case. Whether the Hells Angels, Russian organized crime, the Sicilian Mafia, the *'ndrangheta*, or the Colombian cartels, every police investigation we researched yielded a Canadian connection. Whether researching cases in Los Angeles, the eastern American seaboard, Florida or Europe or South America, we found joint criminal ventures in play, with Canadian organized crime players at the forefront.

Taking a fresh look 10 years later, we see that Canada holds a special place in the underworld. With its lacklustre legislation and lip service to commitment in the fight against organized crime, a decade ago Canada stood as simply a transit country for criminals aiming their operations into the U.S.; it is now a triple-threat country: still a transit point, but also a haven for criminals and a source country for drugs.

The traditional threat to the lucrative U.S. market once came from the south, notably Mexico and Colombia. These countries are, if not complete narco-states, then certainly thoroughly corrupted and co-opted. Drug traffickers and migrant smugglers operate with impunity, protected by both terror and corruption. While Mexican and South American governments pay lip service in their futile and largely illusionary efforts to combat organized crime—often accepting massive anti-drug "bribes" from the Americans to fund their efforts—their results are rarely and barely successful. If there's any success in fighting crime on the southern border of the U.S., it is purely because of American initiatives.

It's on the northern border where the greatest threat to the U.S. lies. Canada, with its loose border and liberal immigration and justice policies, is a prime base for the world's criminal organizations. Safely ensconced above the 49th parallel, criminal groups conduct massive incursions into the American market. They also use Canada as a "safe conduit" to transit drugs into Europe, Eastern Europe, and Israel. Shipments originating in Canada receive much less scrutiny than if they were sent from cocaine-producing countries.

There are several reasons why Canada is a triple threat—haven, transit, and source—from organized crime. The same values, fairness, and emphasis on personal and human rights that makes Canada a desirable destination for the world's refugees and honest immigrants also makes it desirable for gangsters, terrorists and war criminals.

It's very easy to get into Canada and, if you're a criminal or a dictator or a fugitive, it's very hard to be forced out, even if the initial entry itself was illegal. Deportations and extraditions can take several years; in fact, there are organized crime figures and terrorists in Canada who have no expectation of ever being sent back to their home countries. Canadian immigration policies are rife with loopholes. Removing a Portuguese nanny who overstays in the country is a regular occurrence; removing a crime figure can prove impossible.

Once safely ensconced in Canada it is an easy step to get into the U.S. —or to remain north of the border, protected by an array of rights that almost guarantees residency of some form. A criminal organization set up in Canada greatly reduces the risk of being caught due to Canada's weak financial commitment to the fight against organized crime. And, if caught, criminals are offered lenient sentencing, asset forfeiture, and parole guidelines.

There are several cases that point up where the strengths of Canada's humanity and fair play are exploited, without much effort except legal expenses and patience, by international criminals.

The Alfonso Caruana case touches upon many of the problems of Canada's policies. Briefly, Caruana was arrested in Toronto in 1998 after a lengthy investigation into a multimillion-dollar cocaine trafficking network. After 30 years of evading capture in countries around the world, Caruana, who became a Canadian citizen decades ago, had set up his newest initiative from his home north of Toronto. After intense negotiations with the federal government, Caruana pleaded guilty to several charges and was sentenced to 18 years in prison. In spite of having documentation showing as much as 7,500 kilograms of cocaine worth tens of millions of dollars had been smuggled by the Caruana organization, just $623,578 in jewelry, $622,000 in cash, and $585,000 in investment bonds were forfeited to the government. And the investigation—which twice ran out of funding and forced the investigators to go hat in hand for more money—cost an estimated $8.8 million.

The Caruana case involved dozens of traffickers and money launderers, yet only a handful were charged and of those few received minor sentences or didn't go to prison at all. There was clear evidence of political connections at the local level and strong indication of ties to the federal government; there were lawyers who facilitated the conspiracy; there were banking staff who aided in money laundering. None of these avenues was pursued.

In 2001, already in a minimum-medium-security institution, Caruana —who was approaching eligibility for accelerated parole—was arrested on an extradition request from Italy where he's facing 20 years in prison. The accelerated parole was possible because drug trafficking isn't generally considered a violent crime and, in spite of a conviction in Italy, Caruana was considered a first-time offender. He remains in Canada, battling extradition.

Caruana's love affair with Canada was evident throughout the case. He was heard saying he "felt safe" in Canada; he refused to cross into the U.S. under any circumstances. Oreste Pagano, a Neapolitan drug trafficker who turned on Caruana's organization, summed up Alfonso Caruana's feelings about Canada: "He feels very safe in Canada for the reason that, even if he is imprisoned … being a Canadian citizen, after his release, he will be free in every respect," Pagano told his debriefers. "He says even if he gets twenty-five years of jail, which is the maximum, he won't do more than five years. …"

In addition to vowing never to enter the U.S., Caruana was also said to fear Italian justice: "He would accept the sentence … he would accept his guilt in Canada if he had a guarantee that he wouldn't get extradited to Italy," Pagano said. "Caruana told the Canadian prosecutors," being a Canadian citizen, I will accept the sentence, but one sentence only, and you don't extradite me to Italy. …'"

And going to Venezuela, where he'd previously lived, wasn't an option according to Pagano: "Because the fear he had of being in

Venezuela was that, if he was arrested in Venezuela, they would send him to Italy right away."

For Caruana, a top Mafiosi drug trafficker, Canada was a haven that he fully expected would protect him from the governments of the world who had pursued him for 30 years.

Similarly, Vito Rizzuto, dubbed an organized crime boss by the Canadian government, is fighting extradition to New York City where he's wanted on racketeering charges. According to court documents, Rizzuto was allegedly involved in the slaying of three Cosa Nostra bosses in 1981. Rizzuto has several avenues of appeal, should he lose pending court hearings.

The case of Antonio Commisso, arrested near Toronto in the summer of 2005, points up another facet of Canada's reputation in the underworld. Commisso, the head of the Siderno cell of the 'ndrangheta, fled Italy just prior to being sent to prison for 10 years for mafia-related crimes. He quickly made his way to Geneva where he bought an airline ticket to Canada. Upon arrival he didn't bother lying to immigration authorities; he stated his real name and showed his real passport, and was admitted in May 2004. Making his way to Toronto where he obtained a driver's license, he bought a home and obtained credit cards. All in his own name. He was even listed in the telephone directory.

When Italian investigators learned he was in Canada, they notified the Combined Forces Special Enforcement Unit, an RCMP-run team of organized crime investigators. Within weeks they found Commisso living north of Toronto. He was arrested on the Italian warrant and expressed surprise at being taken into custody. After losing an effort to obtain bail—in essence getting an opportunity to continue his flight from justice—he finally agreed to be returned to Italy.

In another notorious—and seemingly endless—case, one of China's most wanted fugitives has found haven in Canada. Lai Changxing was arrested in 1999 after fleeing China ahead of charges he operated the largest corruption and smuggling operation in Chinese history. Chinese authorities, estimating his smuggling network was worth multibillions of dollars, have tried in vain to extradite him. Although the Chinese government has sworn not to execute him if he's found guilty, Lai remains free in Vancouver after a judge determined he had no money to fund flight from Canada. Lai, who has denied any involvement in the corruption scandal, is under house arrest, and is living with his wife and children. He was ordered under a nightly curfew and is forbidden from associating with known gangsters.

In addition to criminal fugitives, there are reportedly more than a hundred war criminals in the country, but because they're protected by Canada's charter of rights and freedoms, the government is unable to release their identities, even though most of them have failed to turn up for hearings and are considered fugitives.

For migrant-smuggling operations, Canada is the perfect way station en route to Gold Mountain—the United States. Migrant groups—called "pig trains"—are regularly funneled into Canada, where the people are warehoused until the completion of their journey can be arranged. If migrants are caught in Canada, or even taken into custody offshore, they're interviewed, documented, and very quickly set free after filing refugee claims. Unscrupulous lawyers hired by the "snakeheads"— overseers of the migrant smuggling operations—arrange their release and then return them to the smugglers. This keeps the migrants from revealing the details of their trip and ensures they'll be able to finish paying off of their transit fees. Few "refugee claimants" remain in Canada long enough to see their cases adjudged; within days or even hours of their release from Canadian immigration custody, they're often across the border and settling their debt to the smugglers.

Telemarketing scammers, frequently run by organized crime or their associates, find Canada a safe and comfortable location to operate "shotgun" telephone blitzes into the U.S. The primary targets are often elderly Americans, lonely people with nothing but time on their hands and their life savings available for plucking. Using suckers' lists, telemarketers in Canada cull the legions of old folks across America and sell them no end of precious metals or bogus lottery winnings. Prosecutions of telemarketers charged in Canada are few, and in the rare instances where cases have gone to trial, the sentences are minor and the money recovered is minimal. With few exceptions, Canadian courts are extremely lenient when sentencing telemarketers or recovering victims' assets.

But Canada's prime service to the underworld is in drug trafficking. Always a transit country and a staging area, Canada has become a source country for both high-grade marijuana and precursor chemicals needed to process synthetic drugs.

As a transit location, Canadian cocaine seizures show that only about 25 percent of the product imported into the country is meant for local consumption; of the remainder, the bulk goes to the U.S. while the rest is shipped to Europe. The control exercised by Canadian organized crime groups at ports is a significant reason for the entry and subsequent exit of drugs. Several investigations and inquiries have uncovered heavy outlaw motorcycle gang and other criminal involvement in Canada's ports of entry.

Heroin brought into the U.S. enters from the south, usually from Colombia via Mexico, whereas in Canada the bulk of the heroin comes from Southeast Asia. But Asian criminal organizations have a steady north-south corridor of heroin into the U.S. eastern seaboard, where the population of addicts is very high. The density of migrant communities in both countries provides cover as well as infrastructure networks for these drug syndicates.

The transit of cocaine and heroin, however, is a minor irritation compared with the growth of Canada's marijuana industry—the famed "B.C. Bud." B.C. Bud is a potent and now legendary product of Canada, grown mostly on the West Coast. But motorcycle gangs and Vietnamese criminal organizations have increasingly set up sophisticated and massive "grow-ops" in several locations along the top border of the U.S. Literally millions of plants are grown in Canada each year, and much of the marijuana is shipped through pipelines into the U.S.

The crossover between criminal initiatives is manifestly clear in the marijuana grow-op trade. Several indoor "farms" have been uncovered in which illegal migrants in transit pay off their fees by babysitting plants. Basically indentured slaves, the migrants are usually the first and only suspects picked up by police during raids. And seldom do the investigations reach much beyond these front-line workers serving out their debt bondage: financiers, lawyers, real estate agents—all usually walk away and set up another operation. And even when the back-end players are caught, their sentences are relatively light: drug trafficking in Canada is seen as a non-violent offence, resulting in early release from custody after a very short sentence.

Efforts to reduce or control the production of marijuana in Canada have been a miserable failure. Between 2001 and 2005, seizures by American authorities—generally estimated to be about 10 percent of the total product being transported—rose by almost 300 percent. Total output, according to an RCMP estimate in 2003, was between 950 and 2,400 tons.

Meanwhile, the availability of marijuana in Canada and of cocaine in the U.S. has led to a barter system that has in turn increased the amount of cocaine being smuggled into Canada. The DEA reports that traffickers sometimes exchange cocaine in the U.S. for Canadian marijuana; the ratio is four to eight pounds of B.C. Bud for a kilo of cocaine. In addition to creating a new drug outlet, the barter system eliminates one stage of the money-laundering trail—the transfer of money itself.

The contrasting attitudes of the Canadian and U.S. governments toward the use of marijuana have caused friction between the two countries. Whereas U.S. authorities take a hard line, the Canadian government seems poised to decriminalize personal use. The stark differences between the two countries' view of marijuana is expected to be a sore point in intergovernmental relations.

But more serious than the marijuana debate is the situation surrounding the production of methamphetamine and synthetic drugs. Long a money-maker for outlaw motorcycle gangs, the relatively recent involvement of Chinese criminal syndicates in the trade—all operations in Canada—is taking global shape.

Several cases have pointed up Canada's weakness in combating the meth trade. Operation Mountain Express, a multilevel law enforcement investigation into the shipping of pseudoephedrine—an ingredient in the production of methamphetamine—from Canada into the U.S., resulted in 300 arrests and the seizure of 30 tons of pseudoephedrine, 181 pounds of methamphetamine, the dismantling of nine clandestine laboratories, and more than $16 million in U.S. currency. Bulk shipments of pseudoephedrine from Canada were key to the production of the drugs.

In April 2003, the U.S. Drug Enforcement Administration and the RCMP announced the arrests of 65 suspects in 10 Canadian and

American cities arising from Operation Northern Star. The 18-month investigation, targeting the illegal importation of pseudoephedrine, was a "top to bottom" effort, attacking suppliers of precursor chemicals, chemical brokers, transporters, manufacturers, distributors, and money launderers.

Precursor drugs are imported into Canada from China and India in powder form and are manufactured into tablets by legitimate companies. Six executives from three Canadian chemical companies were targeted by U.S. and Canadian officials. Police said the firms all sold bulk quantities of pseudoephedrine into the U.S. to customers "with the full knowledge that their sales were intended for the illegal production of the highly addictive and dangerous drug methamphetamine."

The shipments were sent into the U.S. through border points at Michigan and Minnesota aboard tractor-trailers with the chemicals hidden under "cover loads" of legitimate exports such as glassware, bottled water, and chewing gum. One shipment, in a truck whose manifest indicated it was running empty, consisted of 43 million pseudoephedrine tablets, or about 12 tons' worth of chemicals. The chemicals were warehoused in Chicago and other locations before being sent by truck to California, where they were used in illegal drug laboratories. More than 110 million tablets were seized during the investigation. Police didn't put a dollar value on the seizures but noted that a box of 80,000 pseudoephedrine tablets, worth about US$900 in Canada, could be used to process about $100,000 worth of methamphetamine.

Two of the prime organizers of the operation in the U.S. were two Middle Eastern crime groups based in Detroit and Chicago. While at first U.S. authorities said they'd found no terrorist link to the case, they did uncover a connection to a Middle East cell while tracking the financial end of the operation. Alaa Odeh, a Staten Island, New York, deli-grocery operator, was accused of laundering hundreds of thousands of dollars from the precursor chemical operation. Odeh, whose uncle in the Middle East had been arrested by Israeli authorities on suspicion of being a member of the violent Palestinian group Islamic Jihad, ran an underground *hawala* money-transmitting service. Among Odeh's clients were members of the Chicago end of the criminal organization;

$100,000 was shipped through his underground bank to the West Bank cities of Nablus, Ramallah, and Amman, the capital of Jordan, in 2002. Odeh pleaded guilty to two counts of conspiracy and one of unlicensed money transferring.

The involvement of the terrorist group Hezbollah, operating from Canadian bases, has been well documented. In 2002, according to intelligence documents obtained by Stewart Bell of the *National Post*, Hezbollah used Canadian banks to launder tens of thousands of dollars. As well, according to Bell's report, the terrorists use Canada to buy matériel, forge travel documents, raise money, and steal luxury vehicles. Citing a report by the Canadian Security Intelligence Service (CSIS), the *Post* reported that in 1999 and 2000 Hezbollah sent "shopping lists" of equipment to operatives in Vancouver, Toronto, and Montreal. The goods were shipped to Lebanon in courier packages.

Organized crime operations in Canada have also raised money to finance terrorist activities in various parts of the world. The RCMP has documented auto theft rings in Ontario and Quebec that specialize in high-end SUVs that are shipped to the Middle East where they're sold for much higher prices. And during the trial of suspected terrorists involved a massive cigarette smuggling operation in the U.S., a CSIS agent was brought in to testify against the accused. The profits from the cigarette operation, it emerged, were used to purchase matériel for shipment to the Middle East. Meanwhile, a number of probes into Asian organized crime in Canada have found criminal organizations with ties to China, Vietnam, and Hong Kong involved in large-scale production of Ecstasy and other synthetic drugs. Several of the main players in the conspiracies were in Canada on refugee claims or had previously been ordered out and had secretly returned under refugee cover. And the flow of criminal profits out of the former Soviet Union continues to flood into Canada's financial markets.

$$* \quad * \quad *$$

It isn't only in the underworld that organized crime groups find Canada hospitable. When the Russian criminal architects of the YBM scandal wanted to take their fraudulent company into the stock market, they had no difficulty deciding where to start: in Canada. A blue-ribbon committee of directors was signed up and YBM went on a wild ride that, even when the stock collapsed, was treated not as an organized-crime issue but instead as a "due diligence" matter. No criminal charges were laid in Canada.

Several investigations are currently under way in the Toronto and Vancouver stock exchanges, some involving funds from the drug trade, large-scale frauds, and outlaw motorcycle gang investments. The full extent of terrorist financing, much of it though underground banking systems based in Toronto, Montreal, and Vancouver, hasn't been determined but is estimated in the hundreds of millions of dollars.

Politically speaking, organized crime groups also find Canada a good place to do business, as clear evidence from police wiretaps show. In Toronto, a city councillor's daughter worked for a Sicilian Mafia-run company. The incident was documented in police reports filed with the courts, as well as on wiretaps. The councillor, clearly knowing who he was dealing with, asked that his daughter use a rear entrance when she arrived at work. No action was taken against the councillor. Another councillor was documented having a lavish meal at a mafia-run restaurant, the tab paid by a prominent money launderer. A cohort of the Rizzuto crime family of Montreal ran for a major political party in a provincial election. Money donated to several federal politicians was traced to a now-deceased Russian mafia figure. A former politician went into an import business with another Eastern European gangster, as did a disgraced member of Canada's security intelligence service. The list seems endless and almost never results in charges, much less a public exposure of the shady activities.

In spite of Canada's track record as a welcome wagon for criminals, there have been several initiatives that appear to have teeth. Canada's banks, a heavy presence in many of the world's offshore havens, are shedding their reputations as obstructive and often wilful participants in money laundering, and are initiating policies that appear to be helping in the fight against businessmen washing criminal profits. Stock markets are bringing in increasingly stringent due-diligence rules in an effort to keep unsourced funds from polluting the financial sector. The formation of FINTRAC, a financial transactions monitoring group, has initiated several money-laundering investigations against organized crime figures as well as terrorists using Canada as a laundering conduit. The recent money-laundering act—in spite of some flaws—is mostly in line with the world's standards.

But even with laundering legislation, it didn't take long for the weaknesses to become apparent. The case of Simon Rosenfeld, a disgraced lawyer, was explicit as an example of an eyewitness to Canada's attraction to criminals.

Long known to police in Canada and the U.S. for suspected activities as a white-collar criminal, Rosenfeld was the target of an RCMP sting in 2002. Undercover officer Bill Majcher, posing as Bill MacDonald, a front man for a Colombian drug ring, contacted Rosenfeld and said he was in Miami and was interested in doing some "money pickups"—getting money to be laundered. Inspector Majcher flew to Toronto and met with Rosenfeld at his law office in the city's tony Yorkville area.

As the men discussed money laundering during a meal, Rosenfeld was clearly a big booster of Canada. He said the criminal climate in Canada was much more agreeable than it was in the U.S., where terrorism had ramped up enforcement. Using as an example a couple who defrauded financial institutions for $100 million, Rosenfeld said that one of the accused paid off people to get into a country club-style minimum-security jail where he could play golf.

"In Canada, that's the rule," Rosenfeld told Majcher, adding that the man had served only 14 months, whereas in the U.S. he would have received eight to ten years. Another fraud artist convicted in Canada spent a year in a Canadian jail and had a cellphone and a fax machine with a private line; he ordered pizza all the time. Rosenfeld went on to say that the man told him: "I ate well, drank well. I didn't miss a thing."

During another meal, while negotiating Rosenfeld's commission for laundering money, Majcher held up a $1 U.S. bill: "If I give you this one dollar, do we have solicitor–client privilege?" Rosenfeld said they did. Majcher said: "Okay, then, what we're discussing is cocaine money." Between bragging about the leniency of Canadian justice, Rosenfeld told him about hiring Hells Angels as security for his son's bar mitzvah at a swank club. He also referred to "the Russians" and a planned murder. He said he was a friend of American lawyer F. Lee Bailey, had someone in the Mexican government who wanted to launder $40 million, and had sold two illegal handguns to a Toronto police officer.

During their conversations, Majcher said, Rosenfeld "actually spoke to me about the merits and benefits of bringing my criminal enterprise to Canada versus staying in the United States where there are real consequences to criminal conduct." Rosenfeld said laundering in Canada is "20 times" easier than in the U.S. and that he knew of five lawyers in Vancouver who laundered $200,000 a month through trust accounts for a 7 percent commission.

Majcher carried out several transactions with Rosenfeld, and several others were discussed. In one transaction Rosenfeld accepted $250,000 in Canadian currency and $190,000 in U.S. funds, having been told they were the proceeds of drug trafficking. The cash was funneled to a police-controlled bank account in Florida.

Rosenfeld's lawyer, Glen Orr, had a unique defense: his client was a liar and might be "a few cards short of a full deck." "Didn't he sound like he was just on planet Mars?" Orr asked Majcher.

In February 2005 it took a jury four hours to find Rosenfeld guilty of two counts of possessing, transporting, and transmitting money believed to be derived from cocaine trafficking. He was also convicted of attempting to possess proceeds of crime he thought to be illicit.

Crown attorneys Rosemary Warren and George Lennox argued for a five- to seven-year sentence. Warren called Rosenfeld a "Canadian ambassador for money laundering" who, in recorded conversations, mocked Canada's justice system and advertised the country as a safe haven for criminals.

Defense lawyer Orr said that Rosenfeld wasn't a professional money launderer and had been the victim of an RCMP sting operation; that he had been offered, "by a very clever RCMP officer, an opportunity to make money." Rosenfeld, he said, "was wandering around ... like a lost lamb."

Orr suggested a two-year sentence. Justice Tamarin Dunnet sentenced Rosenfeld to three years in prison and a $43,230 fine.

Only when charges are laid is the public alerted to the possibility of lawyers engaging in criminal activities. But the Rosenfeld case is merely the most public instance of lawyers laundering drug money and participating in organized crime. As Inspector Majcher told the court: "My experience is that it's a widespread problem. ... In almost every case we are doing, lawyers are central." In an interview outside the court, *The Globe and Mail* reported that he further commented: "We are seeing, in almost every case we are doing, a willful blindness or negligence on the part of a number of lawyers that have participated with the stock promoters."

Canada has comprehensive money-laundering legislation that requires financial institutions, casinos, real estate agents, and insurers to report all transactions over $10,000 as well as any suspicious transactions. But after a court challenge found that the measures violated solicitor–client privileges, lawyers were exempted from the legislation. And while the Canadian Bar Association says it's working with the government to find ways to bring lawyers into the reporting system, few law enforcement authorities find any reason to expect things to change.

The involvement of lawyers in crimes, particularly related to organized crime syndicates, is widespread but seldom reported; instead, private consultations are made in which the lawyers who are part of the conspiracies are offered a choice: withdraw from the case or be charged with your client.

In a major Canadian–Sicilian mafia drug investigation, police found evidence that a Quebec lawyer was essentially a part of the conspiracy—and may indeed actually be a full member of the crime family. He was told that if he represented the Mafia members charged in the case, he too would be charged. Police uncovered several instances of the man acting as a participant, particularly in the movement of tens of thousands of dollars' worth of property between conspirators. Another case, also involving a Quebec mafia lawyer, found that he was facilitating the criminal organization by using his solicitor–client rights to carry communications between members who were in custody in several jurisdictions.

✳ ✳ ✳

While slowly accumulating the tools needed to do its part in the fight against organized crime, Canada is lacking in one thing: a focused will. Having lengthy sentences on the books is good, but is ultimately useless if it is used as a bargaining tool in return for guilty pleas—pleas that ultimately assist organized crime figures by preventing trials that would reveal the true scope of their activity. Imposing lengthy sentences is also made moot by a parole system that kicks in very quickly after the prison sentence begins.

Asset seizure laws are fine, too, except when the assets are bargained away because the government wants to save the cost of a trial. Canada practices organized crime control with the mind of an accountant.

BIBLIOGRAPHY

A wide range of research sources is available and many can be tracked down with Internet searches or even through organized crime–related chat rooms and websites. While information retrieved through search engines should be checked carefully before using, the interested reader can find leads that will take them into areas they hadn't previously considered.

Of course, books are still the dominant form of research. We have found severa indispensable.

The Russian Mafia: Private Protection in a New Market Economy; by Federico Varese; Oxford University Press, 2001.

Mafia Brotherhoods: Organized Crime, Italian Style; by Letizia Paoli; Oxford University Press, 2003.

Triad Societies in Hong Kong; by W.P. Morgan; The Government Printer at the Government Press, Hong Kong, 1960.

Mafia and Mafiosi: Origin, Power and Myth; by Henner Hess; New York University Press, 1998.

The Sicilian Mafia: The Business of Private Protection; by Diego Gambetta; Harvard University Press, 1998.

President's Commission on Organized Crime; all volumes; U.S. Government Printing Office; 1985.

Profile of Organized Crime: Mid-Atlantic Region (1983), and *Asian Organized Crime*; hearings before the Permanent Subcommittee on Investigations of the Committee on Governmental Affairs, United States Senate; U.S. Government Printing Office, 1991.

INDEX

drug trafficking; synthetic drugs

DEA. *see* law enforcement

debt bondage. *see* migrant smuggling

Denmark, 228–229

Denver, Colorado, 147–148, 164n6

Detroit, 268

di Lauro, Cosimo, 69

di Lauro, Paolo, 69

diplomats, 117–119, 132n6

drug trafficking. *see also* specific drugs
   in Africa, 237
   and Albanian organized crime,
      250–251
   and Asian organized crime, 88,
      111, 231
   in Australia, 230
   in Canada, 261, 265–268
   counterfeits, 256
   global criminal consortium,
      164n7
   and Italian organized crime, 24,
      28, 59, 69, 71–72
   and kidnapping profits, 26
   and Mexican organized crime,
      195, 209
   and outlaw motorcycle gangs,
      218–225, 231, 232n1
   and Russian organized crime,
      137, 146, 159
   in South Africa, 241
   and terrorist groups, 29, 245–
      246, 251

E

East Africa, 239–240

Eastern European organized crime.
   see Russian organized crime

Eastern European Organized Crime
   Task Force (EEOCTF), 151

Ecstasy, 92–100, 111, 169–178, 228,
   230, 231, 269

ELN (National Liberation Army), 74n9,
   246

El Salvadorian gangs, 210–212

embassies, 117–119, 132n6

Escobar, Pablo, 196, 200–201

Esposito, Giuseppe, 49–50

ETA (Basque Fatherland and Liberty),
   29

ethnicity, 2–3

Europe, 203, 228–229

extortion
   and Asian organized crime, 88,
      101, 108, 115
   and cyber crime, 254
   and Irish gangs, 49
   and Israeli organized crime, 169
   and Italian organized crime,
      17–18, 20–22, 25, 37, 51, 58,
      65, 69
   and outlaw motorcycle gangs,
      219–220, 222
   and Russian organized crime, 150

F

Fainberg, Ludwig, 148, 150
Falcone, Giovanni, 1, 43
FARC (Revolutionary Armed Forces of
  Colombia), 203, 246, 248
FBI
  and Asian organized crime, 87
  and C-24, 149–150, 153–154
  and Italian organized crime, 45,
    55–56, 58, 60, 61
Ferro, Vito Cascio, 40
Fifteen Families (fis), 187
financial crimes, 108
Finland, 228
FINTRAC, 270–271
firearms. see arms trafficking
Fisherman, Igor L'Vovich, 161–162
Florida, 53, 171, 197
Fort Frances, Ont., 20–22
14K-Hau, 240
14K-Ngai, 240
14K Triad, 83, 231, 252
France, 29, 170–171
frauds
  credit card, 90, 95
  fuel tax, 146–147
  government, 25
  health insurance, 146
  and the 'ndrangheta, 25
  Nigerian Letter Scam, 238–239
  and outlaw motorcycle gangs,
    219
  and Russian organized crime, 137
  stock exchange, 270
Friedman, Robert, 156

Fujian province, 102, 104. see also
  migrant smuggling
Fuk Ching, 89–90, 102–104, 115

G

Gagliano, Alfonso, 61–62, 78n20
Galante, Carmine, 55, 58
Gambino Family, 45, 57, 62, 184–185,
  186
gambling, 37, 53, 58–59, 65, 101, 111,
  150, 169
GAMTAX, 56
Garcia Escamilla, Dolores Guadalupe,
  210
Garduna, 63
Genovese Family, 41, 56–57, 62
Gentile, Nicola, 44-45
Germany, 29–30, 169, 170, 187–188
Getty, John Paul III, 25
Golden Venture, 102
Goldfish case, 105–106, 131n1
Gomez Bustamante, Hernando, 212n1
government
  anti-government groups, 245–
    253
  Canadian and organized crime,
    261–274
  effect of organized crime on, 49
  and FARC, 246
  and Italian organized crime,
    34–37, 64
  Mexican, 210
  North Korean organized crime,
    116–125

Gratteri, Nicolá, 30–33
Green Dragons, 115
Guangzhou, 81, 85
Gulf Cartel, 205–208
Guyana, 202
Gypsy Jokers motorcycle gang, 230–231

H

Hariri group, 169, 178n1
    hashish, 224
Hells Angels, 219–229. *see also* outlaw
    motorcycle gangs (OMGs)
        in Australia, 230–231
        in Canada, 222–225
        and drug trafficking, 217–218,
        232n1
        in Europe, 228–229
        extortion, 219–220
        Laughlin Run 2002, 221–222
        in New Zealand, 231
Hennessy, David, 49–51
heroin trafficking. *see also* drug
    trafficking; Pizza Connection
        and Albanian organized crime,
        57, 185, 187–188
        and Asian organized crime,
        81–85, 90, 103–108, 120–124
        in Canada, 266
        and Colombian cartels, 202
        and Italian organized crime, 26,
        33, 42–43, 46, 54–55, 68–69,
        71, 78n19

and Mexican organized crime,
    203, 204
in Nigeria, 237–238
and Noorzai, 248–249
and outlaw motorcycle gangs,
    224, 229
and terrorist groups, 246, 247,
    250
Hezbollah, 248, 257n3, 269
Highway 61 motorcycle gang, 231
Hillsville, Penn., 12–18, 73n4
Holland, 29
home invasions, 115, 142
Hong Kong, 82
Honored Society of Calabria. *see*
    'ndrangheta
Houk, Seely, 14–18
human smuggling. *see* migrant
    smuggling
Hyo Sun Park group, 209

I

Ice. *see* methamphetamine trafficking
Ierinò, Vittorio, 27–28
    immigrants. *see also* migrant
        smuggling
        Albanian, 183, 186
        and development of organized
        crime, 48–49
        Italian, 11–14, 19, 49–51, 66–68,
        74n8
        Russian, 137, 141, 142–143, 172
immigration policies, 150–151,
    261–262

India, 107, 119, 129, 132n3, 249–250, 255

Indonesia, 83

Internet, 2, 186, 253–254

Irish gangs, 49, 52

Irish Republican Army (IRA), 28, 246

Islamic groups, 251–252

Israel, 158, 178, 179n3

Israeli organized crime, 169–178, 231, 242

Italian organized crime. *see also* American La Cosa Nostra (LCN); Camorra; *Sacra Corona Unita* (SCU); Sicilian Mafia
    and drug trade, 226–227
    ethnicity of, 3
    joint ventures, 151, 198, 220, 240, 242, 252
    and Prohibition, 52

Italy, 29–30, 251

Ivankov, Vyacheslav, 1, 140–144, 147–148, 150–157, 159, 162n1, 163n4

Izmailovskaya, 209

J

Japan, 129. *see also* Yakuza

Jarush, 169, 178n1

Jerusalem Connection, 170

Jewish organized crime, 49, 52. *see also* Israeli organized crime

Jones, Rod, 70

Juarez Cartel (Carrillo Fuentes Organization), 205, 208

justice system
    in Canada, 33, 58, 77n18, 266, 271–274
    lawyer involvement, 265, 272–273
    and telemarketers, 265
    in U.S., 57

K

Kadriovski, Daut, 187–188

Kahalon, Ya'acov, 174

Kazakhstan, 254–255

Kazkommerts Securities, 254–255

keondal, 112–113

Khun Sa, 126–127, 133n9

kidnapping trade, 25–27, 75n10, 88, 121, 245

Kil Jae-Gyong, 123–124, 132n6

Kim Jong Il, 116–117, 124. *see also* North Korean organized crime

Kin Cheung Wong, 103–108

Kookh Kim Sung Hol, 209

Korean organized crime, 108–109, 112–116, 210. *see also* North Korean organized crime

Korkov, Gennadiy, 142

Kosovo Liberation Army, 251

Kung Lok, 84–85

Kuomintang (KMT), 125

X

Xanax, 256

Y

ya ba. *see* methamphetamine trafficking
Yakuza, 109–112, 113, 122, 209
Yamaguchi-gumi, 110–111
YBM, 157, 161, 162, 269

Z

Zangari, Giovanni and Saverio, 24
Zetas, 208, 212n2
Zezev, Oleg, 254–255
Zito, Rocco, 24, 74n9